Neville Goddard

Your Inner Conversations are Creating Your World

A Collection of 16 Lectures on Imagination and Self Talk

Including

Neville's 1948 Lesson's

&

3 chapters from 3 of his books

"The Coin of Heaven"
"To Him Who Hath"
"Consciousness"

Compiled & Edited
by
David Allen

2015

Published by Shanon Allen
Copyright © 2015 by Shanon Allen / David Allen
All rights reserved. No part of this publication may be reproduced, distributed, or transmitted in any form or by any means, including photocopying, recording, or other electronic or mechanical methods, without the prior written permission of the publisher, except in the case of brief quotations embodied in critical reviews and certain other noncommercial uses permitted by copyright law.
Printed in the United States of America (2)

First Printing, August 2015

ISBN: 978-0-9909643-7-7

Copyright © 2015

Introduction

That you may receive the full benefit of these instructions, let me state now that the Bible has no reference at all to any persons who ever existed or to any event that ever occurred upon earth.

The ancient story tellers were not writing history but an allegorical picture lesson of certain basic principles which they clothed in the garb of history, and they adapted these stories to the limited capacity of a most uncritical and credulous people.

Throughout the centuries we have mistakenly taken personifications for persons, allegory for history, the vehicle that conveyed the instruction, for the instruction, and the gross first sense, for the ultimate sense intended.

From Neville's 1948 Lessons

Visit Us At **NevilleGoddardBooks.com** for a complete listing of all our books and **1000's of Free Books to Read online and download.**

Table of Contents

Page	Lecture / Chapter
7 -	**Lecture 1** Neville Goddard – July, 1951 By Imagination We Become Radio Talk, Station KECA, Los Angele
13 -	**Lecture 2** Neville Goddard – 1954 Awakened Imagination
28 -	**Lecture 3** Neville Goddard – 1955 How To Use Your Imagination
38 -	**Lecture 4** Neville Goddard – 12-1-1959 The Foundation Stone – Imagination
48 -	**Lecture 5** Neville Goddard – (Circa 1960) The Secret of Imagining
56 -	**Lecture 6** Neville Goddard – 3-22-1963 Is Christ Your Imagination
69 -	**Lecture 7** Neville Goddard – 2-13-1967 Imagination, My Slave
83 -	**Lecture 8** Neville Goddard – 6-3-1968 Imagining Creates
94 -	**Lecture 9** Neville Goddard – 10-26-1968 Imagination Fulfills Itself

107 - **Lecture 10**
Neville Goddard – 4-11-1969
The Perfect Image

118 - **Lecture 11**
Neville Goddard – 7-14-1969
Imagination

150 - **Lecture 12**
Neville Goddard – 7-20-1970
The Secret of Imagining

171 - **Lecture 13**
Neville Goddard – 4-26-1971
Control Your Inner Conversations – AKA Mind & Speech

190 - **Lecture 14**
Neville Goddard – 6-21-1971
Secret of Imagination

213 - **Lecture 15**
Neville Goddard – Date Unknown
I AM Reality Called Imagination

232 - **Lecture 16**
Neville Goddard, (1955)
Self-Talk Creates Reality / Mental Diet

243 - **Neville's 1948 Lesson's**
Lesson 1 – Consciousness is the Only Reality
Lesson 2 – Assumptions Harden into Fact
Lesson 3 – Thinking Fourth-Dimensionally
Lesson 4 – No One to Change But Self
Lesson 5 – Remain Faithful to Your Idea
Questions and Answers

419 - **Chapter 1** – The Coin of Heaven
429 - **Chapter 2** – To Him Who Hath
432 - **Chapter 3** – Consciousness

Lecture 1 – By Imagination We Become – Radio Talk

Lecture 1

Neville Goddard July, 1951
By Imagination We Become
Radio Talk, Station KECA, Los Angeles

How many times have we heard someone say, "Oh, it's only his Imagination?"

Only his Imagination . . man's Imagination is the man himself. No man has too little Imagination, but few men have disciplined their Imagination. Imagination is itself indestructible. Therein lies the horror of its misuse. Daily, we pass some stranger on the street and observe him muttering to himself, carrying on an imaginary argument with one not present. He is arguing with vehemence, with fear or with hatred, not realizing that he is setting in motion, by his Imagination, an unpleasant event which he will presently encounter.

The world, as Imagination sees it, is the real world. Not facts, but figments of the Imagination, shape our daily lives. It is the exact and literal minded who live in a fictitious world. Only Imagination can restore the Eden from which experience has driven us out. Imagination is the sense by which we perceived the above, the power by which we resolve vision into being. Every stage of man's progress is made by the exercise of the Imagination.

It is only because men do not perfectly imagine and believe that their results are sometimes uncertain, when they might always be perfectly certain. Determined Imagination is the beginning of all successful operation. The Imagination,

Lecture 1 – By Imagination We Become – Radio Talk

alone, is the means of fulfilling the intention. The man who, at will, can call up whatever image he pleases is, by virtue of the power of his Imagination, least of all subject to caprice. The solitary or captive can, by intensity of Imagination and feeling, affect myriads so that he can act through many men and speak through many voices.

"We should never be certain", wrote William Butler Yeats in his "Idea's of Good and Evil", "that it was not some woman treading in the winepress who began that subtle change in men's minds, or that the passion did not begin in the mind of some shepherd boy, lighting up his eyes for a moment before it ran upon its way."

Let me tell you the story of a very dear friend of mine, at the time the costume designer of the Music Hall in New York. She told me, one day, of her difficulty in working with one of the producers who invariably criticized and rejected her best work unjustly; that he was often rude and seemed deliberately unfair to her.

Upon hearing her story, I reminded her, as I am reminding you, that men can only echo to us that which we whisper to them in secret. I had no doubt but that she silently argued with the producer, not in the flesh, but in quiet moments to herself. She confessed that she did just that each morning as she walked to work. I asked her to change her attitude toward him, to assume that he was congratulating her on her fine designs and she, in turn, was thanking him for his praise and kindness. This young designer took my advice and, as she walked to the theater, she imagined a perfect relationship of the producer praising her work and she, in turn, responding with gratitude for his appreciation.

Lecture 1 – By Imagination We Become – Radio Talk

This she did morning after morning and in a very short while, she discovered for herself that her own attitude determined the scenery of her existence. The behavior of the producer completely reversed itself. He became the most pleasant professional employer she had encountered. His behavior merely echoed the changes that she had whispered within herself. What she did was by the power of Imagination. Her fantasy led his; and she, herself, dictated to him the discourse they eventually had together at the time she was seemingly walking alone.

Let us set ourselves, here and now, a daily exercise of controlling and disciplining our Imagination. What finer beginning than to imagine better than the best we know for a friend. There is no coal of character so dead that it will not glow and flame if but slightly turned.

Don't blame; only resolve. Life, like music, can, by a new setting, turn all its discords into harmonies. Represent your friend to yourself as already expressing that which he desires to be. Let us know that with whatever attitude we approach another, a similar attitude approaches us.

How can we do this? Do what my friend did. To establish rapport, call your friend mentally. Focus your attention on him and mentally call his name just as you would to attract his attention were you to see him on the street. Imagine that he has answered, mentally hear his voice . . imagine that he is telling you of the great good you have desired for him. You, in turn, tell him of your joy in witnessing his good fortune. Having mentally heard that which you wanted to hear, having thrilled to the news heard, go about your daily task.

Lecture 1 – By Imagination We Become – Radio Talk

Your imagined conversation must awaken what it affirmed; the acceptance of the end wills the means. And the wisest reflection could not devise more effective means than those which are willed by the acceptance of the end. However, your conversation with your friend must be in a manner which does not express the slightest doubt as to the truth of what you imagine that you hear and say. If you do not control your Imagination, you will find that you are hearing and saying all that you formerly heard and said.

We are creatures of habit; and habit, though not law, acts like the most compelling law in the world. With this knowledge of the power of Imagination, be as the disciplined man and transform your world by imagining and feeling only what is lovely and of good report. The beautiful idea you awaken in yourself shall not fail to arouse its affinity in others. Do not wait four months for the harvest. Today is the day to practice the control and discipline of your Imagination. Man is only limited by weakness of attention and poverty of Imagination. The great secret is a controlled Imagination and a well sustained attention, firmly and repeatedly focused on the object to be accomplished.

"Now is the acceptable time to give beauty for ashes, joy for mourning, praise for the spirit of heaviness; that they might be called trees of righteousness, the planting of the Lord that He might be glorified."

Now is the time to control our Imagination and attention. By control, I do not mean restraint by will power, but rather cultivation through love and compassion. With so much of the world in discord, we cannot possibly emphasize too strongly the power of imaginative love.

Lecture 1 – By Imagination We Become – Radio Talk

Imaginative Love, that is my subject next Sunday morning, when I shall speak for Dr. Bailes, while he is on his holiday. The services will be held, as always, at the Fox Wilshire Theater, on Wilshire Boulevard, near La Cienega, at 10:30.

"As the world is, so is the individual", should be changed to, "As the individual is, so is the world".

And I hope to be able to bring to each of you present the true meaning of the words of Zechariah, "Speak ye every man the truth to his neighbor and let none of you imagine evil in your hearts against his neighbor"

What a wonderful challenge to you and to me.

"As a man thinketh in his heart, so is he."

As a man imagines, so is he. Hold fast to love in your Imagination. By creating an ideal within your mental sphere, you can approximate yourself to this "ideal image" till you become one and the same with it, thereby transforming yourself into it, or rather, absorbing its qualities into the very core of your being. Never, never, lose sight of the power that is within you. Imaginative love lifts the invisible into sight and gives us water in the desert. It builds for the soul its only fit abiding place.

Beauty, love and all of good report are the garden, but imaginative love is the way into the garden.

Sow an imaginary conversation, you reap an act; Sow an act, you reap a habit; Sow a habit, you reap a character; Sow a character, you reap your destiny.

Lecture 1 – By Imagination We Become – Radio Talk

By Imagination, we are all reaping our destinies, whether they be good, bad, or indifferent.

Imagination has full power of objective realization and every stage of man's progress or regression is made by the exercise of Imagination. I believe, with William Blake, "What seems to be, is, to those to whom it seems to be, and is productive of the most dreadful consequences to those to whom it seems to be, even of torments, despair, and eternal death".

By Imagination and desire, we become what we desire to be. Let us affirm to ourselves that we are what we imagine. If we persist in the assumption that we are what we wish to be, we will become transformed into that which we have imagined ourselves to be. We were born by a natural miracle of love and, for a brief space of time, our needs were all another's care. In that simple truth lies the secret of life. Except by love, we cannot truly live at all.

Our parents, in their separate individualities, have no power to transmit life. So, back we come to the basic truth that life is the offspring of love. Therefore, no love, no life.

Thus, it is rational to say that "God is Love". Love is our birthright. Love is the fundamental necessity of our life.

Do not go seeking for that which you are. Those who go seeking for love only make manifest their own lovelessness and the loveless never find love. Only the loving find love and they never have to seek for it.

Now let us go into the silence.

Lecture 2 – Awakened Imagination

Lecture 2

Neville Goddard 1954
Awakened Imagination

As you have heard, this morning's subject is "Awakened Imagination". It is my theme for the entire series of nineteen lectures. Everything is geared towards the awakening of the Imagination. I doubt if there is any subject on which clear thinking is more rare than the Imagination. The word itself is made to serve all kinds of ideas, many of them directly opposed to one another. But here this morning I hope to convince you that this is the redeeming power in man. This is the power spoken of in the Bible as the Second Man. "the Lord from Heaven".

This is the same power personified for us as a man called Christ Jesus.

In the ancient text it was called Jacob, and there are numberless names in the Bible all leading up and culminating in the grand flower called Christ Jesus.

It may startle you to identify the central figure of the Gospels as human Imagination, but I am quite sure before the series is over, you will be convinced that this what the ancients intended that we should know, but man has misread the Gospels as history and biography and cosmology, and so completely has gone asleep as to the power within himself.

Now this morning I have brought you the means by which this mighty power in us may be awakened.

Lecture 2 – Awakened Imagination

I call it the art of revision. I take my day and I review it in my mind's eye. I start with the first incident in the morning. I go through the day; when I come to any scene in my unfolding day that displeased me, or if it didn't displease me if it was not as perfect as I thought it could have been, I stop right there and I revise it. I rewrite it, and after I have rewritten it so that it conforms to the ideal I wished I had experienced, then I experience that in my Imagination as though I had experienced it in the flesh. I do it over and over until it takes on the tone of reality, and experience convinces me that that moment that I have revised and relived will not recede into my past.

It will advance into my future to confront me as I have revised it. If I do not revise it, these moments, because they never recede and they always advance, will advance to confront me perpetuating that strange, unlovely incident.

But if I refuse to allow the sun to descend upon my wrath, so that at the end of a day I never accept as final the facts of the day, no matter how factual they are, I never accept them, and revising it I repeal the day and bring about corresponding changes in my outer world.

Now, not only will this art of revision accomplish my every objective, but as I begin to revise the day it fulfills its great purpose and its great purpose is to awaken in me the being that men call Christ Jesus, that I call my wonderful human Imagination, and when it awakens it is the eye of God and it turns inward into the world of thought and there I see that what formerly I believed to exist on the outside really exists within myself.

Lecture 2 – Awakened Imagination

No matter what it is, I then discover that the whole of Creation is rooted in me and ends in me as I AM rooted in and end in God. And from that moment on I find my real purpose in life and my real purpose is simply to do the will of Him that sent me, and the will of Him that sent me is this – that of all that he has given me I shall lose nothing but raise it up again.

And what did he give me? He gave me every experience in my life. He gave me you. Every man, woman and child that I meet is a gift to me from my Father, but they fell in me because of my attitude towards society, because of my attitude towards myself.

When I begin to awaken and the eye opens and I see the whole is myself made visible, I then must fulfill my real purpose, which is the will of Him that sent me, and the Will is to raise up those that I allowed in my ignorance when I slept to descend within me.

Then starts the real art of revision; to be the man, regardless of your impressions of that man, regardless of the facts of the case that are all staring you in the face, it is your duty when you become awakened to lift him up within yourself and you will discover that he was never the cause of your displeasure. When you look at him and you are displeased, look within and you will find the source of the displeasure. It did not originate there.

Now let me give you a case history to illustrate this point. I know a few of you were at the banquet and maybe a few of you heard me last Thursday on T.V. but I doubt in this audience of say twenty-three or twenty-four hundred of us, that more than say a hundred and fifty heard it, and even if

Lecture 2 – Awakened Imagination

you heard it you can hear it time and time again for it is this, that if you hear it will cause you to act upon it because as I told you, and I think I did last Sunday, but if I didn't let me tell you now; if you attended the entire nineteen and you became saturated with all that I have to tell you, so that you had all the knowledge you think it takes to achieve your objectives, and you did not apply what you received, it would avail you nothing; but a little knowledge which you carry out in action, you will find to be far more profitable than much knowledge which you neglect to carry out in action. So by repeating this case history this morning, though say a hundred or two hundred of you have heard it, it will help you to remember you must do something about it.

This past May in New York City, there sat a lady who had been coming for years and I made a simple observation that people must become doers of the word and not mere hearers only.

For if a man only hears it and never applies what he hears he will never really prove or disprove what he has heard; and then I told the story of a lady who had only heard me three or four times and how she transformed the life of another, and this lady hearing what one who came only three times and this miracle took place in her life, she went home determined that she would really apply what she had heard over the years, and this is what she did.

Two years before, after a violent quarrel, she was ordered out of her son's home by her daughter-in-law. Her son said "Mother, you need no proof from me that I love you: it's obvious: I think I have proven that every day of my life, but if that is Mary's decision, and I regret it, it must be my decision, for I love Mary and we live in the same house and it

Lecture 2 – Awakened Imagination

is our house: it is our little family, and I am sorry she feels this way about it, but you know these little things that culminate in an explosion as took place today. If that is her decision, it is mine". That was two years ago.

She went home and she realized that night after night for over two years she had allowed the sun to descend upon her wrath. She thought of this wonderful family that she loved and felt herself ostracized from it, expelled from the home of her son. She did nothing about revising it and yet I had been talking revision to my New York audience for the past year.

This is what she did now. She knew the morning's mail brought nothing. This was a Wednesday night. There had been no correspondence in two years. She had sent her grandson at least a dozen gifts in the two years. Not one was ever acknowledged. She knew they had been received for she had insured many of them; so she sat down that night and mentally wrote herself two letters–one from her daughter-in-law, expressing a great kindness for her, saying that she had been missed in the home and asking her when she was coming to see them; then she wrote one from her grandson in which he said "Grandmother, I love you". Then came a little expression of thanks for the last birthday present, which was in April, and then came a feeling of sadness rather because he hadn't seen her and begging her to come and see him soon.

These two short notes she memorized and then, as she was about to sleep, she took her imaginary hands and held these letters and she read them mentally to herself until they woke in her the feeling of joy because she had heard from her family; that she was wanted once more. She read these letters over and over feeling the joy that was hers because

Lecture 2 – Awakened Imagination

she had received them and fell asleep in her project. For seven nights this lady read these two letters. On the morning of the eighth day she received the letter: on the inside there were two letters–one from her grandson and one from her daughter-in-law. These letters were identical with the letters she had mentally written to herself seven days before.

Where was the estrangement? Where was the conflict? Where was the source of the displeasure that was like a running sore over two years? When man's eye is opened he realizes all that he beholds, though it appears without, it is within–within one's own Imagination, of which this world of mortality is but a shadow.

She gave me permission to tell that story. When I told it, and we came to the period of questions and answers, there was a strange reaction from that crowd. They wondered what joy life would hold for any of us if we had to write our own letters; if we had to do everything to ourselves that seemingly is done in joy; that seemingly is spontaneous coming from another; but I don't want to write myself a love letter from my wife, or my sweetheart or my friend. I want that one to feel this way towards me and to express it unknown to me that I may receive a surprise in life.

Well, I am not denying that sleeping man firmly believes that is the way things happen. When a man awakes he realizes that everything he encounters is a part of himself, and what he does not now comprehend, he knows, because the eye is opened, that it is related by affinity to some as yet unrealized force in his own being; that he wrote it but he has forgotten it, that he slapped himself in the face but he has forgotten it; that within himself he started the entire unfolding drama, and he looks out upon a world, and it

Lecture 2 – Awakened Imagination

seems strange to him, because most of us in our sleep are totally unaware of what we are doing from within ourselves.

What that lady did, every man and woman in this audience today can do. It will not take you years to prove it; what I tell you now may startle you; it may seem to be bordering on insanity for the insane believe in the reality of subjective states and the sane man only believes in what the senses will allow, what they will dictate, and I'm going to tell you when you begin to awake, you assert the supremacy of Imagination and you put all things in subjection to it.

You never again bow before the dictates of facts and accept life on the basis of the world without.

To you, Truth is not confined by facts but by the intensity of your Imagination.

So here we find the embodiment of Truth, which I say is human Imagination, standing in the world drama before the embodiment of reason personified as Pontius Pilate. And he is given the authority to question truth and they ask him, "What is the truth?" and Truth remains silent. He refuses to justify any action of his; he refuses to justify anything that was done to him, for he knows no man cometh unto me save I call him: no man takes away my life, I lay it down myself.

You didn't choose me, I have chosen you. For here is Truth seeing nothing hereafter in pure objectivity, but seeing everything subjectively related to himself and he the source of all the actions that take place within his world; so Truth remains absolutely silent and says nothing when reason questions him concerning the true definition of Truth.

Lecture 2 – Awakened Imagination

Because when the eye opens it knows that what is an idea to sleeping man is a fact to the awakened Imagination, an objective fact, not an idea. I entertain the idea of a friend and I make some wonderful concept of him in my mind's eye and when I sleep it seems to be a wish, it seems to be the longing of my heart, but purely subjective, just an idea. And the eye within me opens, and he stands before me embodying the quality that I desired in my sleep to see him express. So what is an idea to sleeping man, the unawakened Imagination, is an objective reality to awakened Imagination.

Now, this exercise calls for, I would say, the active, voluntary use of Imagination as against the passive, involuntary acceptance of appearances.

We never accept as true and as final anything unless it conforms to the ideal we desire to embody within our world, and we do exactly what the grandmother did. But now we start it and we do it daily. You may get your results tomorrow; it may come the day after; it may come in a week, but I assure you they will come.

You do not need some strange laboratory, like our scientists, to prove or disprove this theory.

Here in 1905 a young man startled the scientific world with his equation that no one could even test. It is said not six men lived who could understand his equation. It was 14 years later before Lord Rutherford could devise the means to test that equation and he found that it was true, not 100%, because he did not have the means at his hand to really give it a complete test. It was another 14 years before further tests could be made. And you know the results of that

Lecture 2 – Awakened Imagination

equation that Einstein gave us in 1905. For today man, not knowing the power of his own Imagination, stands startled at the results of that unlocking of energy. But he was the man who said, and I put it in the first page of my new book– "Imagination is more important than knowledge"

That was Albert Einstein.

Imagination is more important than knowledge. For if man accepts as final, the facts that evidence bears witness to, he will never exercise this God-given means of redemption, which is his Imagination.

Now I'm going to ask you to test this: you will not take the three weeks that I am here to prove it or disprove it, but the knowledge of it cannot prove itself, only the application of that knowledge can prove it or disprove it. I know from experience you cannot disprove it.

Take an objective, take a job, take some conversation with your boss, take an increase in salary. You say well, the job doesn't allow it, or maybe the Union will not allow it. I don't care what doesn't allow it.

Yesterday morning's mail brought me one, where, in San Francisco, this captain, a pilot, and he writes me that I saw him backstage after one of my meetings, and there he said, "But Neville, you are up against a stone wall. I am a trained pilot; I have gone all over the world, all over the seven seas; I'm a good pilot and I love the sea, not a thing in this world I want to do but go to sea; yet they restrict me to certain waters because of seniority.

Lecture 2 – Awakened Imagination

No matter what argument I give them the Union is adamant and they have closed the book on my request." I said, "I don't care what they have done, you are transferring the power that rightfully belongs to God, which is your own Imagination, to the shadow you cast upon the screen of space.

"So here, we are in this room; need it remain a room? Can't you use your Imagination to call this a bridge.

This is now a bridge and I am a guest on the bridge of your ship, and you are not in waters restricted by the Union; you are in waters that you desire to sail your ship.

Now close your eyes and feel the rhythm of the ocean and feel with me and commune with me and tell me of your joy in first proving this principle. and secondly in being at sea where you want to be.

He is now in Vancouver on a ship bringing a load of lumber down to Panama. He has a complete list that will take him through the year what this man has to do. He is going into waters legitimately that the Union said he could not go. This doesn't dispense with unions, but it does not put anyone in our place . . no one, kings, queens, presidents, generals, we take no one and enthrone him and put him beyond the power that rightfully belongs to God. So I will not violate the law but things will open that I will never devise.

I will sit in the silence and within myself I will revise the picture. I will hear the very man who told me "No, and that's final" and hear him tell me yes, and a door opens. I don't have to go and pull strings or pull any wires whatsoever.

Lecture 2 – Awakened Imagination

I call upon this wonderful power within myself, which man has forgotten completely because he personified it and called it another man, even though it is a glorious picture of a man but that is not the man: the real man is not in some other world.

When religion speaks, if it's a real religion, it speaks not of another world; it speaks of another man that is latent but unborn in every man that has attunement with another world of meaning, so that man sat and he tuned in with another world of meaning and brought into being a power that he allowed to go to sleep because he read the laws of man too well.

He accepted as final the dictate of facts for they read him the by-laws, they read him the laws of the Union.

And here today he is flying the ocean as he wants to do it.

The grandmother is no longer locked out from the home she loved, but she is in communion, but she was locked out by herself for two years. And he was locked out by himself for well over 18 months, and burning up day after day allowing the sun to descend upon his wrath when he had the power within himself and the key to unlock every door in the world.

I say to each and every one of you I wouldn't take from you your outer comfort, your religion, for all these things are like toys for sleeping man, but I come to awaken within you that which when it awakes it sees an entirely different world.

It sees a world that no man when he sleeps could ever see, and then he starts to raise within himself every being

Lecture 2 – Awakened Imagination

that God gave him; and may I tell you God gave you every man that walks the face of the earth. He also gave it for this purpose that nothing is to be discarded. Everyone in the world must be redeemed and your individual life is the process by which this redemption is brought to pass.

So we don't discard because the thing is unpleasant, we revise it; revising it we repeal it, and as we repeal it, it projects itself on the screen of space bearing witness to the power within us, which is our wonderful human Imagination.

And I say human advisedly–some would have me say the word divine. The very word itself means nothing to man. He has pushed it off from himself completely and divorced himself from the thing that he now bows before and calls by other names. I say human Imagination.

As Blake said "Rivers, mountains, cities, villages all are human". When the eye opens you see them in your own bosom, in your own wonderful bosom they all exist, they are rooted there. Don't let them fall and remain fallen; lift them up for the will of my Father is this, that of all that he has given me I should lose nothing but raise it up again, and I raise it up every time I revise my concept of another and make him conform to the ideal image I myself would like to express in this world. When I do unto him what I would love the world to do unto me, and see in me, I am lifting him up.

And may I tell you what happens to that man when he does it? First of all, he is already turned around within himself. He no longer sees the world in pure objectivity, but the whole world subjectively related to himself, and hang it upon himself. As he lifts it up do you know he blooms within himself. When this eye of mine was first opened I beheld man

Lecture 2 – Awakened Imagination

as the prophet saw him. I saw him as a tree walking: some were only like little antlers of a stag, others were majestic in their foliage, and all that were really awake were in full bloom. These are the trees in the garden of God. As told us in the old ancient way of revision in the 61st chapter of the Book of Isaiah . . "Go and give beauty for ashes, go and give joy for mourning, give the spirit of praise for the spirit of heaviness, that they may become trees of righteousness, plantings to the glory of God."

That is what every man must do, that's revision. I see ash when the business is gone; you can't redeem it, you can't lift it up, conditions are bad and the thing has turned to ash.

Put beauty in its place; see customers, healthy customers, healthy in finances, healthy in the attitude towards you, healthy in every sense of the word. See them loving to shop with you if you are a shopkeeper; if you are a factory worker, don't see anything laying you off, lift it up, put beauty in the place of ash, for that would be ash if you were laid off with a family to feed. If someone is mourning, put joy in the place of mourning; if someone is heavy of spirit, put the spirit of praise in place of the spirit of heaviness, and as you do this and revise the day you turn around, and turning around you turn up, and all the energies that went down when you were sound asleep and really blind now turn up and you become a tree of righteousness, a planting to the glory of God. For I have seen them walking this wonderful earth, which is really the Garden; we have shut ourselves out by our concept of self and we have turned down.

As told us in the Book of Daniel, we were once this glorious tree and it was felled to the very base, and what

Lecture 2 – Awakened Imagination

formerly sheltered the nations and fed the nations and comforted the bird and gave some comfort to the animals from the sun of the day, of the heat of the day; and suddenly some voice said from within, "Let it lie, let it remain as it is, but do not disturb the roots; I will water it with the dew of heaven and as I water it with the dew of heaven it will once more grow again, but this time it will consciously grow, it will know what it really is and who it is. In its past it was majestic but it had no conscious knowledge of its majesty, and I felled it . . that was the descent of man. And now, he will once more spring from within himself and he will be a tree walking, a glorious, wonderful tree.

Now to those who are sound asleep this may seem to you too startling: this may be just as startling as Einstein's equation was; that was startling too. But I tell you I've seen it and I see it . . men are destined to be trees in the garden of God. They are planted on earth for a purpose and they don't always remain men, they are transformed as they turn in and turn up. This is the true meaning of the transfiguration. There is a complete metamorphosis taking place like the grub into the butterfly. You don't remain what you appear to be when man is asleep, and there is no more glorious picture in the world than to see this living animated human being, for every branch within him is represented by an extension of himself called another, and when he lifts the other up that branch not only comes into leafage but it blossoms and the living human blossoms that blossom upon the tree of man who awakens.

So that's my message for you this year; I'll give it to you to stir into being that which sleeps in you, for the son of God sleeps in man and the only purpose of being is to awaken him. So it is not to awaken this, nice as it appears to be, but

Lecture 2 – Awakened Imagination

this man of sense . . is only a casing: it is called the first man, but the first shall be last and the last shall be first. So that which comes into being second, like Jacob coming second from his mother's womb, he takes precedence over his brother Esau who came first. Esau was the one like this, he was made of skin and hair, and Jacob was made a smooth skinned lad, but that one that comes second suddenly becomes the lord of all the nations and that one sleeps in every man born of woman, and it is the duty of a teacher or a true religion to awaken that man, not to talk of another world, not to make promises to be fulfilled beyond the grave, but to tell him as he awakens now he is in heaven and the kingdom is come now, this day, on earth.

For as he awakens, he revises his day and he repeals his day and projects a more beautiful picture onto the screen of space.

Now let us go into the silence.

Lecture 3 – How To Use Your Imagination

Lecture 3

Neville Goddard 1955
How To Use Your Imagination

The purpose of this record, is to show you how to use your Imagination, to achieve your every desire. Most men are totally unaware of the creative power of Imagination and invariably bow before the dictates of "facts" and accepts life on the basis of the world without. But when you discover this creative power within yourself, you will boldly assert the supremacy of Imagination and put all things in subjection to it.

When a man speaks of God-in-man, he is totally unaware that this power, called God-in-man, is man's Imagination. THIS is the creative power in man. There is nothing under heaven, that is not plastic, as potter's clay, to the touch of the shaping spirit of Imagination.

Once a man said to me, "You know, Neville, I love to listen to you talk about Imagination, but as I do so, I invariably touch the chair with my fingers and push my feet into the rug, just to keep my sense of the reality and the profundity of things. Well, undoubtedly he is still touching the chair with his fingers and pushing his feet into the rug.

Well, let me tell you of another one, who didn't touch with her fingers and didn't push that foot of hers onto the board of the street car. It's the story of a young girl just turned seventeen. It was Christmas Eve, and she is sad of heart, for that year she had lost her father in an accident, and she is returning home to what seemed to be an empty

Lecture 3 – How To Use Your Imagination

house. She was untrained to do anything, so got herself a job as a waitress.

This night it's quite late, Christmas Eve, it's raining, the car is full of laughing boys and girls home for their Christmas vacation, and she couldn't conceal the tears. Luckily for her, as I said, it was raining, so she stuck her face into the heavens to mingle her tears with rain. And then holding the rail of the street car, this is what she did: she said, "This is not rain, why, this is spray from the ocean; and this is not the salt of tears that I taste, for this is the salt of the sea in the wind; and this is not San Diego, this is a ship, and I am coming into the Bay of Samoa." And there she felt the reality of all that she had imagined. Then came the end of the journey and all are out.

Ten days later this girl received a letter from a firm in Chicago, saying that her aunt, several years before, when she sailed for Europe, deposited with them, three thousand dollars, with instructions that if she did not return to America, this money should be paid to her niece. They had just received information of the aunt's death and were now acting upon her instructions.

One month later this girl sailed for Samoa. As she came into the bay it was late that night and there was salt of the sea in the wind. It wasn't raining, but there was spray in the air. And she actually felt what she'd felt one month before, only this time she had realized her objective.

Now, this whole record is technique. I want to show you today, how to put your wonderful Imagination right into the feeling of your wish fulfilled, and let it remain there and fall asleep in that state. And I promise you, from my own

Lecture 3 – How To Use Your Imagination

experience, you will realize the state in which you sleep . . if you could actually feel yourself right into the situation of your fulfilled desire and continue therein, until you fall asleep. As you feel yourself right into it, remain in it, until you give it all the tones of reality, until you give it all the sensory vividness of reality.

As you do it, in that state, quietly fall into sleep. And in a way you will never know . . you could never consciously devise the means that would be employed . . you will find yourself moving across a series of events leading you towards the objective realization of this state.

Now, here is a practical technique: The first thing you do, you must know exactly what you want in this world. When you know exactly what you want, make as lifelike a representation as possible of what you would see, and what you would touch, and what you would do, were you physically present and physically moving in such a state.

For example, suppose I wanted a home, but I had no money . . but I still know what I want. I, without taking anything into consideration, I would make as life-like a representation of the home that I would like, with all the things in it that I would want. And then, this night, as I would go to bed, I would in a state, a drowsy, sleepy state, the state that borders upon sleep,

I would imagine that I am actually in such a house, that were I to step off the bed, I would step upon the floor of that house, were I to leave this room, I would enter the room that is adjacent to my imagined room in that house. And while I am touching the furniture and feeling it to be solidly real,

Lecture 3 – How To Use Your Imagination

and while I am moving from one room to the other in my imaginary house, I would go to sound asleep in that state.

And I know that in a way, I could not consciously devise, I would realize my house. I have seen it work time and time again. If I wanted promotion in my business I would ask myself, "What additional responsibilities would be mine, were I to be given this great promotion? What would I do? What would I say? What would I see? How would I act? And then in my Imagination, I would begin to see and touch and do and act, as I would outwardly see and touch and act, were I in that position.

If I now desired the mate of my life, were I now in search of some wonderful girl or some wonderful man, what would I actually find myself doing that would imply that I have found my state? For instance, suppose now I was a lady, one thing I would definitely do, I would wear a wedding ring. I would take my imaginary hands, and I would feel the ring, that I would imagine to be there. And I would keep on feeling it and feeling it until it seemed to me to be solidly real. I would give it all the sensory vividness I am capable of giving anything. And while I am feeling my imaginary ring . . which implies that I am married . . I would sleep.

This story is told us in The Song of Songs, or A Song of Solomon. It is said, "At night on my bed, I sought him whom my soul loveth. I found him whom my soul loveth, and I would not let him go, until I had brought him into my mother's house, right into the chamber of her that conceived me."

If I would take that beautiful poem and put it into modern English, into practical language, it would be this:

Lecture 3 – How To Use Your Imagination

"While sitting in my chair I would feel myself right into the situation of my fulfilled desire, and having felt myself into that state I would not let it go. I would keep that mood alive, and in that mood I would sleep." That is taking it "right into my mother's chamber, into the chamber of her that conceived me."

You know, people are totally unaware, of this fantastic power, of the Imagination, but when man begins to discover this power within him, he never plays the part that he formerly played. He doesn't turn back and become just a reflector of life; from here on in he is the affecter of life. The secret of it, is to center your Imagination in the feeling of the wish fulfilled, and remain therein. For in our capacity, to live IN the feeling of the wish fulfilled, lies our capacity to live the more abundant life.

Most of us are afraid to imagine ourselves as important and noble individuals, secure in our contribution to the world, just because, at the very moment that we start our assumption, reason, and our senses deny, the truth of our assumption. We seem to be in the grip of an unconscious urge, which makes us cling desperately to the world of familiar things, and resist all that threatens to tear us away from our familiar and seemingly safe moorings.

Well, I appeal to you to try it. If you try it, you will discover this great wisdom of the ancients. For they told it to us in their own strange, wonderful, symbolical form. But unfortunately you and I misinterpreted their stories and took it for history, when they intended it as instruction to simply achieve our every objective. You see, Imagination puts us inwardly in touch with the world of states.

Lecture 3 – How To Use Your Imagination

These states are existent, they are present now, but they are mere possibilities while we think OF them. But they become overpoweringly real, when we think FROM them and dwell IN them. You know, there is a wide difference between thinking OF what you want in this world and thinking FROM what you want.

Let me tell you when I first heard of this strange and wonderful power of the Imagination. It was in 1933 in New York City. An old friend of mine taught it to me. He turned to the fourteenth of John, and this is what he read: "In my father's house are many mansions. If it were not so, I would have told you. I go to prepare a place for you, and if I go and prepare a place for you, I will come again and receive you unto myself, that where I AM, there ye may be also."

He explained to me that this central character of the Gospels was human Imagination; that 'mansion' was not a place in some heavenly house, but simply my desire. If I would make a living representation of the state desired, and then enter, that state and abide in that state, I would realize it.

At the time I wanted to make a trip to the island of Barbados in the West Indies, but I had no money. He explained to me that if I would, that night, as I slept in New York City, assume that I was sleeping in my earthly father's house in Barbados and go sound asleep in that state, that I would realize my trip. Well, I took him at his word and tried it.

For one month, night after night as I fell asleep I assumed I was sleeping in my father's home in Barbados. At the end of my month an invitation from my family came

Lecture 3 – How To Use Your Imagination

inviting me to spend the winter in Barbados. I sailed for Barbados, the early part of December of that year.

From then on, I knew I had found this savior, in myself. The old man told me that it would never fail. Even after it happened, I could hardly believe, that it would not have happened anyway. That's how strange this whole thing is. On reflection, it happens so naturally, you begin to feel or to tell yourself, "Well, it would have happened anyway," and you quickly recover from this wonderful experience of yours.

It never failed me, if I would give the mood, the imagined mood, sensory vividness. I could tell you unnumbered case histories to show you how it works, but in essence it is simple: You simply know what you want. When you know what you want, you are thinking of it. That is not enough.

You must now begin to think FROM it. Well, how could I think from it? I am sitting here, and I desire to be elsewhere. How could I, while sitting here physically, put myself in Imagination at a point in space, removed from this room, and make that real to me? Quite easily. My Imagination puts me in touch inwardly, with that state. I imagine that I am actually where I desire to be. How can I tell that I am there? There is one way to prove that I am there. For what a man sees when he describes his world is, as he describes it, relative to himself. So what the world looks like depends entirely upon where I stand when I make my observation.

So if, as I describe my world, it is related to that point in space, I imagine that I am occupying, then I must be there. I am not there physically, no, but I AM there in my Imagination, and my Imagination is my real self!

Lecture 3 – How To Use Your Imagination

And where I go in Imagination and make it real, there I shall go in the flesh, also. When in that state I fall asleep, it is done. I have never seen it fail. So this is the simple technique upon how to use your Imagination, to realize your every objective.

Here is a very healthy and productive exercise for the Imagination, something that you should do daily: Daily relive the day as you wish you had lived it, revising the scenes to make them conform to your ideals. For instance, suppose today's mail brought disappointing news. Revise the letter. Mentally rewrite it and make it conform to the news you wish you had received. Or, suppose you didn't get the letter you wish you had received. Write yourself the letter and imagine that you received such a letter.

Let me tell you a story that took place in New York not very long ago. In my audience sat this lady who had heard me, oh, numerous times, and I was telling the story of revision . . that man, not knowing the power of Imagination, he goes to sleep at the end of his day, tired and exhausted, accepting as final all the events of the day. And I was trying to show that man should, at that moment before he sleeps, he should rewrite the entire day and make it conform to the day he wished he had experienced.

Here is the way a lady wisely used this law of revision: It appears that two years ago she was ordered out of her daughter-in-law's home. For two years there was no correspondence. She had sent her grandson at least two dozen presents in that interval, but not one was ever acknowledged. Having heard the story of revision, this is what she did: As she retired at night, she mentally constructed two letters, one she imagined coming from her

Lecture 3 – How To Use Your Imagination

grandson, and the other from her daughter-in-law. In these letters they expressed deep affection for her and wondered why she had not called to see them.

This she did for seven consecutive nights, holding in her imaginary hand the letter she imagined she had received and reading these letters over and over until it aroused within her the satisfaction of having heard. Then she slept. On the eighth day she received a letter from her daughter-in-law. On the inside there were two letters, one from her grandson and one from the daughter-in-law. They practically duplicated the imaginary letters that this grandmother had written to herself eight days before.

This art of revision can be used in any department of your life. Take the matter of health. Suppose you were ill. Bring before your mind's eye the image of a friend. Put upon that face, an expression which implies, that he or she sees in you, that which you want the whole world to see.

Just imagine he is saying to you that he has never seen you look better, and you reply, "I have never felt better." Suppose your foot was injured. Then do this: Construct mentally, a drama which implies, that you are walking . . that you are doing all the things that you would do if the foot was normal, and do it over and over and over until it takes on the tones of reality. Whenever you do, in your Imagination, that which you would like to do, in the outer world, that you WILL do, in the outer world.

The one requisite is to arouse your attention in a way, and to such intensity, that you become wholly absorbed in the revised action. You will experience an expansion and refinement of the senses by this imaginative exercise and,

Lecture 3 – How To Use Your Imagination

eventually, achieve vision in the inner world. The abundant life promised us, is ours to enjoy now, but not until we have the sense of the creator, as our Imagination, can we experience it.

Persistent Imagination, centered in the feeling of the wish fulfilled, is the secret of all successful operations. This alone is the means of fulfilling the intention. Every stage of man's progress is made by the conscious, voluntary exercise of the Imagination. Then you will understand why all poets have stressed, the importance of controlled, vivid Imagination.

Listen to this one, by the great William Blake:

In your own bosom, you bear your heaven and earth,
And all you behold, though it appears without,
It is within, in your Imagination,
Of which this world of mortality, is but a shadow.

Try it, and you too will prove that your Imagination is the creator.

Now let us go into the silence.

Lecture 4 – The Foundation Stone – Imagination

Lecture 4

Neville Goddard 12-1-1959
The Foundation Stone – Imagination

We believe that man can create anything he desires.

We believe the Universe is infinite response and the one who causes it is the individual perceiver. Nothing is independent of your perception of it.

We are so interwoven we are part of the machine, but as we awake we detach ourselves from this machine and make life as we wish it to be.

"For man is all Imagination and God is man and exists in us and we in him." "The eternal body of man is the Imagination: that is God himself." You can imagine and I can imagine, and if we can be faithful to the state imagined it must appear in our world.

This is not new. This was given centuries ago, for we have it in the Bible; but people do not know how to read the Bible, so they got together and organized it into an "ism."

It is not an "ism," but it is the great plan to free man.

The Bible shows this plan in detail.

We will turn to a few passages and show you what those who wrote it intended we should see.

Lecture 4 – The Foundation Stone – Imagination

"Thus says the Lord God, 'Behold, I am laying in Zion for a foundation a stone, a tested stone, a precious cornerstone, of a sure foundation: He who believes will not be in haste.'" Now, we are told in the Book of Psalms that the world rejected the stone. "The stone which the builders rejected has become the head of the corner." "You cannot lay any other stone." "On this stone you may build gold, silver, hay, or stubble and the day will reveal it." I tell you that this stone is your Imagination, and it is called in the Bible: Christ Jesus, or God, or the Lord.

It is your Imagination, which is one with the Divine Imagination which created, sustains, changes, and even destroys parts of the creation. This is the stone that is tested and it is a sure foundation, and he who believes in it will not be in haste. If I can but imagine and know that imagining creates reality I will not be impatient or lead a superficial life. When a man does not live in his Imagination he will become impatient of the outcome of what he desires, and finally he will become violent in his effort to get things.

Here is one who asks the question: "Who do men say that the Son of Man is?" Some said this and some that, but again he asked: "But who do you say that I AM?" "And Simon Peter replied, 'You are the Christ, the Son of the Living God.' And Jesus answered him, 'Blessed are you, Simon Barjona! For flesh and blood has not revealed this to you, but my Father who is in Heaven. And I tell you, you are Peter, and on this rock I will build my church."

The churches tell you that it means a man called Peter. It is not an individual. The whole thing takes place in the mind of you the individual. You imagine a certain state and it is called Peter. If it were a man called Peter, you would not find

Lecture 4 – The Foundation Stone – Imagination

what you find six verses later. For there he turns to the same character, Peter, and says to him: "Get behind me Satan: You are a hindrance to me; for you are not on the side of God, but of men." That is what every man in the world does. He gets a revelation and he realizes the foundation stone is Imagining. He sees a friend who needs help and he imagines he has what he wants. If he believes it, he is not in haste. He is imagining what he wants and he is not violent, and he is not concerned, and he does not give suggestions to the friend as to what to do physically to bring his desire to pass.

If the foundation stone is true, there is only one power to support it. If he knows that, he will not allow himself to be turned; he will remain faithful to his assumption. But we are told in the Bible story that the one who had been commended, Peter, turned and became violent, and then Jesus said to him, "Get behind me, Satan." You turn back to the ways of men to get things to go as you want them to go. You pull all the wires and therefore you have turned from the only foundation in the world, and that is Christ Jesus, which is human Imagination. If you believe this you will not reject the stone.

"Stone" is "even" . . in Hebrew . . and it means to create, or build, or beget children. Here is a stone in "Zion" (which means a high pinnacle or a barren place). That is man, before the stone is sunk in him. He is the waste, the desert. Sunk in man as his Imagination is the only foundation stone, for there is no other foundation of the living God and he has sunk himself in me. Therefore, I AM the son of the living God, for there is only one and I AM He. If I believe this, I will not be impatient. "He who believes it will not be in haste." This is the Lord's way. I ask you to test it. Bring before your mind's eye what you want to see in this world.

Lecture 4 – The Foundation Stone – Imagination

It may be business or a friend's good fortune. It can be anything, for on this foundation you can put stubble, or wood, or hay. You are building with hay when you say of someone: "I know . . he was no good." They lived in that state concerning another and then it came to pass . . and they say: "I always thought he was like that." Some of us build strange things for another. We were imagining on the only foundation, but we have put stubble on it instead of gold or silver, and the day revealed it, and then we cannot relate what happens to anything we have done.

The Hebrew meaning of the "stone" is to beget children. All the events of my life are my children. Everyone can build on this one foundation. "I am laying in Zion a stone." What stone? God is burying himself in everyone in the world. It is a true stone, a precious cornerstone, and one who believes will not be in haste. I have seen an imaginal act take two years to come forth, but when it appeared . . what a giant! I have seen it come in an hour. But do not be in haste or think there is any other foundation and . . like Peter . . turn to another foundation, growing violent toward those who would lead Jesus to the cross. But Christ said: "I came to move toward the cross. Get behind me, Satan. You are a hindrance to me."

If I am still in the machine, I think the good things come only by accident or chance. Let the wheel turn, for each must go through all the furnaces until he awakens and sees the whole universe as infinite response. The day will come when every person, at a certain degree of awakening, will freeze an activity within himself, and as it comes to a stop within him, that whole section is "dead." The laws of nature are only free action, repeated until they become accepted as a law. Yet you will see leaves in mid-air not falling, and people moving in space will cease to move but will not fall, for as you stopped

Lecture 4 – The Foundation Stone – Imagination

the action within yourself the whole thing stopped. And you will see the whole thing as Zion . . the desert . . and the only thing that makes it alive is the stone buried in it.

But man becomes lost in the things he has made and gives to them the power. For example, through the use of his Imagination he brings money into his world; then he forgets that it was the activity of his mind that did this, and he sees in the money itself the power to get what he desires. But when he awakes he will no longer lose himself in his own creation.

I say to everyone here: there is only one stone. If tonight there is someone very ill who needs your help and you imagine the best for him and then you get news that he is worse tomorrow, do not be impatient, but remain faithful to the one stone laid in Zion. What more can you do after you have imagined? Someone writes to you about a problem. Imagine for them what they desire and then do not turn aside to do anything to make it come true. You remain faithful, and it will create the conditions necessary to bring fulfillment.

You can look at someone with deep concern and want a change. You do not voice it, but lock it in, and then forty-eight hours later there is initiated what you set in motion. And they wonder: "Could my problem be traced to so-and-so?" Just the very thing you had been thinking! You entertained their problem with deep concern, and then you will ask: "Did you influence me or did I influence you? When did you entertain this thought?" And they say: "Just now," and then you say: "Forty-eight hours ago I entertained this thought, but I did not say it aloud." That makes no difference. All things by a law divine in one another's beings

Lecture 4 – The Foundation Stone – Imagination

mingle. We all influence each other. We are all interpenetrated, and the more one is deeply concerned for another, the more he is penetrated by another.

I say the universe is infinite response, but it also gives back more than you imagine. It is pressed down and running over. Therefore, to be negative can be frightening. The good will come back a thousand fold, but so will the negative. But if I am optimistic and do not waver, I will bring that also pressed down and running over. It is something wonderful; it will come like a gusher. The world responds more than it takes, and it gives to the individual more than he imagines . . good or bad.

I say to everyone that the greatest of books is the Bible, but people have organized it, and even say they have found the remains of Peter or some other Biblical character. Peter is not a man, but a state. You rise up to the crown of it all and that is Christ. States are permanent but I am not fixed; I AM a living moving being. I can be praised for one state and then I see a morning headline, say, and move from that true foundation, and then the power rebukes me as Satan, for I reacted instead of acted.

Would you like to be in the state called Peter, the one addressed in Matthew 16? How? Let me say, and mean it: "My Imagination is God and there is no other." It is one with the supreme power and let me live in that state, and then I am being addressed: "You are blessed, Simon Barjona." It means the depth of my being is giving it to me. Can I do it? The day that you do it and remember you did it, at that moment you are relating that story. When Peter confessed: "Thou art the Christ," that is the stone on which the whole

Lecture 4 – The Foundation Stone – Imagination

thing rests, but when he got away from that and reacted, then he was called Satan, or the re-actor.

God is begetting sons by means of the stone. He buries himself in every man in the world, but he is rejected. I can tell you these things here, but if I told them across the airways I would be immediately turned off. People cannot believe they are responsible for their imaginal acts. They do not want to believe it. I cannot be free of the results of what I imagine. Go out determined to prove it, and having proved it, keep the stone alive. There is no other stone. "No other can any man lay, which is Christ Jesus," But on this build anything . . but build gold, do not build hay or stubble. I want everyone here to test it. Take someone who is really distressed, and if you believe in the foundation you will leave here tonight without any concern for them, even if you receive wires stating things are worse. It might take a week or a month, but that which you have imagined, if you remain faithful to the stone, will come.

I have seen a man looking at a building . . which is an inanimate thing . . and you would say it could not respond. How can he look at it and see his name on it when he does not have a nickel? But he did it. I know the man. [Neville's brother] and in a way he could not have devised, the building became his. Let no one tell you that something cannot respond, but when we are still part of the machine, we cannot quite see that we are the cause of everything in our world, and we hope good fortune will smile on us. Then when you set something bad in motion, as the machine turns you cannot see what caused it, but when you become awake you can control the machine. It responds to the imaginal acts of the awakened man, for the awakened man is in control.

Lecture 4 – The Foundation Stone – Imagination

A thrill is in store for you when you can finally stop all activity and the whole thing will freeze. You will know what the so-called wise men say, but you will hear only these words: "I thank you Father that you have hid these things from the wise and pious and revealed them unto babes." For you will know that it is the perceiver who is making everything alive. For you will find that nothing is independent of the mind of the perceiver. A truly awakened teacher could freeze certain sections for the edification of his students if he chose.

By normal standards everything would die if you suspended activity; but it does not die, for there is nothing outside of your perception of it. Take your boss or an employee and represent them to yourself as you want them to be, and believe in the reality of the foundation stone, and then you will not make haste to bring it to pass. For Imagination is creating reality, and in a way no one knows it will be brought to pass if you remain faithful to that foundation stone. It makes no difference who you are or what you have. The man who cannot always sign a check to realize a dream is better off, for he is more awake; for he must use the talent God gave him, which is God himself. If I can always put pressure on someone to get what I want, I will never know I am this machine. But if I have to do it all within myself, then I know.

A story was told me tonight of a man who had lost his wife at the birth of his son, and the child was taken to St. Louis to be brought up by his wife's sister. This man had tried for seven years to get enough ahead to take a trip to St. Louis to see the child. He constantly tried to see himself getting a job with more money so he could make the trip. He was told that by the right use of this law he should only see

Lecture 4 – The Foundation Stone – Imagination

himself with his child and let the way be left to God. Following this he was given a job that took him from Los Angeles to New Orleans. But that was not near St. Louis. He took the job and persisted in his dream, and in three months he was transferred to the St. Louis run and given a twenty-four hour layover there every week.

The best thing that ever happened to me was when I was fired from Macy's during the depression. I might be captain of the elevators if I had stayed there. My father lost everything he owned, and that proved to be the beginning of the great dream he brought to pass. One person believed in him and he started on that, and when he made his exit last October, he had given to his community much that no one had ever given before. The blackest day of his life turned out to be the bright day of his life. No matter what you have done, forget it. You are God and God is untarnished, for he is all imagining.

Now, you start to imagine and make it something of which you can be proud. Make it big. If it is truly the stone being laid in Zion, do not turn to any argument of man. You be faithful, and whatever you put on the stone as an imaginal activity will come into your world. Of course, you may go back to the world of men, like Peter. He denied the stone three times but he did then return to it again. You may do that, but in the end you will learn, for in the depth of your being the words are being said: "Get behind me, Satan." But I have seen people forget. I have seen them rise from nothing to great heights and then say: "It would have happened anyway." They do not believe that their imaginal activity was the foundation on which they built that structure. There is only one stone and that is your wonderful Imagination.

Lecture 4 – The Foundation Stone – Imagination

This works better if you do not try to aid it on the outside, for it is not flesh and blood that revealed it to you. You got it from the Christ.

Now let us go into the silence.

Lecture 5 – The Secret of Imagining

Lecture 5

Neville Goddard – (Circa 1960)
The Secret of Imagining

It may seem incredible, but it is true, the world in which we live, is the world of Imagination. In fact, life itself is an activity of imagining. All that we behold, though it appears without, it is within, in our Imagination, of which this world of mortality, is but a shadow. Nothing appears or continues in being, by a power of its own. Events happen, because comparatively stable imaginal activity created them, and they continue in being, only as long as they receive such support.

Therefore the secret of imagining, is the greatest of all problems, to the solution of which, everyone should aspire. For supreme power, supreme wisdom and supreme joy, lie in the solution of this great mystery. When man solves the mystery of imagining, he will have discovered the secret of causation, and that is, imagining creates reality. Divine imagining and human imagining are not two powers at all, but one. The valid distinction which exists between them, lies not in the substance which they operate, but in the degree of intensity of the operant power itself.

Acting at high tension, an imaginal act, is an immediate objective fact. Keyed low, an imaginal act, is realized in the time processed.

Human history, with its forms of government, its revolutions, its wars, and in fact the rise and fall of nations, could be written in terms of the imaginal activities of men and women. All imaginative men and women, are forever

Lecture 5 – The Secret of Imagining

casting forth enchantment, and all passive men and women, who have no powerful imaginative lives, are continually passing under the spell of their power. If Imagination is the only thing that acts, or is, in existing beings or men, as Blake believes, then we should never be certain it was not some woman, treading in the wine press, who began that subtle change in men's minds, or that the passion, because of which the Earth has been drenched in blood, did not begin in the Imagination of some Sheppard boy lighting up his eye for a moment, before it ran upon its way.

The future, is the imaginal activity of man, in its creative march, imagining is the creative power, not only of the poet, the artist, the actor and orator, but of the scientist, the inventor, the merchant and the artisan. It's of use in unrestrained, unlovely image making, is obvious. But its abuse in undo repression, breathes of sterility, which robs a man of actual wealth of experience. Imagining novel solutions, to ever more complex problems, is far more noble than to restrain or kill out the desire. Light is the continuing solution of a continuously synthetic problem. Imagining creates events.

Our world, created out of men's imagining, comprise unnumbered warring beliefs. Therefore there can never be a perfect stable or static state. Today's events are bound to disturb our yesterdays established order. Imaginative men and women invariably unsettle a pre-existing peace of mind. Hold fast to your ideal in your Imagination, nothing can take it from you, but your failure to persist in imagining the ideal realized. Imagine only such states that are of value or promise well. To attempt to change circumstances, before we change our imaginal activity, is to struggle against the very nature of things. There can be no outer change, until there is

Lecture 5 – The Secret of Imagining

first an imaginal change. Everything we do unaccompanied by an imaginal change, is but futile readjustment of surfaces.

Imagining the wish fulfilled brings about a union, with that state, and during that union, we behave in keeping with our imaginal change. This shows us that an imaginal change will result in a change of behavior. However, our ordinary imaginal alterations, as we pass from one state to another, are not transformations, because each of them is so rapidly succeeded by another, in the reverse direction. But whenever one state grows so stable, as to become our constant mood, our habitual attitude, then that habitual state defines our character and is a true transformation.

Now let me call your attention to the design on the cover of this record. You will notice a man sitting on a park bench, imagining himself being in a home. This is the secret of those who lie in bed awake, while they dream things true. They know how to live in their own dream house, until in fact, they do. Man, through the medium of a controlled waking dream, can predetermine his future. That imaginal activity, of living in the feeling of the wish fulfilled, leads man across a bridge of incidents, to the fulfillment of the dream.

If we live in the dream, thinking from it, and not of it, then the creative power of imagining will answer our adventurous fancy and the wish fulfilled will break in upon us and take us unaware. Man is all Imagination, Therefore man must be, where he is, in Imagination, for his Imagination is himself.

To realize that Imagination is not something tied to the senses, or enclosed within the special boundary of the body,

Lecture 5 – The Secret of Imagining

is most important. For though man moves about in space, by movement of his physical body, he need not be so restricted. He can move by a change in what he is aware of. However real the scene, on which sight rests, man can gaze in one never before witnessed. He can always remove the mountain, if it upsets his concept of what life ought to be.

This ability to mentally move, from things as they are, to things as they ought to be, is one of the most important discoveries that man can make. It reveals man as the center of imagining, with powers of intervention, which enable him to alter the course of observed events. Moving from success to success, through a series of mental transformations, of nature, of others and himself.

How does he do it? Self abandonment, that is the secret. He has to abandon himself mentally to his wish fulfilled, in his love for that state, and in so doing, live in the new state and no more in the old state. Now we can't commit ourselves to what we do not love, so the secret of self commission is Faith plus Love. Faith is believing what is incredible. We commit ourselves to the feeling of the wish fulfilled. In Faith, that this act of self commission, will become a reality, and it will, because imagining creates reality. Imagination is both conservative and transformative. It is conservative, when it builds its world from images supplied by memory, and the evidence of the senses.

It is creatively transformative when it imagines things as they ought to be, building its world out of the generous dreams of fancy. In the procession of images, the ones that take precedent, naturally are those of the senses. Nevertheless a present sense impression is only an image, it does not differ in nature from a memory image or the image

Lecture 5 – The Secret of Imagining

of a wish. What makes a present sense impression so objectively real, is the individuals Imagination functioning in it and thinking from it. Whereas in a memory of it or a wish, the individual's Imagination is not functioning in it and thinking from it, but is functioning out of it and thinking of it.

If the individual would enter into the image, in his Imagination, as a design on the cover of this record suggests, then would he know what it is to be creatively transformative, then would he realize his wish and then he would be happy.

Every image can be embodied, but unless man himself enters the image and thinks from it, it is incapable of birth. Therefore it is the height of folly, to expect the wish to be realized, by the mere passage of time. That which requires imaginative occupancy, to produce its effect, obviously cannot be effective, without such occupancy.

We cannot be in one image and not suffer the consequences of not being in another. Imagination is spiritual sensation. Enter the image of the wish fulfilled, then give it sensory vividness and tones of reality, by mentally acting, as you would act, were it a physical fact. Now this is what I mean by spiritual sensation. Imagine that you are holding a rose in your hand, smell it, do you detect the odor of roses?

Well if the rose is not here, why is its fragrance in the air? To spiritual sensation, that is, to imaginal sight, sound, scent, taste and touch, man can give to image, sensory vividness. If he does, all things will conspire to aid his harvesting and on reflection, he will see how subtle with a

Lecture 5 – The Secret of Imagining

thread, that led to his goal. He could have never devised the means, which is imaginal activity, which is used to fulfill itself.

If man longs to escape from his present sense sensation, to transform his present life, into a dream of might well be, he has but to imagine that he is already what he wants to be and then feel the way he would expect to feel, under such circumstances. Let him, like the make believe of a child, who has been making the world after its own heart, create his world out of pure dreams of fancy. Let him mentally enter into his dream, let him mentally do what he would actually do, were it physically true. He will discover that dreams are realized, not by the rich, but by the imaginative.

Nothing stands between man and the fulfillment of his dream, but facts, and facts are the creations of imagining. If man changes his imagining, he will change the facts . Man and his past, are one continuous structure. This structure contains all of the facts, which have been conserved and still operate below the threshold of his surface mind. For him, it is merely history, for him it seems unalterable, a dead and permanently fixed past, but for itself it is living, it is part of the living age.

He cannot leave behind him the mistakes of the past, for nothing disappears. Everything that has been is still in existence. The past still exists, and it gives . . and still gives . . its results. Man must go back in memory, seek for and destroy the causes of evil, however far back they lie. This going into the past and replaying a scene of the past in Imagination as it ought to have been played the first time, I call revision . . and revision results in repeal.

Lecture 5 – The Secret of Imagining

Changing our life means changing the past.

The causes of any present evil, are the unrevised scenes of the past. The past and the present form the whole structure of man; it is carrying all of its contents with it. Any alteration of content will result in an alteration in the present and future. Live nobly . . so that mind can store a past well worthy of recall. Should you fail to do so, remember, the first act of correction or cure is always . . "revise." If the past is recreated into the present, so will the revised past be recreated into the present, or else the promise... that though your sins are like scarlet, they shall be as white as snow, is a lie.

The question may arise as to how, by representing others to ourselves, as better than they really were, or mentally rewriting a letter to make it conform to our wish, or by revising the scene of an accident, the interview with the employer, and so on . . could change what seems to be the unalterable facts of the past, but remember my claims for imagining: Imagining Creates Reality.

What it makes, it can unmake. It is not only conservative, building a life from images supplied by memory, it is also creatively transformative, altering a theme already in being. The parable of the unjust steward, gives the answer to this question. We can alter our world by means of a certain "illegal" practice, by means of a falsification of the facts, that is, by means of a certain intentional alteration of that which we have experienced. All this is done in one's own Imagination. This is a form of falsehood which not only is not condemned, but is actually approved in the gospel teaching. By means of such a falsehood, a man destroys the causes of evil and acquires friends and on the strength of this revision

Lecture 5 – The Secret of Imagining

proves, judging by the high praise the unjust steward received from his master, that he is deserving of confidence.

Because imagining creates reality, we can carry revision to the extreme and revise a scene, that would be otherwise, unforgivable. We learn to distinguish between man . . who is all Imagination, from those states into which he may enter.

An unjust steward, looking at another's distress, will represent the other to himself, as he ought to be seen, were he himself in need, he would, like the man on the cover of this record, enter his dream house, in his Imagination and imagine what he would see and how things would seem and how people would act, after these things should be.

Then, in this state he would fall asleep, feeling the way he would expect to feel, under such circumstances. Would that all the Lord's people, were unjust stewards, mentally falsifying the facts of life, to deliver individuals, forevermore. For the imaginal change goes forward, until at length the altered pattern is realized on the heights of attainment. Our future is our imaginal activity in its creative march. Imagine better than the best you know.

Now let us go into the silence.

Lecture 6 – Is Christ Your Imagination

Lecture 6

Neville Goddard 03-22-1963
Is Christ Your Imagination

Tonight's subject is in the form of a question: "Is Christ your Imagination?" When we ask the question we expect the answer in terms of our current background of thought, and quite often that is not adequate to frame the answer. Now, I am asking the question, and in order to answer myself, I should really clarify the terms, "Imagination" and "Christ" I think there will be no problem tonight if I define . . say . . "Imagination." I think you will agree with me when I define "Christ."

If I say to that, that Imagination is the power of performing mental images, you wouldn't quarrel with that. Sitting here tonight, you can think of anything and see it mentally. You may not see it as graphically as you see it in its present form, in the room at the moment, but you could see it vividly in the mind's eye and discriminate. Think of a tree, a horse, and you know the difference between one and the other, and they are two separate objects in your mind's eye. Well, that is the power of Imagination.

When it comes to Christ . . and there are hundreds of millions in the world that call themselves Christians . . the very use of the word instantly conjures, in the mind's eye, a person. They think of Christ as a person, and no two have the same mental picture of this person. I know, many, many years ago in New York City, this French artist went to the library on 42nd street and brought up 46 different pictures of Christ and screened them with his little lantern. No two

Lecture 6 – Is Christ Your Imagination

were alike, and each artist claimed that this was an inspired picture, as it was presented to him, and he painted the picture.

There were blond and blue-eyed pictures, dark swarthy skin; there were those with a very black skin . . all 46 pictures were projected as so-called originals. So, man has been conditioned to believe that Christ is a person. So I ask the question: "Is Christ your Imagination?" Can I personify the Imagination? I will.

Let us go back to the Bible. What does the Bible say of Christ? In Paul's first letter to the Corinthians (I will just give you the highlights) he defines Christ as: "The power and the wisdom of God." In John 1 (which brings Christology to its height, as far as the Bible goes . . there is no single book that takes the secret of Christ and brings it to this height as you will find in the Gospel of John) . . in the Gospel of John, speaking now of this presence that was with God, his meaning, his power: "By Him all things were made and without Him was not anything made that was made." It is the power and yet it is wisdom. So here is a creative power.

If I take that now and analyze myself in another world, the sign goes to the end of the second letter to the Corinthians. He calls upon all of us who would read that letter: "Test yourself. Do you not realize that Jesus Christ is in thee?" Here we are told: "All things were made by Him." He is the power of God and the wisdom of God. Every attribute of God is personified. So his power is personified, and may I confess I have seen that power . . and it is a man. I have seen that wisdom . . and it is a man. And when you stand in the presence of that personified aspect of infinite being, you know you are standing in the presence of infinite might. It is

Lecture 6 – Is Christ Your Imagination

not just power, it is almightiness, and you stand in the presence . . and yet it is a man. So here he calls it the power and the wisdom.

Now he asks me, and you who read his letter, to test ourselves: "Test yourself, do you not realize that Jesus Christ is in thee." And he made all these things . . well then, let us put him to the test in us. I say he is our Imagination, that is the power, the creative power of the universe. Look around. Do you know anything in the world of man that man has created . . from the clothes that he wears to the homes that he inhabits . . that wasn't first imagined? Do you know of anything in this world that is now proved as fact, as a concrete reality, that wasn't first imagined . . only imagined, and then it externalized?

Yes, using hands, using implements of the world, but it first began as an image, and an image is simply the product of this reforming image-making faculty in man, which is man's Imagination. Now, if "All things were made by him and without him was not anything made that was made," I can't come to any other conclusion than the fact that Christ of scripture, is my Imagination.

Now who is Jesus? If Christ is the power and the wisdom of God, and God sunk himself in us, that was his sacrifice. He actually became us that we may live; for were it not for this sacrifice of God, to actually limit himself to the state called "man," man would . . like the earth . . wear out like a garment. As we are told in Isaiah 51:6: "Lift up your eyes to the heavens, and look at the earth beneath; for the heavens will vanish like smoke, the earth will wear out like a garment, and they who dwell in it will do likewise; but my salvation will be forever and my deliverance will never be

Lecture 6 – Is Christ Your Imagination

ended." That word "salvation" means Jesus. The word "Jesus" is "Jehovah saves." That is salvation. That is forever. Were it not that God became man that man may become God, to save man and lift him up to immortality, because the promise is: "The earth will wear out like a garment."

Our scientists tell us today that the sun is melting in radiation. If it took unnumbered billions of years, if it started a process of melting, no matter how long it takes it has an end, and with its end we have our end as part of the system. So we, walking the earth, always have an end. To stop that process of bringing man to an end: "My salvation will be forever and my deliverance will never have an end."

So, God became man that man may become God. In becoming man (as God is the only creative power in the world) what in me creates? My Imagination. I may not have the talent to put it on paper, I may not have the ability to execute it the way artists can, but I can imagine it. I can imagine a book and the joy of having a book. I can imagine a picture. Without being an artist I can dream. I cannot conceive of a picture that a man can paint on canvas that is more alive than my dream, yet I can't put a thing on canvas.

But I go to sleep and I can dream. And what is doing it, if not my Imagination? And here when I lose the conscious faculty, this restricted area, I can actually dream. Dream as no artist in the world conveys; put color upon it, put motion upon it, and have the most wonderful drama . . and that is my Imagination.

But this is not the only power and wisdom of God. In the greatest of all the New Testament, which is John, John does not emphasize the power. He states in the beginning . . yes,

Lecture 6 – Is Christ Your Imagination

he declares might as power . . but the emphasis is not on power; it is on redemption and revelation. Revelation in John's gospel is an act of God in self-revealing. So, in the first chapter he tells us what this power will do for us. First of all there are two endings to John.

Let us take the real ending, which is the 20th chapter, the first ending, and whoever the writer is, who calls himself John: "Now Jesus did many other signs that are not written in this book; but these are written that you may believe that Jesus is the Christ . . and believing have life in his name." He is the power and the wisdom of God.

That is what the author is telling us in the very end. Many signs he did, but in spite of the number of the signs and the character of the signs, it did not evoke faith. The whole teaching of the Gospel of John is based upon faith and unbelief in him. Either one or the other. Have faith in him, or you disbelieve in him, and few believed in him . . few, we are told, even his disciples. only a few believed and they imperfectly.

Well now, who is Jesus? Christ is the power and the wisdom, but who is Jesus? We have this wonderful thought expressed in Paul's letter to the Philippians. "Though he was in the form of God, he did not consider equality with God a thing to be grasped, but he emptied himself, taking the form of a slave, being born in the likeness of men." That identifies man with a slave, every man. "And being found in human form he humbled himself and became obedient unto death, even death on a cross. Therefore God has highly exalted him and bestowed on him the name" (not an indefinite article) "which is above every name, that at the name of Jesus every knee should bow, in heaven and on earth and under the

Lecture 6 – Is Christ Your Imagination

earth, and every tongue confess that Jesus Christ is Lord, to the glory of God the Father." He gave him the name, and it is above every name, and at that name every power in the world must bend, at the name of names. That is the name called Jesus, which is Jehovah. Jesus simply is Jehovah's name.

Every child born of woman in this world one day wears that name. There is only one name, only one being: Jesus. You go through the same story as told us in the gospel . . everyone will . . and when he passes through this series of events, that name is conferred. Conferred on the risen Christ. That power is latent in man, that is man's Imagination. Where it is lifted up, on that risen Christ, the name Jesus . . the divine name, Jesus . . is conferred, and that individual then enters a new age.

An entirely different age that is immortal, eternal, because until the end of that age we are still subject to being worn out like a garment . . as told us in the 51st chapter of Isaiah. So everyone is moving on that wheel that is being worn out, wearing out like a garment and vanishing like smoke, like the heavens. But not one will fail, for God redeems us and God resurrects us, one after the other, lifts us up and confers on that risen Christ the name . . the name, Jesus.

When Blake was asked quite innocently about the mysterious name: "What do you think of Jesus?" without batting an eye, Blake replied: "Jesus is the only God," and then hastened to add: "But so am I, and so are you." So in the end, all believed the name where the power . . all Christ in man . . is lifted up, lifted up so that the whole vast wonderful being that was sunk in man is now awake. What that body is like, I can't describe it to anyone. I can't find

Lecture 6 – Is Christ Your Imagination

words to describe the glory that is yours, for everyone. It certainly isn't this, I assure you, yet I will know you and you will know me in eternity. But for all the sameness of identity we will actually know each other. There will be a radical discontinuity of form (not the form I now wear here today and have for the last fifty-eight years) . . but identity . . yes, you will know me.

But how to display the glory of the being that you are when you are resurrected? This is shown us by the Sadducees, who do not believe in the resurrection. They are the modern scientists. The Sadducees of 2,000 years ago were the wise men. The Pharisees were the priesthood of the world. The Sadducees were the intellectual giants of that day and they . . any more than today . . could not even believe in survival, far less resurrection. Like the world today puts the two words together and they speak of survival as resurrection . . and they are not. Survival is continuity; resurrection is discontinuity. You leave the field completely and enter the worlds of eternity.

So they ask the question based upon the law of Moses, and Moses said: "If a man's brother dies, leaving a wife but no children, the man must take the wife and raise up children for his brother. Now there were seven brothers; the first took a wife, and died without children; the second and the third took her, and likewise all seven left no children and died. Afterward the woman also died. In the resurrection, therefore, whose wife will the woman be?". It is a fable, because they did not believe in the resurrection. "And Jesus said to them, "The sons of this age marry and are given in marriage; but those who are accounted worthy to attain to that age and to the resurrection from the dead neither marry nor are given in marriage, for they cannot die anymore,

Lecture 6 – Is Christ Your Imagination

because they are equal to angels and are sons of God, being sons of the resurrection."

They are completely above the organization of sex. What we call sex here, this garment of flesh, are shadows thrown by this fabulous being above. And the body you really have, you are told (as I quoted earlier): "Being in the form of God, did not count equality with God a thing to be grasped, but emptied himself, taking the form of a slave, being born in the likeness of men, didn't think it strange. And being found in human form he humbled himself and became obedient unto death, even death on a cross." And then to find himself with all the limitations of man, all the weaknesses of man, everything that is man? Then God exalted him at the end when he resurrected him and gives him the name. That name is conferred only at resurrection.

So, everyone will get it, for everyone will be resurrected. Then you will not be wearing these bodies, wonderful as they are for us, filled with all the passions of the world, and they are all wonderful . . but it is not the body you will wear. You will be completely above the organization of sex. No need for this kind of creativity. Imagination becomes completely awake and you will create at will, and your imaginal act will become an immediate objective fact. And what we call reality today, all this fabulous world of ours . . may I tell you I have seen it . . it is all Imagination.

When man has played his part and God has completed his purpose (which is to bring forth from us himself and make us all gods with him) then these garments . . made up of all the elements that feel so permanent and so wonderful . . they will vanish like smoke. There isn't an element that wasn't brought into being by the creative power of God, by

Lecture 6 – Is Christ Your Imagination

his own wonderful divine imagining, and it is sustained in me because he sustains it by his imaginal act. When he ceases that imaginal act all the elements will melt, all vanish, and the world will be as though it never existed. But you and I will be lifted up above it all into an entirely different world, an eternal world.

So is Christ your Imagination? I say Christ is the power and the wisdom of God, and this power and this wisdom creates everything in the world. I can trace to my own being an imaginal act that became fact, then I repeated it and it became fact. If I can repeat it and repeat it, and these imaginal acts externalize themselves in facts, then I have found it. Found that power in myself, for the Bible calls him Christ and personifies it and speaks of this presence as a man . . but that man is Jesus. Jesus Christ is simply the resurrected being that is God now, because he has resurrected the power within him, which is Christ. Now he is called "the Lord," and everything should bow before him when it happens. I say to you: the day will come you will have the experience, and you will be startled. No one will believe you; they aren't going to believe you anymore than they believed the first person to whom it happened. He is the first that rose from the dead, but no one believed him. Up to the very end who would believe the story?

They were looking for a different kind of Messiah, a conquering hero who would come just like a man out of some glorious background of warriors, and then conquer the enemy of Israel and lead Israel to some victorious end. They always look for that kind of a Messiah. We have them all over the world today, these false Messiah's who promise the nations they will lead them to some victory, even a little temporary victory. That's not Messiah. Messiah hasn't a

Lecture 6 – Is Christ Your Imagination

thing to do with this world; he is resurrected out of this world. This world is vanishing, wearing out just like a garment. Christ in man is the power and the wisdom; and then, that in man that is man's Imagination, becomes a mercy because he exercises it lovingly.

If I read John correctly, not only my salvation is dependent on it; I must actually believe in him. Who is the being? My own Imagination. If I don't believe and test it . . even though I fail . . well then, I don't believe in Christ, for Christ is really my Imagination, your Imagination. So you imagine something lovely of another, and if you don't believe in the reality of that Imagination, then you don't believe in Christ. Though you can go to church every day and give ten per cent of your income to the church of your choice . . all these things are lovely, give them if you feel that way about it . . but that is not Christ. That is not believing in Christ.

To believe in Christ is to see someone in this world, and have a sweet feeling towards that one that hasn't yet realized how to be lovely, something without his knowledge. Then represent him to yourself as though it were true, and believe in the reality of what you have done mentally. Believe in Christ, for all things are possible to Christ. Bring him before your mind's eye and see him as he would like to be seen by himself, as he would like the world to see him. But you do it and believe in the reality of what you have done. That is believing in Christ.

You will be surprised beyond measure how it works. At that very moment, because: "All things by a law Divine in one another's being mingle." At that very moment that you interfere with his life, you reshuffle the entire deck, and all things will completely rearrange to mirror the change that is

Lecture 6 – Is Christ Your Imagination

going to take place in him; and everyone in this world who can aid that change will be used to bring it about without their knowledge or consent. You don't need the consent of any being in the world; if they can be used to externalize what you have imagined, they will be used. And when you least expect it, because you believe in Him, then God resurrects you. Then you will live it out, and you stand bewildered when you see what God did for you.

Everything claimed of him that you thought, that your mother taught you, happened 2000 years ago . . it is happening. It didn't stop. Go back and read Paul's letter to Timothy: "Those who teach that the resurrection is past are misleading the faithful." It isn't a past: it took place in one, and it is taking place in unnumbered. It's all over, the crucifixion is over, yes . . but not the resurrection.

The resurrection is taking place in everyone that is called and lifted up. As we are called, God's mightiest act is performed. and we are lifted up and pass through the series of events leading into the kingdom of heaven. Though we seemingly remain here still wearing this garment for a little while, the garment will be shown you that you will occupy. You can't describe it to anyone, even to your own satisfaction. It is such a living thing, so luminous; it is just light, like the rainbow. You can't describe it to any being in this world who thinks only in terms of a garment of flesh.

Now we are told in the 1st chapter of John . . he is speaking of an entirely different kind of birth: "And those who believe in his name will be born, not of blood, nor the will of the flesh nor of the will of man, but of God." Not born in any that this (the body) is born. "Flesh and blood cannot inherit the kingdom of God," only Spirit. When you are born,

Lecture 6 – Is Christ Your Imagination

you are self-begotten. You have actually no parents. You come right out of a grain, the mystery of the grain of wheat that falls into the ground. If it doesn't fall into the ground it remains alone; if it falls into the ground, it bears much fruit. The mystery of life through death, for God actually died to become you, to become me.

God is divine Imagination and he limits himself to the very limit of contraction, called human Imagination, and actually dies in the sense that all the power and all the memory of his glorious being had to be completely forgotten. So the cry on the cross is true: "My God, my God, why hast thou forsaken me." He himself has cried out, because he so completely gave himself to us he suffered total amnesia, complete forgetfulness of his divinity as he became us, and that was divine imagining becoming human imagining.

Then we, building our little world . . lovely as it is to many of us . . it is so different, and the power we exercise is so fragile, compared with that same power when raised up, when lifted up and the great name which is above all names is conferred upon us. And the day will come, without loss of identity you will bear the name "Jesus." Everyone is destined to be Christ Jesus . . that power, with the name exercising infinite power . . without loss of identity. We will know each other and all glorified, everyone. There is no limitation to the gift. Some will exercise it more than others, but certainly the gift is the same, the gift of Christ Jesus.

So my question, as far as I am personally concerned: "Is Christ your Imagination?" I say: yes. And yet don't limit it only to power and wisdom, for the emphasis is not on power and wisdom . . it is on redemption, revelation. He reveals himself, and in that very first chapter, the prologue of John.

Lecture 6 – Is Christ Your Imagination

The first eighteen verses are the prologue, and in the very last of the 18th verses he shows you the revelation: "No man has seen God at any time, but the son in the bosom of the father, he has made him known."

No one has seen him, but in the bosom of the father there is a son, and he reveals the father. Then we are told in the 10th chapter of Luke: "No one knows the son except the father. No one knows the father except the son and anyone to whom the son chooses to reveal him." There will come that moment in time when the son reveals you, and you will know your name is Jesus Christ the Lord, for the son is going to call you, "My Lord." He is actually going to call you his father, his Lord, the rock of his salvation, and then you will know who you are.

I can tell you from now to the ends of time, but I can't tell you the condition that experience will carry when it happens. And when it happens to you, it will make no difference to you if all the wise people in the world rise in opposition and tell you: you started from some grand little amoeba. It will make no difference to you whatsoever. This is revelation, and the whole thing is lifted . . the veil is lifted . . and now you know why you couldn't see the face of the father. You can see him only reflected in the Son. There is no mirror to reflect the consciousness of the Son. You can't see your face because you are mirrored on earth; but that is not the face, and you only know your face in the beauty of your son. So, everyone in the world is destined to bear the name of Christ Jesus, the Lord.

Now let us go into the silence.

Lecture 7 – Imagination, My Slave

Lecture 7

Neville Goddard 2-13-1967
Imagination, My Slave

I would like to make this series as productive and as helpful as the fall series. For I feel in the fall series that we reached a very high watermark. Not only in what we've accomplished in the world of Caesar but in the spiritual life. Everything here is geared toward a center and that center is God and where are we in relationship to God.

So, we accomplish not only the changes we desire in this outer world, but the real change between the surface mind of ours and the deeper self, which is God. And to accomplish that, I must ask you to do what we did last fall: to share with me your dreams and your visions, and your experiences as you apply this law to accomplish changes in this outer world. That makes it far more real, more wonderful. And if you will share with me, things, we'll all be mutually encouraged by each other's faith.

If you have the faith enough to apply it . . when you come up against it, then tell me what happened, so I can then, from the platform tell others. It will encourage those who are present to try it and, therefore, increase their faith. So share with me your dreams. For God is speaking to man through the medium of dreams and when I chose the word God, here, let me make it quite clear. When I use the word Lord, God, Jehovah, Jesus, Christ, I AM, Imagination, to me they are synonymous and interchangeable.

Lecture 7 – Imagination, My Slave

I do not have a God stuck off in space that differs from the one I speak of as I AM. When I speak of Imagination, I speak of God; I speak of Jehovah; I speak of Jesus; I speak of Christ. So, these terms, to me, are synonymous and interchangeable. When I say that Jesus Christ is my deeper self, I could say Imagination is my deeper self and yet my slave for purposes of his own. I personify Imagination for I AM a person, and my real being is all Imagination.

Therefore, Imagination, to me, is a person. But this deeper self, and for purposes of his own, he is my slave. So I say he waits upon me, upon you, he waits upon all of us . . swiftly, impersonally, without any effort whatsoever. When our will is evil or when it is good; it makes no difference to the deep of myself. I AM in a state and I AM thinking unlovely thoughts; but he waits upon me just as quickly. And he will conjure for me images of evil out of the nowhere. Let me change the state and feel myself in a state of love, of good, and the same presence will conjure for me, instantly, images of love.

So he waits upon me so quickly; so swiftly. No matter what I AM on the surface of this being, he conjures and radiates through me, upon the screen of space, all that I AM imagining. So I say the entire outer world is solely produced through imagining. If my outer world is produced solely through imagining, then I cannot change the outer world without changing the imagining.

How long will it take? As long as it takes me to change the state I'm imagining. So I imagine I AM this, that, or the other. I don't like what I'm seeing and I hate to admit it's caused by what I'm imagining. If it is caused by imagining, it will take no longer to change it than it takes me to change

Lecture 7 – Imagination, My Slave

what I AM imagining. Is it true? I ask you to test it. See if it works . . if there is evidence for it, does it really matter what the world thinks? If tonight you test it, and it proves itself in performance, will it really matter what anyone in this world thinks about this concept? Not if it proves itself in performance. So I ask you to test it.

Tonight I will share with you one man's experience. One of his many responsibilities in his present job is publishing a magazine. It's very high quality in workmanship and it's brought out in four colors. Before the last issue was to be prepared he became bored and tired with it and did nothing about the content of the magazine. Two weeks before the date of publication, here he was without anything and he had to start from scratch to get the magazine out in two weeks . . practically impossible.

Sitting in his office he said, although it didn't mean anything to him, if it came out or not, it means so much to so many people, especially his boss, he was being extremely selfish. Something happened in him and he became completely fired with bringing it out. He said it seemed that stories, art, articles . . everything . . just came through the walls. He wrote three short pieces himself with so much enthusiasm. He then edited all the articles, stories, all the things to be used and then the men who had never worked on this publication before were assigned to get the whole thing out.

Photographers were taken off their jobs and sent out on assignments and his printers, typographers and everyone else concerned worked three shifts of the two weeks left and they brought it out.

Lecture 7 – Imagination, My Slave

How did it start? Before he started, this is what he did. He knew he couldn't bring out a magazine in four colors in two weeks without any stories, articles, editorial comment, etc., so he created a scene in which he saw his boss holding the issue, with the date sign on it. His boss had an expression on his face that implied complete satisfaction with what he was seeing. Then he heard his boss tell him it was the best issue they had ever published.

During that two-week interval, when his mind would falter, he went back to that one picture of his boss and heard him praise him for the work he had done. He held to the end. The end is where we begin. The end is my beginning. We're always imagining ahead of our efforts. We go to the end . . no matter what it is we want . . we go to the end. And it calls everything in this world to fulfill itself.

Came the day when the magazine was published. His boss praised him like he'd never praised him before. He said it was the best issue they had ever brought out . . just as he had imagined it. And as he had imagined it, it happened in the outer world as fact. When the magazine was out and mailed he went by his boss's office and his boss was happy but skeptical. His boss said he felt they had mailed it out a few days too early . . two weeks to bring out a four-color magazine and his boss felt it was mailed a few days too soon!

The above story and the following stories are related. His dry cleaner, whom he likes very much, lost the trousers to his best and most expensive suit. He was beside himself and although the cleaner searched his plant three times, he couldn't find the pants. The cleaner told him to make out a claim but he didn't want money, he wanted his pants.

Lecture 7 – Imagination, My Slave

On the next day, driving to and from his work, he felt the fabric of those trousers on his leg. He also felt it with his imaginary fingers. The next day the dry cleaner called his wife to tell her he had found the pants pinned to a suit that was ready for delivery to another person. So the pants were returned.

So here is the picture and listen to it carefully and apply it to what you will hear this night. It was the Christmas season, and he felt very generous and extravagant; he bought dozens of presents and made out dozens of checks. One day a merchant called his wife to tell her a check she had given him had bounced. She called and told him, and he was beside himself. He knew he had hundreds of dollars more than was necessary in his account. He knew there must have been a mistake. But when he checked his bank statement, which had come a few days before, his face was red and he was humiliated. He had made an enormous error in subtraction and there were no funds.

There was no place for him to turn and the next paycheck was weeks off. Where could he turn to get the money immediately? He wrestled with the problem long after bedtime. He thought of going to his bank the next day, and explain what happened; and then he knew he must have some imaginary image that he could believe. HE MUST HAVE AN IMAGINARY IMAGE HE COULD BELIEVE IN . . an imaginal act he could believe in.

He said he could believe in imagining that God was bringing it to pass in the best way for everyone involved; those whom he had unwittingly deceived; those whom he had planned to send presents to and now could not; for everyone involved, everything would be all right.

Lecture 7 – Imagination, My Slave

So he fell asleep in the assumption that God was bringing about the best solution for everyone involved.

The next morning when he got up and started toward the bank, he wasn't altogether sure, so he went back to that assumption that God is bringing about the best solution for everyone. He went to the bank and the cashier sent him to a Vice President who listened to his story and told him he should see the Assistant Manager, who asked him nothing. He just looked him over and asked when he thought he could aright this situation. He told the manager the date of his paycheck and he said, all right, all the checks will be taken care of. He didn't ask him how many checks were yet to be taken care of!

Two days later he received an extra bonus from his boss almost ten times the amount of money due for his checks and one of the reasons was because of the outstanding work he had done on the magazine. And when he received the check he was wearing the suit . . lost pants and all!

The next day he went to the bank and made a deposit and he was wearing the suit, and he thought it would be only decent to stop and thank the Assistant Manager for his kindness. He recognized on his face a certain sadness. The Manager said it was because they had not been able to do anything for him as no new checks had come in for them to take care of.

At the end of the letter he said I must tell you imagining creates reality. There is nothing I can do or say to you but "thanks". And it seems so inadequate.

Lecture 7 – Imagination, My Slave

May I tell him, and you, there is nothing you can do for me more than to share with me such experiences. Nothing you can do would please me more. If he had sent me a check, I would have spent it. I have spent everything I have ever earned or what was given me except what my father gave me. And if that were not the family estate I would have spent it long ago.

But I can't spend experiences. I can only share them. I can tell my friends in New York, in Barbados, in San Francisco. This is like the stories in the Bible. This is taking God's principle and proving it. For his Imagination is God. Your Imagination is God. Let me repeat it. God, Jehovah, the Lord God, Jesus, Christ, I AM, Imagination, they are all interchangeable.

So I say that imagining is like the creative power in me. "The great creative power of the universe is like imagining in me and underlies all of my faculties, including my perception. But it streams into my surface mind least disguised in the form of productive fancy."

So when he sat there and there was no magazine, no articles . . not a thing . . and he felt embarrassed and selfish, and that he was letting down all those people who depended on him, he took the end. That's productive fancy. He saw his boss reading the magazine and heard him say it was the best issue yet. He found a scene in which he could believe and all the articles and stories, and art came pouring in. Everything moved forward to the fulfillment of that state.

So, I tell you, imagining does create reality. If you would find God, stop thinking of a little term. You know what he is. He's your own human Imagination and he's speaking to you

Lecture 7 – Imagination, My Slave

moment after moment through desire. He is speaking in the depths of your soul, through dreams and through visions, and you can tell through your dreams and visions what level you are on relative to God. Everything is relative to God. It isn't relative to anything on the outside world for all that is shadows. It's all relative to God

So where do I stand relative to him? Everything, the most insignificant dream to the outer world, has profound significance to you to whom it is spoken and to God who speaks it to you. And the God in you is your own self. Let me repeat: Jesus Christ is my deeper self and yet my slave. He is the one enslaved in me for purposes of his own and he waits upon me as impartially and as swiftly when my ideas and my thoughts, and my desires are evil as when they are good. He will conjure for me in the twinkling of an eye, ideas of good and evil by the call of my desire. Also, let me wish something and instantly the idea is accomplished. They'll say it came out of your wonderful Imagination. I say that is Jehovah, if you prefer, rather than Jesus Christ. I tell you it is the LORD God. It is your own wonderful human Imagination. That is God. And when you learn to fall in love with it, because he's enslaved himself . . poured himself . . in you, for you aren't really two, you are an extension of himself being called back level by level by level until finally you are one; you aren't two.

So we are called back from an expulsion. It was a self-expulsion, and we are now called back through these infinite levels of awareness and he reveals to us, through the medium of dreams, the level on which we stand. I take scriptures and find out where I stand by a simple dream. Study scripture.

Lecture 7 – Imagination, My Slave

Paul said, "Learn from us to live by scripture". Is it there? Does it parallel your dream in any way? It doesn't have to be exactly the same thing. He's always talking to you and calling you back to himself through layer after layer until finally you reach home. You and He are one.

So this man had to have something, not only to imagine, but something he could believe. I can imagine anything. You can imagine anything. Is there something you can't imagine? Don't tell me. I can tell you the most fantastic story in the world and you can understand me, but you may not believe me. Therefore it means nothing. So he said he must find something he can imagine that he can believe in. He wanted a scene that would cause no embarrassment to anyone. He could believe in God. He could believe that God is bringing to pass now, in the best possible way for everyone involved, a solution to the situation. He knew God would do it in the best way possible. And so he went about his business the next day in the state that God would do it. He didn't question how, he knew God would do it. And in the end he received a check that was ten times the amount he needed to liquidate all the checks he had passed.

So I say, go to the end. The end is where we begin. You can go on casting shadows and trying to change shadows, and you'll go on forever and ever and you will never change that which is in the shadow. But simply remove the object, which is a state of consciousness, out of the shadow into another desirable light, and remain in it until it casts a shadow.

The shadow will not take long. You are the light of the world. "I AM the light of the world." Do you think another one is speaking? God is speaking. When I say God is speaking I

Lecture 7 – Imagination, My Slave

mean your Imagination. Your Imagination is the light of the world. He takes the light to illumine the state and the world outside is only a reflection. It's an act bearing witness to the state in which I have moved. I move into a state. I remain in that state and cast my shadow on the screen of space. When you say, suppose he does this, or that, you are giving all your power, which rightly belongs to you, to the shadow world where it does not belong.

So it's entirely up to you. If you test it tonight it will prove itself in the testing.

So please share with me your letter. Paul asks that those who heard it, those who receive the letter, to share with him, that all of them might be encouraged by each other's faith. So, if man has faith enough to try it, though tomorrow morning is the deadline, based upon Caesar's world, you can try it tonight and move into a different state so that if you have a prospective meeting with someone in the morning, a meeting in which the other person would ordinarily say "if you don't do this or that or else", then in the morning that person may not feel well, or maybe he had to go somewhere else, or maybe he's just forgotten. A thousand and one things could happen to prevent that unpleasant meeting. But everything must happen based upon what you are doing.

You are the causative power. But bear in mind that because you are the causative power, it doesn't work by itself. It works only because you are the operant power.

The next lecture will be Remembrance of Things Future. This is Ecclesiastes one hundred percent, as few in this world will accept it. Remembrance of Things Future: to show you who you really are. I tell you that you are God. I'm not

Lecture 7 – Imagination, My Slave

here to flatter you. You and I are one. God is one and here, fragmented on the surface of his dream. And then we are called back to the core. All are called back, and we are one. For we come back one by one by one. The entire outer world is solely produced by imagining. "All that you behold, though it appears without, it is within, in your Imagination, of which this world of mortality is but a shadow."

And if it is a shadow, then let me find that which is causing the shadow. And the cause of the shadow is your imaginal activity. What are we imagining, that is the cause of the shadow that we think so objectively real and is so completely independent of our conception of it. All these things seem so completely independent of our conception of it and they are all cast by our own imaginal activity.

So you get into a state of wealth or health or the state of being wanted, etc; any state, and while you remain in the state, they can do their best to rub out the shadows you are casting but they cannot rub out the cause of it all and it always reproduces itself. The whole vast world is reproducing itself, based upon the state that you occupy.

So they can't rub anything out that you are doing by rubbing out things that you do. No matter what they are doing in the outer world, it is what you are doing within yourself.

Man is all Imagination, and God is man and exists in us and we in him. The eternal body of man is the Imagination and that is God himself, the divine body of Jesus. And we, on the surface, are his master. All are the members of this one divine body and only this one body, all gathered into the unity in the one body, which is God. Call it God or Jehovah,

Lecture 7 – Imagination, My Slave

or Jesus Christ or I AM. You can say I AM or Imagination in a group like this that understands and get behind names and surfaces. But in the outer world I wouldn't use it because they wouldn't understand.

And so, if you would use the word Jehovah or Jesus, it jumps up there! But it's not living in space. It doesn't appear in time, away up there thousands of years ago in time. But it jumps if you use the word Jehovah or Jesus. But if you use the word I AM, it can't jump. There's no place you can go. You can't go outside the present moment. And if you actually show people what you mean by it, that I AM is the creative power and you create by imagining, then it's got to be here. You just can't get outside this present moment of time when you use these terms. But you can only use them in a group like this.

I AM completely awake and have been sent to tell you what I am now telling you. I'm not talking to another being, I'm only talking to myself; all are wonderful aspects of myself. All. All being withdrawn out of me. All coming back through infinite levels of awareness to the one being that I AM.

What is the most practical in this world is the most profoundly spiritual. Tie them together and reverse them. What is the most profoundly spiritual is the most practical. So he is a practical person, yet the world would call him a dreamer... sitting there doing nothing, a four-color magazine to be done and only two weeks before the deadline. Then everything is thrown in his face and he's working three shifts, and everything is at his disposal . . everything is completed and the magazine is mailed "a few days too early".

Lecture 7 – Imagination, My Slave

But just imagine the terrific intensity on his part that he gets a bonus check that is ten times the amount of money he had drawn against his checking account.

So I ask you to continue sharing with me your experiences and your dreams. That is the only way you can say thanks.

(Neville mentions here, that in future lectures, he will tell the visions of Bob Cruther and his wife and he will explain the depth of meaning in Jan's dream. He says that there is so much more to it than she is aware of.)

Question: A woman, from time to time, works with psychologically disturbed children. To them their world is real. How can she correlate their real world of theirs with the real world she creates for herself and not be one of them?

Answer: No man comes unto me except I call him. And he can only call his own. He can't call another. So here is a disturbance in my world in something that is detached from me, asking for help. I'm going to change my world. I'm going to change that shadow. But it really is reflecting some disturbance in me so I'm going to change it. No matter what the outside world thinks, there are more fashions in the world of medicine than there are in the world of clothes. The most highly flung concept of the imbalanced, or unbalanced, people is simply changeable because it is only a theory. The whole thing is in the eye of the beholder. They come to you for help. Don't try to instantly find out what is causing it. Rearrange the whole thing.

Suppose an individual now sees the world in what we would call a natural way. Persuade yourself that they do and

Lecture 7 – Imagination, My Slave

if you can believe it, that person will conform to the image. You don't treat the shadow from the outside; you treat it from the inside.

If the child is born blind, who sinned? No one. Neither the child nor his parents but that the will of God be made manifest. No one did wrong. People cannot understand that. They cannot understand that God is love, infinite love, and he can't hurt another for there is no other . . only himself.

So, in this case, it will not only depend on the imaginal act, but on one's ability to believe in the reality of the imaginal act. The potency of the imaginal act is its implication, not the imaginal act. Its potency is its implication. What does it imply? Create a scene implying the child is normal and believe it.

Neville tells the story of the teacher in New York with a problem child who was to be expelled from school. The teacher applied the principal of imagining against almost impossible odds and the situation was completely changed. The child graduated; she was not expelled and all the unpleasantness that was there before, disappeared.

If you take the people in this world, including all the doctors, physicians, vegetarians, those who drink excessively and eat excessively . . they all have the same length of time to continue. Few men take care to live well, many to live long. Yet it is within the power of any man to live well; but it is not within the power of any man to live long.

Now let us go into the silence.

Lecture 8 – Imagining Creates

Lecture 8

Neville Goddard 6-3-1968
Imagining Creates

The creator of the world works in the depth of your soul, underlying all of your faculties, including perception and streams into your surface mind least disguised in the form of creative fancy. Watch your thoughts, and you will catch Him in the act of creating, for He is your very Self. Every moment of time you are imagining what you are conscious of, and if you do not forget what you are imagining and it comes to pass, you have found the creative cause of your world.

Because God is pure Imagination and the only creator, if you imagine a state and bring it to pass, you have found Him. Remember: God is your consciousness, your I AM; so when you are imagining, God is doing it. If you imagine and forget what you imagine, you may not recognize your harvest when it appears. It may be good, bad, or indifferent, but if you forget how it came into being, you have not found God.

You do not have to be rich to be happy but you must be imaginative. You could have great wealth and be afraid of tomorrow's needs, or have nothing and travel the world over, for all things exist in your own wonderful human Imagination.

Let me tell you a story of a lady I know who traveled in her Imagination. When this lady was about sixteen she lived in Northern California. She was devoted to her father, who lived high, wide and handsome. He supplied all of the family's needs very well until the day he was killed. Then,

Lecture 8 – Imagining Creates

overnight, the family discovered they had nothing! Her mother, feeling she could not stand being ridiculed, moved the family to San Francisco, where the girl . . although possessing outstanding artistic talent . . found employment as a waitress in order to help the family.

Taking the streetcar home from work that first Christmas Eve, she found the car filled with young boys and girls, singing and happy, and she could not restrain the tears. Lucky for her it was raining, so she extended her face to the heavens and let the rain mingle with her tears. As she tasted the salt of her tears she said to herself: "This is not a streetcar, but a ship and I am not tasting my tears, but the salt of the sea in the wind."

While she physically held the rail of the streetcar, she mentally touched the rail of a ship moving into Samoa. Physically tasting the salt of her tears she imagined it was the salt of the sea. As the streetcar reached its destination, she was entering the bay of Samoa, feeling the moonlight shining on her body and hearing a voice say: "Isn't it a heavenly night."

Two weeks later this girl received a check for $3,000 from a law firm in Chicago. It seems that two years before, her aunt had left the United States, requesting that if she did not return, the money was to be given to her niece.

Within one month, the girl was on a ship sailing for Samoa. Coming into the bay, she saw a ship plowing through the water leaving lovely white foam in its path. As the moonlight touched the wake, its spray touched her face and a man standing near said: "Isn't it a heavenly night." At that

Lecture 8 – Imagining Creates

moment her outer senses experienced what she had used her inner senses to make real!

Now, Imagination . . being spiritual sensation . . is the creator of the world. With her five senses (sight, sound, scent, taste, and touch) she transformed a streetcar in San Francisco into a ship in the South Pacific, and within one month she physically fulfilled her imaginal act.

Many will say that was just coincidence, but it was not! It is reality, but how do I get you to believe me? But whether you believe me or not, I know from experience that God and you are one grand Imagination, and there is no other God! One day, Imagination in you will awaken and you . . fully aware of who you really are . . will know that all things are subject to you. That is your destiny.

The present moment is a formed imaginal act. Arrest it, and you can change it in yourself by following the advice given in the 18th chapter of the Book of Jeremiah:

'Arise! Go down to the potter's house and I will let you hear my words.' So I went down to the potter's house and there he was working at his wheel. The image in his hand was misshapen, but he reworked it into another image as it seemed good to the potter to do."

The word translated "potter," means Imagination, and we are told that the Lord is not only our Father, but the potter, and we are the clay in his hands!

Remember the day your boss criticized you, and you are molding an image of yourself based upon what he said. Being undesirable, that image is misshapen. Unable to discard

Lecture 8 – Imagining Creates

yourself, go down to the potter's house by taking the same scene and reshaping yourself by remembering the day your boss congratulated you on your accomplishments. Will this act change your world? Yes! I tell you: the God of the universe is shaping you morning, noon, and night, as you accept words, actions, and events from seeming others.

I urge you to shape your world from within and no longer from without. Describe yourself as you would like to be seen by others and believe your words. Walk in the assumption they are true and . . because no power can thwart God . . what He is imagining, you will experience.

You are not someone apart from God, for I AM cannot be divided. The Lord, our God, is one I AM, not two! If God's I AM and your I AM is the same I AM, define what you would like to be. Then believe you are the Lord! Be like the lady who transformed a streetcar into a cruise. Lose yourself in your new state, while your world on the outside remains, momentarily, the same.

Now, your reasoning mind may say she did have an aunt who had the presence of mind to die and leave her $3,000 at that particular time. And being young she did not consider the future; but I tell you: this is how the law works. It never fails if you will go all out and believe that your human Imagination is God.

Because God cannot die, he is a God of the living! So when the garment you now wear comes to its end, you . . the being living in it . . will continue to live. You will still be in a world just like this one until you awaken from the dream of life. Then you will move into an entirely different age, to

Lecture 8 – Imagining Creates

realize the oneness of the being that you really are. Until then, believe what I am telling you, for it is true.

When you imagine for a seeming other you are blessed, for there is no other and you are giving your imaginal gift to yourself!

Hear your friend tell you his good news, see the joy on his face, feel the thrill of fulfillment, and let it take place in your world. And as it does, recognize your harvest. Realize you are responsible for its consummation.

The world is yourself pushed out. Ask yourself what you want and then give it to yourself! Do not question how it will come about; just go your way, knowing that the evidence of what you have done must appear, and it will.

Last year, while I was in Barbados, a friend received a call from his mother telling him that his brother had killed a man. As he replaced the phone, a vision appeared in which a woman said: "Find Neville and he will give you the rainbow in the sky." My friend called me in Barbados, and when I heard his story I said: "It is done. God is infinite mercy, and there is nothing but forgiveness of sin."

When the spirit of Christ is formed in you, you will forgive a person, no matter what he has done. Pharaoh would not let his people go because God had hardened his heart, so how can you condemn Pharaoh for something God did? Tonight my friend told me his mother had called to tell him his brother had been set free.

I will tell you now, that no one can reach the end of the journey without having killed someone. Everyone must play

Lecture 8 – Imagining Creates

every part, so that when memory returns he may forgive all. The part of the thief, the murderer, the rapist and the one raped . . every state will be experienced. Anything man can do is recorded in scripture, and to fulfill scripture man must do everything.

Had I not played every part, I would not have been born from above. My friend, who loves his brother and could not understand how he could do such a thing, has murdered, as we all have. We must do everything the world condemns in order for the spirit of Christ . . which is continual forgiveness of sin . . to be formed within us. And when this happens to you, you will see no one to condemn. It is not that you are indifferent to war or murder, but you will see the world as a play with you . . the author . . playing all the parts.

Remember: you don't have to abide by anything you dislike. It is but a vessel in your hand which is not properly shaped. Go down to the potter's house and rework it into another vessel as it seems good for you, the potter, to do.

You cannot only rework your concept of self into a new one, but you can rework another. If one is not well or does not earn enough to pay his expenses, the concept is misshapen. You don't ask the vessel if you may rework it, rather you feel as though you have witnessed the change or heard the good news.

There must be action, for an idea alone produces nothing. You must act within yourself by entering the idea. When someone calls or makes a request of you, you must act upon it by producing a motor element within yourself. It may be the sound of their voice telling you it has already happened. Or you may feel the touch of his hand. Whatever

Lecture 8 – Imagining Creates

you do, it must be something that takes the desire from being an idea and moves it into the creative state of fulfillment.

The very first creative act recorded in scripture is when the spirit of the Lord moved upon the face of the waters. Here is motion. If you would like to be elsewhere, all you need to do is close your senses to the room you now occupy and sense the room where you would like to be. Open your eyes, and your senses will deny any change, for yours was a psychological motion. By closing your eyes the obvious here vanishes, and through the act of assumption, there becomes here. Seeing the world related to your new position, you breathe reality into the state and, having moved from where you are to where you want to be, you have created it.

I know this doesn't make sense, but as Douglas said: "The secret of imagining is the greatest of all problems, to the solution of which every mystic aspires, for supreme power, supreme wisdom, and supreme delight lie in the solution of this far-off mystery."

How is this mystery unraveled? By claiming you are all Imagination. Then wrapping yourself in space, and mentally seeing your world relative to your assumed position in space. Do that and you have moved.

President Hoover once said: "Human history, through its many forms of governments, its revolutions, its wars . . in fact the rise and fall of nations . . could be written in terms of the rise and fall of ideas implanted in the minds of men."

Here you see that the change of governments is the result of the change of ideas implanted in the mind. Can you

Lecture 8 – Imagining Creates

now see how we are implanting the horrors of the world? Read the morning paper, watch television, or listen to the radio, and you will observe how their words frighten you in order to get your attention. See a headline that someone was murdered and you stop to read it. See another, saying things are fine, and you ignore it, as it would mean nothing. Read the scandal sheet, telling of some prominent person who has been unfaithful and you enjoy a bit of gossip. All of these are ideas implanted in the mind, which cause the rise and fall of nations.

I tell you: imagining creates reality! If you want to change your life you must become aware of the ideas you are planting in the mind of others! When you meet someone who is negative, put a lovely idea in its place. Then, whenever you think of him, imagine he is telling you something lovely. And, because you now walk in a world that is not disturbed by his negative state, when he finds himself no longer thinking negative thoughts, he will never know you were its source. You will know it and that is all that is important.

Become aware of the thoughts you are thinking and you will know a more pleasant life. It makes no difference what others do; plant loving, kind thoughts and you will be blessed in the doing.

Believe me: Here was a child of sixteen who transformed her tears into the salt spray of the sea, a streetcar into a ship, and San Francisco into Samoa. She is blessed, for when it came to pass, she never forgot her moment of despair when she imagined a state and it came to pass.

I ask you now to believe in the invisible God who became you. When you say "I AM", you think of the face you wear,

Lecture 8 – Imagining Creates

but you are not it. You are so much greater than it could ever be.

One day, God's son David will look into the eyes of the being you really are and call you father. He will not call you by the name of the mask you wear, for David is the express image of your invisibility. Recognizing you as his eternal father, David signifies that your journey into the world of death is at its end. And from that moment on you will share your experiences with anyone who will listen and save everyone you meet.

You will save one who is unemployed by mentally hearing him tell you he is now gainfully employed and making more money than ever before. Having heard his good news, you will subjectively appropriate your objective hope and never turn back by doubting the reality of what you have done. You will simply watch it come to pass. Then you will know that you have found him of whom Moses and the law and the prophets wrote: Jesus of Nazareth, who is the Lord God, and the Father of all!

I have disclosed the one and only source of the phenomena of life. Everything that has ever happened, is happening, or will happen to you, comes from God, who is your own wonderful human Imagination. I urge you to use it wisely.

Now a lady wrote me, saying she heard a voice cursing her, and . . not understanding . . she questioned self and heard the words: "Because I want you."

In the Book of Galatians, Paul tells those who have arrived at the end of their journey, to reject all laws and

Lecture 8 – Imagining Creates

institutions which would interfere with the direct communication with their individual God.

In the spirit world, all organized societies are personified. Rivers, mountains, cities . . everything is human, for God is Man. Even the Los Angeles Woman's Club building is personified in the spirit world. Representing a need of the ladies who own it, when seen in the spirit world, and trying to detach yourself from it, it will curse you, for it wants to feed on you.

So when you leave religious institutions, organizations, customs, and laws that would interfere with your individual direct communion with your God, they will curse you, for they will have lost you. Just leave them alone. I have seen them all and they are nothing more than shadows. Once I saw a monstrous witch in a cave teaching little children the black arts. When she saw me she screamed: "O Man of God, what have you to do with me?"

The Bible tells the same story. Those who teach the black arts and how to hurt people, those who would control your mind and make you dependent upon them, are only personifications of organizations who keep you from contacting the only God who is within you.

Every orthodox religious group would enslave you for the rest of eternity if they could; but when you leave that belief, its personification will curse your leaving, but their curse means nothing. They cannot touch you when you completely reject any intermediary between yourself and God.

Lecture 8 – Imagining Creates

Now to come back to tonight's theme: Imagining creates reality! Have you imagined something and it hasn't come to pass? Then what are you imagining right now?

Are you imagining you are John Brown? You were not born knowing you were John Brown. You were born and others began to call you John. As time passed you began to assume you were John Brown and began to respond when you heard the name John.

When you imagined being secure did you forget the feeling? Are you imagining you are secure now? You may have no evidence that you are secure, but as you allow others to tell you how much you are loved and wanted, how successful and famous you are, you will begin to assume it, and Imagination will have created its reality. Try it, for that reality you already are!

Now let us go into the silence.

Lecture 9 – Imagination Fulfills Itself

Lecture 9

Neville Goddard 10-26-1968
Imagination Fulfills Itself

I say Imagination creates reality, and if this premise is true then Imagination fulfills itself in what your life becomes. Although I have changed the words, what I am saying is not new. Scripture says it in this manner: "Whatsoever you desire, believe you have received it and you will." This statement goes back two thousand years, yet even before that Jeremiah tells of the same principle in his story of the potter and his clay.

But until Imagination becomes a part of your normal, natural currency of thought, you will not act consciously. Like breathing, this awareness must become so much a part of you that you will not turn to the left or the right to praise or blame anyone. When you know this presence it will not matter if you started life behind the eight-ball, or in a palace; as a poor, or a rich child; you will realize that life is always externalizing what you are imagining.

Lacking the knowledge of this principle, you can reproduce your environment . . be it pleasant or unpleasant . . forever and ever, as you feed your Imagination on what your senses dictate. But knowing this principle, you can ignore the present, and untethered by the so-called facts of life, you can imagine the present as you desire it to be and feed upon your desire, rather than its omission.

Now, Imagination cannot be observed as we see objects in space, for Imagination is their reality. Fawcett gives the

Lecture 9 – Imagination Fulfills Itself

name, "God" to the cause of the universe, saying: "God, the creator, is like pure imagining in ourselves. He works in the depths of our soul underlying all of our faculties, including perception, and streams into our surface mind least disguised in the form of productive fancy."

Listen to your thoughts and you will hear God's words! A thought that is not felt produces nothing. But a thought producing motor elements reproduces itself! Catch God in a moment of a motor element such as anger, fear, or frustration, being congratulated or congratulating, and you will know what is going to happen in your world. Unless, of course you arrest your thoughts and revise them. Most of us, however, are not aware of what we are doing, so we do not observe the creator. But we can catch him as he streams into our surface mind least disguised in the form of productive fancy.

If, while riding the bus, driving the car, sitting at home, or standing at a bar, you hear a remark and react by moving on the inside, that remark will fulfill itself in what your life becomes. This principle sets you free, if you are willing to assume its responsibility.

But whether you assume it or not, you will fulfill your every motor element thought anyway. So in the end you will not sympathize or condemn, but simply tell those who may be going through an unpleasant experience of this principle, and . . if they accept it . . let the principle work in their lives.

Now, the average person in America is either Christian or Jew. Ask any one of them if they believe that imagining creates reality, and the chances are they will give you a negative response. But although they do not know it, if they

Lecture 9 – Imagination Fulfills Itself

believe in God they believe in Imagination. They may read scripture and accept the words on the surface, but their meaning has not become a part of their thinking.

Last night, for instance, I heard Billy Graham for the first time. Here were thousands of people in the audience listening to a thousand-member choir sing the song, "Oh, how I love Jesus." Now, I don't want to be critical, but when I heard Billy Graham speak I realized that he had not the slightest concept of Jesus, far less his second coming. He said: "If Jesus should come now, just imagine, there would be no more cancer, no more heart failures, and no more death."

Billy Graham believes heaven is made up of flesh and blood bodies in excrementitious states. And they would have to have bathrooms there, if there were no more death. If you were still in a body, that is excrementitious. You would have to take in food which is given you, and what you could not assimilate you would have to expel. And, unless you lost all sense of shame and reverted to the animal world, you would have to have a bathroom. I listened to this man and asked myself: is this the man who was entertained at the White House and received by the Pope at the Vatican? (On the other hand, the Pope is equally silly concerning the mystery of Christ.)

Then at the end of the program, there was an appeal for money. He will give you two books which you hadn't asked for. One interprets the Bible and the other interprets the first one. All you need do is send in your donation to this simple address: Billy Graham, Minneapolis, Minn. "But," said he: "this program is costing us $500,000, and we don't have that sort of money. So if you are alone please send in a

Lecture 9 – Imagination Fulfills Itself

contribution. But if you are not alone then take up a collection among all who are with you and send it in." Now, this goes on night after night for one solid week! He is a grand and wonderful being, but he has no concept of the mystery of Christ.

Now, I want to show you what I mean when I say you can be exactly what you want to be. Let me begin by telling you that for the last couple of months I have felt like the devil, yet I knew I was responsible for the hell I found myself in. The doctor gave me every possible test, and when I saw him yesterday he told me I was a dilemma.

Do you know what a dilemma is? It's an argument presenting two or more alternatives equally conclusive against an opponent. In other words, if you start on the assumption that whatever you choose your conclusion will be wrong, you have a dilemma. You can use anything as a dilemma. That's me. My blood indicated one thing in a certain test and the opposite in another. The tests only confirmed what I already knew: that the cause of my discomfort lay in the depth of my soul and not in any secondary cause . . such as a thyroid, heart, liver, kidney, or anything outside of myself.

I AM wearing a body, but it is not me. I put myself into this body, which limits me. I AM its operant power. It cannot be causeful, as it only reflects what I AM entertaining in my Imagination. I must not justify it, condemn, or excuse myself in any way. Knowing I did not feel well, I changed my feeling, and when the tests (which I had taken to please the one I love) came back, I learned I was a dilemma.

Lecture 9 – Imagination Fulfills Itself

I ask you to take the same responsibility. To not pass the buck to any person, organization, situation, or circumstance, but to discover for yourself that imagining truly does create reality. If the cause of all life is God, then God must be all Imagination. And because you can imagine, then . . like God . . you are pure Imagination in yourself. Regardless of what reason and your senses deny, you can imagine anything and bring it to pass if this premise is true.

Now let me share a few wonderful letters I recently received. A lady writes: "In July my car needed repair. As I signed the credit slip agreeing to pay the cost of $62, I imagined it was a check, for I never sign a check unless there is money in the bank to cover it. August and September passed with no request for payment. In September a man stopped by and, eager to sell his house, asked me to list it for him. I told him that I was no longer in the business and recommended my former broker. I forgot all about it, but in October, just before the car repair statement arrived, I received a referral commission from my former broker in the amount of $68 . . six dollars more than the cost of the repair of my car.

Here the money . . like the story in the 6th chapter of Luke . . came to her pressed down, shaken together, and running over. Everyone in the ancient world had a big pocket where grain was placed and pressed down until it ran over. Just like the baker's dozen this lady received her $62 . . plus.

Then she said: "For some time now my favorite chair has needed new upholstery. Choosing the material and pattern was easy, but the cost of $87 had to be imagined. So rather than limit myself to an exact figure, I simply imagined my chair as already newly upholstered. While sitting in it, I

Lecture 9 – Imagination Fulfills Itself

denied its worn cover, and when thinking of it while in another part of the house, I always saw it as I desired it to be.

In early September, while on vacation, our neighbor had a heart attack. His wife, desiring to be with her husband, asked if their son could stay with us until their return. Since he and our son were playmates and inseparable, John stayed with us for five beautiful weeks, and when his mother asked how much she owed me I kiddingly said, 'Nothing! But, some day when you have an old, worn out hundred dollar bill tucked in your billfold and you don't know what to do with it, you can give it to me.' And the lady replied 'That's exactly what my husband and I agreed to do,' and from her billfold she took a folded hundred dollar bill and gave it to me. That money paid for the chair's new cover, plus an additional $13." Again we see the money came to her pressed down, shaken together, and running over.

When you apply this principle towards the seeming other you are applying it towards yourself, because there is no other. We are told that when Job forgot himself in his love for his friends and prayed for them, his own captivity was lifted. Then all that he seemingly had lost was returned, multiplied one hundredfold.

As you forgive another by thinking of him as you would like him to be and persuading yourself of the reality of your imaginal act, you are forgiving him for what he appears to be by putting him into an entirely different state. Do that and you are substituting a noble concept for an ignoble one. That's forgiveness! Forgiveness tests the individual's ability to enter into and partake of the nature of the opposite. A priest will say: I forgive you, yet when he passes you on the

Lecture 9 – Imagination Fulfills Itself

street he remembers what was confessed. If he can remember, he has not forgiven! The memory of what was done or said must be replaced by something else, so that the former can no longer be remembered.

If the present Mrs. Onassis remains Mrs. Kennedy in your eyes you have not forgiven her, because you are still seeing her in the old state. Forgive her by so losing yourself in the idea of her new state that it is all you can remember, and not the former one. Keep thinking of her in the former state and you have pulled her back into it, for there are only states, externalized.

Now here is another story: My friend went to Pittsburgh this summer to visit a childhood friend, who expressed a desire for a new Baldwin organ. Now, owning an inexpensive organ, my friend told her that every time she sat down to play, to imagine seeing the word, "Baldwin" across the front of the organ and claim it is their top-of-the-line model and paid for. This she promised to do.

Now, the friend's father had departed this world, and when she received a check for $4,500 from his estate, she spent it on necessary home repairs. But when another check in the amount of $3,500 arrived from the estate, she decided to buy her organ. Although the Baldwin top-of-the-line model was priced at $5,000, she was told that it would be going on sale for $4,000, plus they would give her a $1,000 trade-in allowance on her present organ . . making the total cost to be $3,000. Contracting for the organ of her dreams, she agreed to pay the $3,000 and the organ was installed.

Although a torrential rain had caused the roof of their home to need replacement, the estimate of $1,700 was

Lecture 9 – Imagination Fulfills Itself

delayed; so when it arrived, my friend received a call from her friend asking why the roofer had waited to give his estimate until after the Baldwin had been purchased. Then my friend told her the story of my friend Ann, who lived in New York City.

Ann was a member of the world's oldest profession, that of being a lady of the evening. She often came to my meetings, but this day we met on the corner of Broadway and 72nd Street, where she told me this story. One day, while walking by a hat shop, she fell in love with a beautiful hat in its window with a price tag indicating a cost of $17.50. Wanting it so much, she decided to apply this principle, so in her Imagination she placed the hat on her head, and as she walked up Broadway she felt the hat on her head. She would not look in a store window and be disillusioned, and when she arrived home she imagined taking off the hat and placing it on the top shelf before looking in the mirror.

Ten days later a friend called and invited her to lunch. When she arrived, the friend handed her a hat box, saying: "I don't know what possessed me, but I bought this hat and when I brought it home I realized I had made a mistake. I do not like it on me but I think it would look lovely on you, Ann." Opening the box she reached in and brought out . . not a hat, but the hat.

Then Ann said to me: "Why didn't God give me the money to buy the hat, instead of giving it to me through a friend?" I asked her if she felt obligated to her friend, and when she shook her head, No, I asked how much she usually paid for a hat. When she told me $4 or $5, I asked if she had ever purchased a $17 hat before. Again the answer was No, and when she admitted to owing two weeks' rent, I said: "If

Lecture 9 – Imagination Fulfills Itself

while admiring the hat you found a hundred dollar bill on the sidewalk, would you have bought the hat? I'll answer for you, no you would not. You would have paid your rent and perhaps bought some groceries, but you would not have purchased the hat. Tell me Ann, how much money must God give you to get you to buy a $17 hat? If he gave you a thousand dollars you wouldn't have bought it, for you are not in the habit of buying such expensive hats, so God knows best how to give you the hat you desired."

After telling the story, my friend asked: "How much money must God give you to buy the organ? You have the organ because you imagined it. Now, apply the same principle towards the new roof, for Imagination will not fail you. Here is a principle the lady used for her organ, but when a new roof was needed she forgot the source of the phenomena of life. Reason came in and told her all of the money from her father's estate was gone. If you will let it, reason will take this divine gift from you and leave you poor, indeed. For you have the gift of possessing whatever you imagine, if you are faithful to that which you have assumed!

Now, a lady wrote, saying: "I dreamed I was in a large department store with a dear friend who agreed to watch my purse while I shopped. But when I returned, my friend was gone and my purse was sitting in a paper bag on the floor. Upon opening the purse I discovered that $30, and a small card which I carry designating that I am an ordained Unity minister, was missing. I awoke wondering why anyone would want that card."

The card contained the central object of truth in her dream. She has paid the thirty pieces of silver . . the price paid for truth . . and now she has transcended any

Lecture 9 – Imagination Fulfills Itself

ordination in this world. As nice as Unity and all of these groups are, they are playing their parts on certain levels of consciousness. But this lady has gone beyond any man-made ism, be it Unity, Christian Science, or Science of Mind. All of these are man-made doctrines, not based on vision. She was shown that she had paid the price for Christ; and the little card which gave her title to a certain level of consciousness has been removed, for she has transcended the psychological level and entered the third level of the ark of life . . the level of vision. She has found Christ because she has paid the price.

May I tell you: you have the power within to create anything! Let people be what they want to be, while you set goals for yourself. It doesn't matter what has happened in your life or what the evidence of your senses tells you, the power of the universe is in you. That power is the Lord Christ Jesus, whose name is I AM. You will never know it however unless you test him, for only then will you realize that Jesus Christ is in you. I was taught Christ was on the outside somewhere in space. But I took the challenge and tested myself, to discover that I AM creative. That I create from within and that my life is the fulfillment of my own imaginal acts. I haven't always been wise in my choice, for Imagination is always fulfilling its imaginal state and I have imagined unlovely things and reaped them by becoming the fulfillment of what I was imagining.

Then I became more alert and discovered I could catch Christ as he streamed into my mind least disguised in the form of a creative fancy. If my thoughts were motor driven and they were unpleasant, I knew what to expect unless I revised them. But whether they were pleasant or unpleasant, I knew I would fulfill them.

Lecture 9 – Imagination Fulfills Itself

Envy no one. If a man has $500 million and a girl stands at the top of the social ladder it is because God, in them, had the desire and is fulfilling it. Blake was right when he titled his wonderful picture: "More! More! is the cry of the fool. Less than all is not enough." Scripture tells us: "All thine are mine and mine are thine," for all that God is, is yours, as you inherit God. He is your possession, so whatever God is, when you inherit him less than all is not enough. But the cry of "more" is the cry of the fool, for as long as he wants more he never has enough.

Mrs. Onassis draws from a trust fund of over $20 million. You would think that was enough, but you can adjust yourself to a way of life where it would not be. There are the demands of charities, plus . . if you desire to be one of the ten best-dressed in the land, you must have a fortune to gratify that desire.

There is nothing wrong with it. I personally have no desire to be named among the externally well dressed. I hope I am internally well dressed. I hope my light is blinding. I hope my garment is so powerful one cannot stand in its presence unless qualified to be there. And if I modify my garment to suit the level upon which another stands, that he may see the being I represent, I do . . but certainly not on the outside.

I tell you: imagining creates reality. Believe me, for it is true. Fawcett was right when he said," The secret of imagining is the greatest of all problems to the solution of which the mystic aspires, for supreme power, supreme wisdom and supreme delight lie in the far off solution of this mystery.

Lecture 9 – Imagination Fulfills Itself

A friend of mine sent Mr. Fawcett my book, and called his attention to the chapter called, "Revision". He also sent a copy to one who was a physicist at one of our great universities. The physicist felt that since the statements recorded there were not scientifically provable, the book was not worthy of his library. While the old gentleman . . who was a philosopher and teacher at Oxford University . . wrote the sweetest letter, saying: "I do not know who Neville is, but having read the chapter on revision as you requested, I know that he could only have received it from the brothers. No one but the divine society could have dictated this chapter." Here was a man filled with praise for a thought the scientist ridiculed because it was beyond his grasp.

I ask you to take me seriously. Imagination will fulfill itself, so do not limit yourself by anything that is now happening, no matter what it is. Knowing what you want, conceive a scene which would imply you have it. Persuade yourself of its truth and walk blindly on in that assumption. Believe it is real. Believe it is true and it will come to pass. Imagination will not fail you if you dare to assume and persist in your assumption, for Imagination will fulfill itself in what your life becomes.

Now, you may know of someone who had an assumption but died before it was realized. May I tell you: death does not terminate life. The world does not cease to be at the moment in time when your senses cease to register it. Instead, you are restored to life to continue your journey, and your dreams . . unrealized here . . will be realized there. You can't stop it, for imagining is forever creating reality.

When my brother, Lawrence, was making his exit from this world, I told my sister-in-law that there was marriage in

Lecture 9 – Imagination Fulfills Itself

the next world and she . . in a very light vein . . said: "I don't want to go now, but do you think Lawrence will be waiting for me so we can get married again?" Well I answered in the same light vein, saying: "God is merciful." I'll let it be at that and you can give any interpretation you want to regarding what I have said. But just imagine two people who have spent their life fighting like cats and dogs . . wanting to perpetuate it? No. God is merciful. He really is. Once you have experienced an unhappy state you would have to be a stupid idiot to repeat it. But after the resurrection there is no giving or taking in marriage, for you are above the organization of sex . . away beyond it.

Now let us go into the silence.

Lecture 10 – The Perfect Image

Lecture 10

Neville Goddard 04-11-1969
The Perfect Image

"He is our peace, who will make us both one by breaking down the wall of hostility, that he may create in himself one new man in place of the two, so bringing peace." This being of peace is a person, not a doctrine or philosophy. He is a person who breaks down the wall of hostility between you who are seated here and your true identity, who is a son of God, one with his Father.

Now, a lady wrote, saying: "I saw myself in vision as radiantly perfect, yet I knew that we were two. Remembering the words 'Be ye perfect,' I knew that at one time I was not, but now my present reflection is one of perfection. Then I awoke, got out of bed and stumbled into the door, then lost my temper and yelled at my children for pouring soap on my nice clean carpet. So it must have happened in some other dimension of my being, for I certainly am not perfect here." She is right.

While we wear these garments of flesh and blood, we lose our temper; we run into doors and do all the things people do here. Did not the perfect one, who was the pattern man, call Herod "that fox," and the scribes and Pharisees "Whited sepulchers, outwardly beautiful and inwardly full of hypocrisy and iniquity"? While you are here, encased in your body of flesh and blood, certainly you will lose your temper. Maybe not as you did before you were perfect, but you will to some degree as long as you remain here.

Lecture 10 – The Perfect Image

Now, how does he who is our peace, break down the wall of perdition and make the two of us one? By fulfilling his primal wish, which was: "Let us make man in our image, after our likeness." God fell asleep to his true awareness and began a good work in you, which he will bring to completion on the day of Jesus Christ . . who is described as being the perfect image of God, one who reflects and radiates God's glory. When his good work is finished, in you, then you . . the image . . will be superimposed upon him, and you will know yourself to be the Father. There is only God in the world. Having taken upon himself the limitation of man (as you are) he is working you into his image from within. And when you . . the made, are as perfect as he . . the Maker, you rise as one man, enhanced by reason of the experience of making an image which radiates and reflects your glory. So her vision was perfect, all based upon scripture.

Here is another beautiful one. This lady said, "I found myself in a forest, sitting on the ground leaning against a tree, when I heard a voice calling, 'Father, Father,' but I did not answer, because I did not want to be discovered. Suddenly you appeared, dressed as a shepherd boy, and said to me: 'Why did you not answer me? I have been searching for you.' And I replied: 'You are always searching and finding me, in spite of the fact that the Good Book says I can rest on the Sabbath day.' Then you looked at me and smiled the smile of an indulgent father; yet strangely enough, I . . very female . . felt I was the father."

In the 4th chapter of Galatians it is said: "When the time had fully come, God sent forth the Spirit of his Son into our hearts, crying: 'Abba! Father!' But the Father, sound asleep in Man, doesn't want to be found, although the Son is always calling: "Rouse thyself, why sleepest thou, O Lord! Awake!"

Lecture 10 – The Perfect Image

And when one who is called the Son of God awakens to Fatherhood, he is sent into the world to awaken his brothers, but finds they still want to postpone the day of waking, still wanting to hold onto these little garments of flesh and blood. But I will always find you and will not let you rest, for "Truly, truly I say unto you, the dead will hear the voice of the son of God and those who hear it will live." This lady heard the voice and recognized it, so she is not far from waking. Sent as a shepherd boy, the son of God does the Father's will by calling the Father (in Man) to awaken and rise from the dead.

God entered this world for the sole purpose of making you perfect as he is perfect. When his work is finished, he will superimpose himself upon that image and they will be perfectly one. This lady knew she was perfect. She recalled the words: "Be ye perfect." The completed sentence is: "as your Father in heaven is perfect." Yes, be ye perfect for then you become one with your Maker; awake from this dream of life and resurrect from this world of death into a world of eternal life. Without the resurrection you would know infinite circuitry, repeating the same states over and over again. But, after moving around the circle unnumbered times, the perfect image is formed, removing you from the circle to enter a spiral and move up as the person who created it all.

You can join every doctrine, sign every contract between people and nations; yet you will not know perfection until He (in you) finds you perfect and the two of you become one. So, he who is your peace will make you one with him by breaking down the dividing wall of hostility. Then, without telling others you walk knowing who you really are. If you tell the world, they will only laugh at you because . . while in this world, like my friend who had the vision . . you will run into a door and lose your temper. Everyone is here for a definite

Lecture 10 – The Perfect Image

purpose, which is revealed through revelations, thereby giving purpose to the whole of life. Without purpose, what does the world have to offer? If you owned everything that you could buy with money, if you had all the money necessary to live comfortably . . and your soul is called, what would it matter?

The world may call you dead, cremate your body and scatter your ashes, but you are immortal and cannot die. Rather than being dead, you are in a world just like this one, mentally walking the same tracks over again and again. Oh, maybe you will not experience the same situations, but your world will be just as solidly real. You will return to a lovely twenty-year-old form, to marry, and age, and lose your temper as you bump into a door . . until your image is so perfect it is superimposed upon its Maker. Then up you go to know yourself to be the one body, one Spirit, one Lord, one God and Father of all.

That is the great living body of the Risen Lord. It seems incredible, but it is true. You are destined to know yourself to be the creator of the world. You are destined to share in the unity of that one body, that one Spirit, that one Lord, that one God and Father of all. I know, for I have experienced it. I was sent back to tell my experiences in the hope that those who are on the verge of moving into the same body, as the same Spirit, may hear my words and be encouraged by them.

Paul makes the statement: "I stand before you on trial for the hope in that promise that God made to our fathers. O King Agrippa, why should it seem incredible to any of you that God raised the dead? Is this not the promise to our fathers?" Search the scriptures and you will find that the promise was made in the 46th chapter of Genesis. "The Lord

Lecture 10 – The Perfect Image

spoke to Israel in visions of the night saying, 'Jacob, Jacob.'" (As you know, Jacob's name was changed to Israel which means, a man who rules as God because he knows he is God.) Jacob answers: "Here I AM" and the Lord said: "I AM God, the God of your father. Fear not to go down into Egypt, for there I will make of you a great nation. I will go down with you into Egypt and I will also bring you out again." Egypt is not a little place in North Africa; this world of death is Egypt, where everything appears, waxes, wanes, and vanishes. I have gone down into Egypt with you and I will keep my promise and bring you up. When this world was coming to its end, Paul stood in chains before the prince whose kingdom was fading; but he could not let go of it, and said: "Why do you think it incredible that God raises the dead?" and the king could not answer.

I tell you: God literally assumed the weaknesses and limitations of the flesh, in order to know you and to make you into his image. And when that image is perfect as He is perfect, you are no longer two, but one. Then you awake from the dream of life and ascend into your true being, called the kingdom of heaven.

Our commonwealth is in heaven and we are sojourners in this strange land where we are enslaved. But have faith and set your hope fully upon that moment in time when the image is perfect. Then it will be unveiled within you to reveal you as the being who made it. Though you are the made, you are the Maker; for the Maker breaks down the wall of hostility between you, making you and He one. Then you return to your heavenly state as the one who came down, but greatly enhanced because of your journey into Egypt.

Lecture 10 – The Perfect Image

Having purposely imposed this limitation upon myself, I felt as though I were speaking to another, making requests of him and thanking him for their fulfillment. Now I have no sense of another. I feel only as the one who formed me into his likeness; for when I awoke He and I were not two anymore, but one. This lady saw me clothed as a shepherd boy. She saw correctly; for although the Father and the son are one, it is the Spirit of his son who is sent into the heart, crying: "Father, Father." She heard the cry and knew herself to be not only Man, but a father; yet in this world she is very much a lady.

She heard my call, yet not wanting to be disturbed she did not respond; but may I tell you, the son of God will never let the Father rest. He is forever calling: "Awake you sleeper! Why sleepest thou, O Lord?" But the Father in you cannot awaken until he has completed his work. He began it in you and will bring it to completion at the day of Jesus Christ.

That day, the image of God himself is formed in you, and you awake to express that image by radiating and reflecting God's glory. Night after night I am crying and crying to the Father in all; and those who hear my voice will begin to awaken from the dream of life and start their journey back to the being they were before that the world was, to find themselves to be more glorious, more wonderful, than they were when they descended.

Tonight some friends are here who haven't heard me speak in a number of years. When they were last with me I was speaking only of the law, as the promise had not fulfilled itself in me. So for their sake let me say: the promise is the law on a higher level, and the law is very simple.

Lecture 10 – The Perfect Image

There are infinite number of states. The state of health, the state of sickness, the state of wealth, the state of poverty, the state of being known, the state of being unknown . . all are only states and everyone is always in a state. We all have one state in which we are very comfortable, so we return to it moment after moment. That state constitutes our dwelling place. If it is not a pleasant state, we can always get out of it. How this is done is the secret I will now share with you. All states are mental. You cannot remove yourself from your present state by pulling strings on the outside. You must mentally adjust your thoughts to proceed from the desired state, all within yourself. You fell into your present state either deliberately or unwittingly; and because you are its life, the state became alive and grew like a tree, bearing its fruit which you do not like. Its fruit may be that of poverty, or distress, heartache, or pain.

There are all kinds of unlovely fruit. But you can detach yourself from your unlovely harvest by making an adjustment in your human Imagination. Ask yourself what you would like to harvest. When you know what it is, ask yourself how you would feel if your desire was ready to harvest right now. When you know the feeling, try to catch it. In my own case I find it easier to catch the feeling by imagining I am with people I know well and they are seeing me as they would if my desire were now a fact. And when the feeling of reality possesses me, I fall asleep in that assumption.

At that moment I have entered a state. Now, I must make that state as natural as I have made my present state. I must consciously return to my new state constantly. I must feel its naturalness, like my own bed at night. At first the new state seems unnatural, like wearing a new suit or hat. Although no

Lecture 10 – The Perfect Image

one knows your suit is new, you are so conscious of it you think everyone is looking at you. You are aware of its fit and its feeling until it becomes comfortable. So it is with your new state. At first you are conscious of its strangeness; but with regular wearing, the new state becomes comfortable, and its naturalness causes you to constantly return to it, thereby making it real.

Now most of us, knowing what we want, construct it in our minds eye, but never occupy it. We never move into the state and remain there. I call this perpetual construction, deferred occupancy. I could dream of owning a lovely home and hope to go there one day; but if I do not occupy it now, in my Imagination, I postpone it to another day. I may wish my friend had a better job. I may have imagined him having it; but if I don't occupy that state by believing he is already there, I have merely constructed the state for him but not occupied it. All day long I can wish he or she were different; but if I don't go into the state and view him from it, I don't occupy the state, so he remains in the unlovely state relative to me. This is the world in which we live.

You can't conceive of a thing that is not part of a state, but the life of any state is in the individual who occupies it. Life cannot be given to a state from without, because God's name is "I AM." It is not "You are" or "They are." God's eternal name is I AM! That is the life of the world. If you would make a state alive, you must be in it. If you are in a lovely, gentle, kind state, you are seeing another as lovely, living graciously, and enjoying life to the utmost.

Now, to make that state natural, you must see everyone in your world as lovely, kind, and gentle. Others may not see them in that light, but it doesn't really matter what they

Lecture 10 – The Perfect Image

think. I am quite sure if I took a survey of what people think of me, no two would agree. Some would say I am a deceiver, while others I am the nearest thing to God. I would find a range stretching from the devil to God, all based upon the state in which the person is in when called upon to define me.

You can be what you want to be if you know and apply this principle, but you are the operant power. It does not operate itself. You may know the law from A to Z, but knowing is not enough. Knowledge must be acted upon. "I AM" is the operant power in you. Put your awareness in the center of your desire. Persist, and your desire will be objectified. Learn to use the law, because there is a long interval between the law and the promise. Those who heard me prior to 1959 are unfamiliar with my experiences since that time, and my words may seem strange to you. I cannot deny the law, for I came not to destroy the law and the prophets, but to fulfill them. This I have done.

I have told you that in the resurrection, Man is above the organization of sex, and that Man can change his sex at will. This week I received a letter telling of a vision which testifies to the truth of this statement. This gentleman is married to a lovely girl and is every bit a man, yet this is his experience. He said, "I found myself lying on a bed feeling as though I am a woman. Desiring a man of oriental descent and olive skin, I assumed I had found him. Instantly he appeared and, although no act was performed, I felt the thrill of imagining and instant fulfillment of my imaginal act. Then I awoke."

This man's vision verifies what I have been telling you: that in the resurrection Man changes his sexual garments at will, and being above the organization of sex, he does not

Lecture 10 – The Perfect Image

need the divine image of male/female to create. I think his vision is marvelous. When he returned to this world, he was surprised at the experience; but I say to all: you are destined to know you are every being in the world, bar none!

Like the lady who is so feminine, responding when a shepherd boy called her "father". Although she would not answer my call, she knew I would always find her. I always will, for I . . the Word of God . . was sent as the son of God, and I shall not return to my father void. I must bring back that purpose for which he sent me. I stirred the feeling of the fatherhood of God in her, and I will take back with me those that my father gave me.

But while you are in this world of Caesar, it is important that you master the law. Think of everyone as representing a state. There is no such thing as a good man or a bad man, only good or bad states as you conceive them to be; but the occupant of every state is God. Blake said in his "Vision Of The Last Judgment": "On this it will be seen that I do not consider either the just or the wicked to be in a supreme state, but to everyone of them states of the sleep which the soul may fall into in its deadly dreams of good and evil when it leaves Paradise following the serpent."

Identify yourself with a state and you are pronounced by others to be either good or evil; but you are only in a state. Tonight if you are unemployed, or find it difficult to get a promotion in your present employment, remember: the solution to your present state is still a state!

I hope I have made it clear how to move into states. It is done through the act of assumption with feeling and persistence. Assume health. Stand in its center and clothe

Lecture 10 – The Perfect Image

yourself with its feeling. Persist in claiming a healthy body and a healthy mind, and your assumption will harden into fact as you move into and objectify the state of health.

Now let us go into the silence.

Lecture 11 – Imagination

Lecture 11

Neville Goddard 7-14-1969
Imagination

Tonight's subject is Imagination. You read in the 17th chapter of the book of Acts, a story of Paul coming through to the Athenians, and he calls upon these men, for he saw the inscription over and over. He said: "As I passed by . . I saw an altar with this inscription, 'To an unknown god.' This therefore that you worship as unknown, I proclaim unto you."

"He is not far from each of us, for in him we live and move and have our being."

The great Blake said it differently. This is what Blake said: "All that you behold; though it appears without, it is within, in your Imagination, of which this World of Mortality is but a Shadow."

Then he said: "Babel mocks . . ." We are all familiar with what Babel represents: the confusion of tongues, no two believing in the same god. Not yet speaking different languages but speaking one tongue, they have different concepts of the creative power of the universe. And so he said:

Babel mocks saying, there is no God, nor Son of God That thou O Human Imagination, O Divine Body art all A delusion, but I know thee O Lord...

Lecture 11 – Imagination

He equates God and his son with the human Imagination. To him and to the speaker, Divine Imagination is identical with the word "Jesus." So, when I think of Jesus I do not see a being outside of my own wonderful human Imagination.

Are we not told in Scripture: "With God all things are possible"? We are also told in Scripture: "All things are possible to him who believes." That is Scripture, now. The power of believing is God himself.

So, God in man is man's own wonderful human Imagination.

It's difficult for man to make the adjustment, having been trained to turn on the outside to some god that he worships. We go to church and the mind turns outward to some god, and he paints a word picture of someone before whom we must bend our knee and cross ourselves.

But that's not what Scripture really teaches.

Scripture teaches that the power that creates the entire universe is not without man, but within man, as man's own wonderful human Imagination.

That is the creative power of the world.

All things exist in the human Imagination, so if the word "God" would turn you out, try to make the adjustment within yourself and begin to believe that the God of Christendom, the Lord Jesus of Christendom, is your own Imagination.

Lecture 11 – Imagination

If all things are possible to God, and God is your Imagination, then it should be possible for you.

Now, I ask the question. I think I have told it simply enough how you can test it, how you can enter into a state. I think I have told it to the satisfaction of most people that we are the operant power. To hear it, to recite it, commit it to memory, is not enough. We have to apply it, for we are the operant power.

A few days before I closed in Los Angeles, I retired quite early, maybe 9:30 or 10:00 o'clock and I communed with myself. To whom would I turn?"So," I said to myself, "I have said everything that I have heard from within myself, everything that I have experienced concerning the Law, I have told. I have told what I have experienced concerning the Promise. Could I tell them something more about the Law that would make it a little bit more simple? What can I say that I haven't said?"

So, I asked the depth of my own being to show me, to show me exactly what I could say that I haven't said. Well, in the wee hours of the morning, a little after 4:00 o'clock, as I was coming through from the depths of my own being, here is the experience: I am on a spacecraft headed for the moon.

Now, it is all in one's Imagination, for the dreamer is one's Imagination.

That is the cause of all. Now, first of all, let me say that everything in this world contains within itself the capacity for symbolic significance.

Lecture 11 – Imagination

So, the moon has within itself the capacity for some symbolic significance. I am headed for the moon.

Now, you have heard the expression time and time again: "Oh, he is reaching for the moon." It could be an ambition based upon your social desire. You want to transcend the limitation of your world where you were born. Or it could be some financial ambition, and friends who know your limitations will say of you: "He is reaching for the moon." Or it could be some tyrant trying to conquer the earth. We have had a Hitler, a Stalin, Alexander the Great, and Napoleon. All these were reaching to conquer the earth, reaching for the moon. Now we are actually on the verge of stepping on the moon, and so we will hit this object in space.

But forget that part of it. I am asking for light so that I can throw some light upon the Law, how to realize my objective in this world in a more simple way than I have so far succeeded in telling it, and this is the vision: I am on this craft and I am headed for the moon. There are others on the craft with me. Instead of landing on the moon, I went into the moon through a very, very large tunnel . . a tunnel wider than the depth of this room. The object is dead, dead as dead can be.

I say to someone on the craft: "May I get off?" and he said: "Certainly." I stepped off onto this dead body in space, the moon. There were little objects for sale, objects made on earth and placed on the moon to sell to tourists. They were cheap, cheap beyond measure, made of clay: little cups, little saucers, little plates, little ornaments but the cheapest of cheap! You can't conceive anything cheaper in appearance and in quality.

Lecture 11 – Imagination

There they were, made on earth to sell on the moon, just like some sideshow at a carnival. I picked them up, examined them, and thought: "Here, a quarter of a million miles away, man made these things, put them on the moon to sell to tourists." What was the significance of the vision? All of man's ambitions are like clay. They will all turn to dust.

A man died here the other day in Texas. He started out as a poor boy and left an estate of five hundred million dollars, but he left the estate. He had reached the nice, ripe age of seventy-five, but he left every penny behind him. And those who now have billions, they will leave every penny behind them, just as though it is made of dust.

Nevertheless, I asked the question of myself and the depth of my own being answered: so what is the significance of the dream? Tell man, not that he shouldn't have what he wants, certainly he should have it; it is going to be dropped anyway, but he can get it. So, what other point was driven home to me?

This is the point: instead of landing on the moon, I went into the moon.

Blake makes the statement, "If the spectator could enter into the images in his Imagination, approach them on the fiery chariot of his contemplative thought, if he could make a friend and companion of any one of these images in his Imagination" well, he emphasized "enter into the image," not to contemplate it as something on the outside. I contemplate now New York City. I am seeing it from San Francisco. If my desire this night is to be in New York City, I say I can't afford the time, or maybe I can't afford it because of lack of funds,

Lecture 11 – Imagination

or maybe my commitments will tie me here? I don't know, yet my desire is to be in New York City.

I must, if I would realize it in spite of the limitations that now surround me (money, lack of time, obligations, call it what you will, I still want to be in New York City. I must enter into the image that is now something on the surface of the mind 'out there,' 3,000 miles away. Standing here, I must shut out the belief that I am in San Francisco.

Knowing New York City quite well, I would assume I am standing in a most familiar part of New York City and let it surround me. I must be in it, and then think of San Francisco. I must now see it 3,000 miles to the west of me, as I now see New York City 3,000 miles to the east of me. If I go into that state and dwell in it and make it natural, though I remain in it only for a little while, a minute or so, then I open my eyes, 'I am shocked' to find that I am still here. I came back here. I have done it. I have entered into the state of my desire and I will move across a bridge of incidents, a series of events that will lead me and compel me to take a journey to New York City.

Now, this I have used only as a spatial example. You can take it in a financial sense, take it in the social world; take it in any way whatsoever. That is what came to me a few days before I closed. For if I could find something more simple to tell them than I think I have told them, this would be it:

To enter into the state and not simply think of the state.

Thinking *from* it differs from thinking *of* it. I must learn to think from it.

Lecture 11 – Imagination

A man who this night came into a million dollars, from that moment that man is made aware that he has a million, when prior to that he had nothing. He is thinking from the consciousness of having a million dollars. He is not thinking of it; he is walking in the consciousness of having a million dollars. He's not hoping for it, wishing for it; he is actually in it. That is what the vision revealed to me.

Even though at the end of my journey I will leave my things behind me and they will all be as though they were made of clay . . all cheaply made, at that, every man, not knowing this, in fact, how many know it or care to know it? They still want to realize their earthly dreams, and I am all for it; I teach it. But I cannot change the Promise. The Promise is fixed. That is something that will come to every being in this world, for it has been predetermined. But when we are here in this world of Caesar, I can cushion the blows, the inevitable blows, by learning the technique of Law and how to apply it, how to use it.

Now, the thing I quoted earlier, Blake said in this quote from "Jerusalem": "Although I behold Thee not . . ." Well, here it's perfectly true; I do not observe imagining as I do objects. Imagining is the reality that we name this power called God. So I don't observe imagining; I observe objects, but I don't observe the power in them. That's the greatest secret in the world.

The secret of imagining is the secret of God. Anyone who finds it finds supreme power, supreme wisdom, supreme delight. Everyone should aspire after this secret and try to unravel it, for whatever you find about your own wonderful human Imagination, you are finding about God for your Imagination and God are one and the same. There is no

Lecture 11 – Imagination

other God. You imagined yourself into this world, and you'll imagine yourself out of it.

You came into the world for a purpose, and when the purpose is fulfilled you will detach yourself from it and return to the being that you were prior to your descent into this world. "Man is all Imagination and God is Man and Exists in us and we in Him. The Eternal Body of Man is the Imagination and that is God Himself."

Now, I am not saying it is the easiest thing in the world for you to accept this. It will come to those who have never heard it before as blasphemy. It will come as a shock, an awful shock, when man who is trained to believe in an external God to whom he bows, to whom he prays then to discover that He is not on the outside at all.

As we are told in Scripture: "Do you not know that you are the temple of God, and the Spirit of God dwells in you," and God is spirit. Well, if God is spirit, and his spirit dwells in you, you can't divide it into different kinds of spirit. God is spirit and his spirit dwells in me. Now, if his spirit dwells in me, I try to find out what that spirit is in me that I can call by another name that is more intimate. Well, I have found it and the spirit of God, which is God himself in me, is my Imagination. And if all things are possible to God and if I can but believe that they are possible to me, well then it's entirely up to me to find out how to believe it.

I imagine, as do you. We cannot imagine differently. All difference lies in content.

So, my response to the eternal question: "Who am I?" will determine the circumstances of my life. Who am I? Am I the

Lecture 11 – Imagination

little one that was born on a tiny little unknown island with no social, intellectual, financial background? Must I accept the limitations of birth? Well most people do. But have I read Scripture? Did I read the words that I AM the temple of the living God, and the spirit of that God dwells in me and all things are possible to that God? Well, I should not allow anything to interfere with my discovery of that spirit in me that is called the "Spirit of God," for if all things are possible to him and he dwells in me, I must make every effort to locate him.

Well, I have located him, and he is my Imagination and I do not differ from any person born of woman. The Imagination in every one is God. But if they have been trained to believe in their little beings and my own tiny little Imagination, people will say: "Oh, that's just his Imagination."

We are going to the moon. A man imagined it a hundred years ago, Jules Verne. He even imagined the nation that would do it. He said the Yankee know-how, their engineers will contrive the means to get there first. He wrote that 100 years ago, and no matter how others try, we will get there first. We are on the verge of it, but he had to imagine it first.

What is now true was once only imagined. We are in a room. It seems so real. Well, this was once only imagined. You are wearing dresses, you are wearing all kinds of things, but they had to be imagined first. You go to a tailor or your dressmaker and you pick out the material that you like. It's just a plain piece of cloth. Then you tell your dressmaker or I tell my tailor what kind of a suit I want. So I allow him with his know-how, to take my vision of the kind of a suit that I

Lecture 11 – Imagination

want. Having picked out the material, he executes it. Now what is then proven when I put it on was first only imagined?

A man imagines a desire, say for wealth. When he becomes wealthy he may forget the means by which it came about and think all the external forces that were used to bring it to pass are the causes. They had to play the part that they played because he imagined what he imagined.

So, I don't differ in the act of imagining from you or any being in the world. The only difference will have to lie in the content of my imagining. What am I imaging? If I imagine something little and feel sorry for myself? Alright, life will prove that I had every reason in the world to feel sorry for myself, because the blows will come to me. And I will turn to the one who gave the blows and blame him or blame them, when the blame (if any) is in myself; for had I not imagined what I have imagined, I could not encounter the conditions that I encountered. This is the Law of Scripture.

We are told: Don't fool yourselves. "Be not deceived. God is not mocked." God is your Imagination; he's not mocked. "As a man sows, so shall he reap." Well, what am I sowing? I AM sowing everything that I AM imagining. That is what I AM sowing, for the only thing I can 'sow' is what I imagine. So, will I now change from an external god to the internal God and find him in myself as my own wonderful human Imagination?

Let Babel rant and say there is no God. Let Babel say there is no Son of God. Then comes that wonderful statement of the prophet, who sees that: "You, O Human Imagination, Divine Body called my Human Imagination, the Body of the Lord Jesus Christ, buried in me."

Lecture 11 – Imagination

And were he not buried in me I couldn't even breathe, I couldn't think. But one day he will rise in me and as he rises in me, I AM. I AM He now, but do not know it. When he rises in me I know it then because I rise, not "he" rises. He has become me to the point that we aren't two; we are one.

So, he suffers us.

I say: "I AM in pain." Well, his name is "I AM." That is my Imagination.

I don't say: "My body is weeping," I say: "I AM weeping."

I don't say: "My body is tired," I say: "I AM tired."

So, is not Blake right when he says: "Thou sufferest with me"? Though I do not behold . . I can't quite see you as something external. I could not in eternity see myself as something external. I must see it only by reflection and the world undevoutly reflects what I am doing within myself. The day will come I will actually see myself, but not as something external to myself. I will know myself only by reason of the son who stands before me and calls me, "Father."

Then I am looking right into the face of the Son of God, and he will call me "Father." Then, and only then, will I know who I Am.

Everyone will have that experience. One day you will actually see the Son of God, and this relationship is something so deep and so profound there is no uncertainty whatsoever in you when you are confronted. He stands before you, and you see him and you know he is your son and he knows you are his father and there is no uncertainty

Lecture 11 – Imagination

whatsoever. Only then do you know who you are, that you are God the Father.

Everyone, one day, will have that experience, everyone. I am speaking from experience. I am not theorizing. I am not speculating, but until that day comes let us discover God within ourselves as our own wonderful human Imagination and then test it. "For all things are possible to God; and all things are possible to him that believes."

Well, I can believe but have I made all things come to pass? It can only be my lack of belief if that statement is true. So how then to believe when reason denies it, when my senses deny it?

So reason cannot be the God of whom I speak, for reason will deny it. Doubt cannot be the God of whom I speak for doubt is called in Scripture the devil, 'the demon' and he finds rest only in the human Imagination, the Imagination that will entertain him that's where he went.

If I will have no room in my Imagination for doubt then I am on the road to learning the art of believing. How to believe when reason denies it, when my senses deny it? Well, entering into the image is the most delightful thing in the world. You can try it tonight when we go into the silence. Try it in the simplest little way: putting yourself elsewhere by making 'elsewhere' here, making "there" here and "then" now. And you can do it. It's not difficult if you'll try it.

Let me repeat: we are the operant power. Knowing it is one thing and doing it is another and the minute you try it, you can do it.

Lecture 11 – Imagination

Well then, wait. The minute you do it and open your eyes, in the twinkle of an eye you're back here and you will say to yourself, "I didn't do anything; I just did a simple little thing in my Imagination. How on earth could that produce the result when I've just assumed that I've done it?" Well, wait and see if a little bridge of incidents does not quickly appear, compelling you to walk across that bridge of incidents towards the fulfillment of what you have done. It works that way and after you have proven it, the whole world can rise in opposition and it makes no difference to you, you've done it. After you've done it, you keep on doing it and become all the more rooted in who God really is and you'll walk with your head up, walk as you ought to walk as one in whom God dwells.

There's no place in the world more holy than where you are. For wherever you are God is there. There's no church built with human hands comparable to the temple of God and "ye are the Temple of the Living God and the Spirit of God dwells in you." What temple in this world made with human hands could compare to this temple when no hand could make it? It comes into the world and it's a temple of the Living God.

But again, if this is the first time you've heard a thought of this nature, if it's the first time you've been exposed to it, I am not telling you it is not a shock and it's not difficult to accept. It isn't difficult to grasp, but difficult to accept after the training most of us here have had. I know I had it. I was raised in a very wonderful Christian orthodox home, where Sunday school was in order not once a week, but twice a week, grace at the table, Mother reading Scripture to us and interpreting Scripture based upon her concept, which was a secular concept.

Lecture 11 – Imagination

To her the Bible was secular history, things that actually happened in her world. She didn't realize that she, as the whole vast world was mistaking personification for persons and the vehicle that conveys the instruction for the instruction itself and the gross perspective for the ultimate sense intended. But Mother was raised that way and she made her exit from this world in that belief.

So, when I was exposed to this at the age of twenty or twenty-two, I must confess I couldn't sleep. It was so completely different that it turned me inside out. I wondered if I'd done the wrong thing to visit this friend. I wondered what on earth have I done? I felt I was a sinful being even to entertain the thought. I had to wrestle with myself and finally, when I put it to the test and it proved itself in performance then I knew that I'd found him.

But you can't find him and not share it with others, as told in Scripture: So Philip found him and he goes and he shares it with Nathaniel. Andrew found him and he goes and shares it with his brother, Peter. Peter didn't find him; his brother found him and then shared it. So here, we find and we share it. I have found him. All I can do is share him, in the hope that you will accept him.

I know this much: if you believe to the point of acceptance, life will be marvelous for you, perfectly wonderful for this is the one secret in the world that everyone should aspire to solve, for God is that pure imaging in ourselves. He underlies all of our faculties including our perception, but he streams into our surface mind least disguised in the form of productive fantasy. I sit here and have a daydream. Well, that's God in action, but then someone breaks it and I forget it. I didn't occupy it; I simply had a daydream but without

Lecture 11 – Imagination

occupancy. That's one of the greatest fallacies of the world, 'perpetual construction'. It's a daydream, deferred occupancy.

I don't occupy it, I don't go in and possess it and make it mine. If I, in my Imagination, could go right in and possess it and make it mine... If I, in my Imagination, could go right in and possess it and clothe myself with the feeling of the wish fulfilled, actually clothe myself with it by assuming that it's done now, until I feel natural in that assumption and that assumption though at the moment denied by my senses, if persisted in will harden into fact. [a statement made by Anthony Eden at the Guild Hall when he was Prime Minister of England]. So, this is our great secret concerning imagining.

If you doubt it tonight, I would only ask you not to deny it to the point of not trying it, but hold it in abeyance and try it now. Just try it, even if you want to disprove it. I tell you, you will not disprove it. You will in the attempt to disprove it, prove it. And then slowly you will come to completely accept it and then you will walk in the company of God.

You won't have to wait for Sunday morning to meet him in a church or any time of day. No matter where you are, you could be standing in a bar enjoying a drink, having fun at a dance and you are in the company of God. It makes no difference where you are once you know God and God is your own wonderful human Imagination and you'll become extremely discriminating because you'll know you can't entertain these ideas with complete acceptance of them and not reap them in your world.

Lecture 11 – Imagination

And who wants to reap the tears forever? So, you become ever more discriminating. Don't think for one second that you'll live a loose life. No. You'll become a far more wonderful person in the world. You hear a piece of gossip, it doesn't interest you.

Today in the morning paper, many people turned right away to the gossip columnist and wondered who is living with whom and they love it. They don't know the people and they will go right out and repeat what this person is paid to print, because it is like almost peeking through the keyhole of someone else's door.

He can't maintain that job. He's paid to be a gossip hound and people read it. Others read only the obituaries to see who's dead. You will not read those pages. You will simply suddenly dwell upon the noble things. Not only for yourself will you do it, your circle will widen. You will. You will think of a friend and if he is distressed, you represent him to yourself as you would like him to be. If he's unemployed, you represent him to yourself as gainfully employed. If he is earning less than what it really takes to live well in this world with his obligations, you represent him to yourself as living well and earning a decent living and assuming full responsibility of his job and you push him in your mind's eye.

So you widen your circle. It's sort of self perpetuating; you take in all because, eventually, "all that you behold, tho it appears Without it is Within, In your Imagination of which this World of Mortality is but a Shadow."

So, you can't exclude anyone. If you exclude one, it's your own failure. But you don't sit down and work with that

Lecture 11 – Imagination

one to make it so. You simply assume that it is so. You plant it as lightly as you would if you sowed a field. You don't go out and trample it, you sow the field and it comes up.

Well, this is what I mean by 'Imagination.' I identify my own wonderful human Imagination, when I say 'I', I am speaking of all, for everyone imagines, so I identify our Imagination with God. That to me is the Lord Jesus. He is buried in us and one day he will rise in us, not as something external to ourselves but he will rise in us as us, after we've gone through the furnaces of experience in this world of Caesar.

Now there's no room for a final death with Christ in man, for Christ resurrects. You say good-bye to a friend who has gone through the gate we call 'death,' but he cannot die. Nothing dies in this world for God is the God of the living. But nothing dies, because the immortal you cannot die and the immortal you is far more real than the garment of flesh and blood that it wears in the world of Caesar.

This is the limit of contraction for a purpose, but when this is burned in the furnace (cremated) you, the occupant, are not burned in the furnace. You are restored, clothed as you are now only the body is young, not a baby, a young body about twenty.

I encounter them all the time and they are young, though when I said good-bye through the gate of 'death,' they were seventy or eighty, my father, eighty-five when he said good-bye, my mother, sixty-one. I met them in their twenties. I am much, much older. I am. I meet them, and they grow. They grow there too; they don't remain twenty. You grow there and you are just as afraid as you are here; and you marry there

Lecture 11 – Imagination

too and strive there too and die there too, to find yourself restored once more.

And the journey continues until you resurrect. Resurrection is a departure from this age into that age called "the Kingdom of Heaven," but only when he in you resurrects as you, will you leave this world of Caesar. But while you are in it, why not learn his law because the blows are inevitable. Learn the law, that you may cushion the blows.

So, when I know what I want to cushion the problems of the moment, then I will apply it and apply this principle towards anything in my world. And the principle is this: First, you start with desire. Who is desiring? Well, I AM. Well, who is "I AM"? That's God. "That is my name forever and forever," as we are told in the book of Exodus. "Go tell them I AM has sent you. This is my name for all generations, forever and forever." Therefore, who is feeling? I AM. Well, that's God! Who is desiring? I AM. Well, that's God and "all things are possible to him.".

All right, start right there.

Could I continue desiring if I had it? No I couldn't. If I wanted this room to lecture in when I came here and then I got confirmation from the management that I am allowed to speak in the Marines' Memorial for ten days and the dates are set, could I write him a second letter pleading with him? Could I in any way hope after I had realized it? No, I simply walk in the assumption that I have it. So, when I requested that I have this room for 10 talks, it was granted and from then on I had no more desire for it. The desire was realized.

Lecture 11 – Imagination

I had to wait the normal time, the interval of a month, well it was a month ago that I accepted it. Then I came a month later to fulfill it. Well, the same thing is true in all that you do in this world. You simply dare to assume the feeling of the wish fulfilled until it seems natural, until it takes on the tones of reality and when it does, it's done.

And now, trust God. Well, who is God? Your own wonderful human Imagination! Did you imagine it? Well, that's God! Now trust him. Don't turn to any outside power.

The church has just demoted something like a hundred saints, after making fortunes selling little pictures of them. I wonder how many still wear St. Nicholas? They treated him as a saint. It's like treating Santa Claus as a saint. And all these saints . . the saint of the road, to protect you against an accident, now they say he never lived. If he never lived why did they ever start it and yet, hundreds of years ago they started this nonsense, so unnumbered millions of these little icons, little medals.

Down south our Cardinal admitted that tens of thousands of these little medals, he had put his seal of approval, the Seal of the Cardinal, on the reverse side of that little medal. When they asked him: "Well, now do you regret it?" he said: "No, it was acceptable then and I did it in good faith." But whoever started that nonsense started it for a commercial reason and they made unnumbered millions, hundreds of millions in selling them to the many. And what number of millions of people wore them and are still wearing them . . and he never existed! They mount them on the front of their car, on their little trucks, on their bikes and now to discover at this late date...

Lecture 11 – Imagination

I've gone out with these friends of mine to greet three fellows who came back from the war. One was a marine; he lost one foot and the arm was completely smashed, one arm. His brother was going into the priesthood and he came back deaf; he was in the army. Another was in the army; he came back with TB. And their mother told me in all innocence and they went along with the mother. "Were it not for St. Christopher they would not have returned." She really believed it, and they believe it and one was three years going for the priesthood when the war broke and he thought it better to serve his country than to become a priest. Then when he came out he gave up completely and got married and has a nice little family. But he believed it and they believed it and the father and the mother believed it.

They entertained me very well, but they knew that I was not safe because I was a Protestant. "Christian" meant nothing to them because you either are a Roman Catholic or you are not a Christian. So, I said to my wife, "What will they think when they find out that I am not a Roman Catholic?" She said, "It doesn't really matter. They love me dearly and I am not one. They know you can't be saved anyway, so what?" So, we all go and have fun. My wife was very, very honest about it for the simple reason her father was that family's closest friend.

And these came back, one with a foot missing, a crushed shoulder. Well, I was in the army too, not as long as these fellows were, but I didn't come back fragmented. I used this principle to get out of the army and I got out honorably discharged. I didn't run away. The very one who said "No" to my request was the very Colonel who called me nine days after I began to apply this principle. I did it quite simply. I made up my mind that I wanted to get out of the army and

Lecture 11 – Imagination

then I thought, if I were out, where would I be? Well, I wouldn't be here picking up pots and doing all these things in the army and being trained. I would be a civilian in New York City in my own apartment with my little girl and my wife.

My son was a Marine and he was already in Guadalcanal. He volunteered with my consent for he wasn't more than seventeen when I gave my permission for him to join the Marines.

But having tasted the army life, I wanted no part of it. I was thirty-eight. So, I simply assumed I was a civilian living in New York City with my wife and my little girl, who was only a few months old and the same Colonel who had disapproved my application called me in and said: "Goddard, you still want to get out of the army?" I said: "Yes, sir." And he asked a thousand questions and to each I said: "Yes, sir." Then he said, "All right, bring me in a new application," and that day I was honorably discharged and on a train headed for the fulfillment of my dream.

I simply knew what I wanted; I didn't ask any one's permission. I went to sleep in the barracks with all the boys all around. I didn't tell them what I was doing. As far as they were concerned I was sleeping on that cot. As far as I was concerned I was sleeping in New York City. I went to bed physically on a cot, but in my Imagination in my own bed in New York City. When I thought of Camp Polk, Louisiana it was way down south and I am up here in New York City. And, then the same man who disapproved was the one who actually granted me honorable discharge.

Lecture 11 – Imagination

I am speaking from experience; I am not theorizing. I didn't hurt anyone. No one was hurt by my application of God's Law. Are we not told: "Whatever you desire, believe that you have received it, and you will?" You will read that in the 11th chapter of the book of Mark: "Whatever you desire . . ." He didn't say, if it's good for you. He leaves us entirely to make our decision. He actually acquaints us with the law, and leaves us to our decision. So, I was left to my decision. I wanted to get out. The Colonel could tell me nothing to persuade me to change my opinion. If he had said, "No," that was final, I couldn't appeal to some higher echelon.

I could take it only to my commanding officer. Well, he was my commanding officer, and he disapproved it. Well, I came back, I had the paper in my hand, "Disapproved." I went to bed, without his permission, and slept in New York City. I went to bed without anyone in the barracks knowing what I was doing. They saw a man called Neville Goddard sleeping in that bunk but they didn't know I wasn't there, for where could I be save in Imagination? If I am not sleeping here in Imagination, I am not here.

You see the garment that I am wearing, but you would have to find out where I AM in Imagination to actually know where I am. You can see the garment, but is the garment the man? I was sleeping in Imagination which is God and "all things are possible to him." Well then, "He" changed the Colonel's decision. He changed his mind. Who is "He"? My Imagination.

God is one. There aren't a million little gods running around. There is only one God. "Hear, O Israel: The Lord our God, the Lord is one."

Lecture 11 – Imagination

Don't look for a second god; there aren't any second gods. And that one God became humanity and in man that one God is man's own wonderful human Imagination: that one God. So it's the 'one' made up of 'others' and that is exactly what the word Elohim means. The word translated 'God' in Scripture is Elohim and Elohim is a compound unity. It's a plural word, one made up of others. We are the 'others' and all collectively make the one Lord, which is called 'I AM.' Well, don't you know that you are, and don't you say: "I AM"? That's God. And can't you imagine? Well, imaging is God in action.

So, what are you imagining? You determine that. For, as I said earlier, I imagine, as do you. We cannot imagine differently. All differences lie in content. What is my response to the eternal question, "Who am I?" That response determines the conditions of my life. Am I a little unknown being, struggling for a dollar to pay rent, to buy food? Well, all right, that's what will happen to me. And there's no being on the outside to change it! I've got to bring about the change within myself. I can borrow money and beg for money and if I remain in that little concept of myself, I will be unable to pay back and will always have to keep looking for someone else to borrow from while I remain in the consciousness of being a little unwanted non-entity.

Let me remain at that moment just what I am and change it now, begin to change my response to the question, "Who am I?" And if God dwells in me I ought to be important, not against someone else in the world. That doesn't make any difference to me what they are. Grant them exactly what they want. If they want riches, let them. What does it matter? If they want to be in the social world at the very top, let them be. No envy whatsoever! If they want to be important in the

Lecture 11 – Imagination

eyes of the world, let them be important. You have different values. You are in union with God and God is within you and what better companion could you have in this world than to walk in the company of God, walk with him not only on Sunday morning, but every day of the week, knowing who he is?

So, we have to make the decision. "Choose this day whom you will serve." Will I serve a false god or will I serve the one and only living God? And that one and only living God is your Imagination . . my Imagination . . and that is the immortal man that cannot die.

Now let us go into the silence.

Good!

When you completely accept this, you will discover you need no intermediary between yourself and God . . none! He became you, that you may become God!

Now, are there any questions, please?

Q. [Inaudible]

Neville: I would not say that every dream needs an interpretation. Most of them do, for the universal language, regardless of what tongue you use to express yourself . . there is a universal language, and that is the language of symbolism. Unfortunately, we are all past masters at misinterpretation, but there is a language that is a universal language of symbolism. So, I say, everything in this world contains within itself the capacity for symbolic significance.

Lecture 11 – Imagination

So, in my vision of the moon I asked for light concerning the law . . how I could tell those that I am trying to teach, a more simple way to realize their objective in this world. And then that night came the vision. It was a very simple presentation, for here the moon is something that man aspires to reach. Long before we entertained the thought seriously of reaching the moon, we used it as an expression, "He is reaching for the moon." And you would say about someone who has no background to even aspire: Why he is crazy! Here is this man without any educational background, and he hopes one day to leave his imprint in the world concerning that which only an educated man can do. Well, they say, "He is reaching for the moon." So, the moon is only a symbol of anyone's desire.

[The same man continued his question.]

Neville: I find myself intuitive enough to interpret the dream of another. I asked down south (I haven't the time here, it would take more time than I am allotted here for two weeks) but down south they write me letters asking me to explain a dream, which they find difficult to interpret for themselves. And as they grow (and we outgrow in this world) they turn to me for the interpretation of a dream that seems to have no meaning. But every dream has meaning. As we are told in the 12th chapter of the book of Numbers: "God makes himself known unto man in a vision and speaks to him in a dream." Well, if God is my Imagination, and all dreams proceed from my Imagination (that is, my dreams and your dreams) therefore, I must learn the language that it is using to convey to my surface mind this message. So, I cannot discount the simplest dream. It may be produced by some undigested piece of beef, but I don't look upon a dream as the result of any undigested piece of beef. I look upon the

Lecture 11 – Imagination

dream as my own being . . the depth of my being . . attempting to reveal something to me in the language of dreams. When it comes to vision, that is something entirely different. This is vision. A vision is just like this, real beyond measure.

Question: As regards symbolism, I came across a book that contradicted the whole idea. In other words, this mysticism . . they say to deny yourself and all images, and leave yourself open and empty to God, and that this is the only way you can have a mystical union.

Neville: First of all, I would not accept that, and I would not say that any person's individual approach is the only way. So, any man who writes a book (and may I tell you, ninety-nine per cent of the books written are a waste of paper) but because a thing is printed, the other person, because he sees it in print, thinks he must be a wise person. "Look, he has a book," but it is sheer nonsense from beginning to end.

[The man continued with his question]: It was not just one person; it was several who called themselves, "The Friends of God." I don't know whether you have ...

Neville: Well, for instance, today we have enormous groups of people calling themselves by other names. We just had a huge, big one in New York City where the Yankee Stadium couldn't hold the crowd, and Yankee Stadium can take care of 75,000-odd people in the stands alone. But they were allowed to come down on the grass. Well, if the stands can take care of 70-odd thousand and the field certainly holds many, many more, they estimated they had about 300,000. They called themselves by a very wonderful name

Lecture 11 – Imagination

in Scripture, and ask any one of the 300,000 who were there to get up and testify from experience about their name. They called themselves "Witnesses." Well, if you are a witness, witness to what? Have you witnessed the birth of God in you? Have you witnessed any of these great mysteries of Scripture?

One of these "Witnesses" came to my door about a year ago (in fact, four of them, but only one came up the stairs). I was busy at the time reading my Bible. I spend hours every day with the Bible. Well, this was about 4:30 or 5:00 o'clock in the afternoon. She came to the door with her Bible all marked up with little pieces of paper, and then, on the street (looking to see what reception she was going to get) there were about three or four down on the sidewalk. She came up and asked me if I would open the door to let her in to explain God's Word to me. I said: "I am sorry, but you came without an appointment, and I am busy. In fact, I am reading his Word right now." And then something led to something else, and I said: "I am sorry, I am busy, and I have no time to entertain you or to discuss anything with you."

Then she started quoting; she wouldn't allow me to brush her off this way, so she started quoting some Scripture. She said, "Do you know what it means?" So, I told her my interpretation of the passage she quoted, and she said to me, "What are you? A Mormon, or something?" So, she was going to have her way, and that's all you can do. So, I said: "I am awfully sorry, my lady, but I cannot give you any more of my time unless it is by appointment. You can't come and ring my doorbell and expect admittance. You can't do it. I have a family, and we live a very quiet and nice life, and we don't have interruptions this way." So, she went on down and they gabbed and pointed their finger up: "Mark that one

Lecture 11 – Imagination

off; he's going to hell." So, what can you do with people? I mean, leave them alone. You cannot take a man by his nose and put him into a state of consciousness if he resists it. We are told in Scripture, "I will send a famine upon the world; it will not be a hunger for bread or a thirst for water, but for the hearing of the word of God." Well, until that famine is sent upon you by the God within you, the word is not within you. You are more interested in making an extra dollar.

I can't give one person all the questions. I've got to get to someone else.

Q. [Inaudible]

Neville: Ultimately we turn to the One, but we are brothers, as spoken of in Scripture, these words, "He has set bounds to the people, according to the numbers of the sons of God." So, we are brothers; it takes all to make the one. I will never in eternity lose my identity, neither will you, and yet we are one. You are the same God. Of the same son you are the father, as I AM the father. That shows the unity of our being. If you are the father of my son and that one son I know to be my son, and everyone is going to be the father of that son, there is only one Father.

So, Scripture teaches, "There is only one body, one spirit, one hope, one Lord, one faith, one baptism, one God and Father of all" (Ephesians 4:4-6) only one, yet no one is going to lose their identity. I am expanding my identity but there is no loss. When I am embraced by the risen Lord as he wore the "human form divine," which is Love, I answered the question. He asked me to name the greatest thing in the world. When I said, "Love," he embraced me and we fused and became one spirit, one body but I didn't lose my identity.

Lecture 11 – Imagination

When we separated from that union, I came out as Neville, only within myself I was conscious of a greater self, fully aware of the greater self, without loss of identity. So, everyone here is destined to discover the fatherhood of God as himself through the Son calling him, "Father." Everyone.

Q. [Inaudible]

Neville: My dear, we have eaten of the tree of the knowledge of good and evil. We have enormous pressures in the world to make the world good. We will never bring about an unbalance of good and evil. It is always borne on this tree. This is the tree of the knowledge of good and evil, and it bears equal number of fruit. So, they have all the efforts in the world to make it a better world. They are up the wrong tree. We'll get off this tree of good and evil one day and eat of the tree of life . . when that day comes which comes with the resurrection. And the resurrection is not a collective thing; it is an individual experience. We are called out of this state one by one by one, to unite into a single body, who is the risen Lord. So, everyone is favored.

Ten million dollars for this, a hundred million dollars for that and then just wait a little while, and then at the end of a year a little investigation: a committee is formed to find that those who got the hundred million to dispense it for good, they pocketed it themselves. All of a sudden: "Where is the twenty-seven million dollars in oil gone?" Why, twenty-seven million dollars in oil can't be accounted for.

Somebody had it. They didn't spill it in Santa Barbara. [Ed. note: reference to oil blowout in 1969.] That came out of the sea. So, where are the twenty-seven million? Only that week twenty-seven million dollars worth of oil for our boys in

Lecture 11 – Imagination

Vietnam and they can't account for it. You see, you find this in every walk of life: good and evil. So don't try to burn it out; you'll not stop the tree from bearing good and evil. You go along your own way in all the lovely things in the world and grant the others to do what they want to do. They are going to do it anyway. When I speak, I want to help everyone in this world, individually. I am not for the crowd, to make them all this so-called 'good.' "No one can come unto me, unless my Father call him." and "I and my Father are one." Not one could be here tonight if my Father didn't call him. Even those who may never come again were called. This is your first little blow, little explosion.

Q. [Inaudible]

Neville: Why, certainly, you can help anyone in this world, and you will get to the point where you will help everyone. But you are not going to change the nature of the tree. This tree bears good and evil. This is the nature of this world. And all of a sudden you will come out of it and you will eat of the tree of life, and you will see this world so differently, you will be shocked beyond measure.

Q. [Inaudible]

Neville: My dear, the world is dead and people don't know it. Dead, dead as dead can be, even though they are walking it. The day will come that you will have this experience. You will know that what you are feeling within you, you could arrest; and as you look at the people round about you, you arrest their activity within you, and every one stands still. I don't mean they are standing still like soldiers at attention when they can still blink their eyes and move the body; I mean they are dead! They can't move an eye. They are not

Lecture 11 – Imagination

aware that they are standing still. And if you arrested that motion for 1,000 years, when you released it they would continue on their intention and not know for one moment that they were still for 1,000 years. This is all part of the structure of the universe.

All that is taking place in the world belongs to the eternal structure of the universe. You didn't get created; you are part of the eternal structure. All marriages, all divorces, all love, wayward love, lovely friendships, hates it is all part of the eternal structure of the universe.

So, when we speak of creation, I don't mean erecting a little man of clay. Man was always a part of the structure of the universe. I am not speaking of the creation of life. We are only animated bodies now. The day is coming that we will become life-giving spirits. Then you will see the whole vast world is a dead body, as dead as the moon and all the relationships are worked out in detail. If one could but see with the awakened eye as the child comes through the womb, the whole pattern of its life is there.

Q. [Inaudible]

Neville: Because it's a dead body. It is now animated by the spirit of God, which is called breath, for the word "breath," the word "wind," and the word "spirit," are one and the same, both in Greek and in Hebrew. So, it breathes the breath of life into man's body. It is the spirit that possesses the body, that then becomes an animated body . . a living being, but not a life-giving spirit. That one's the act of creation.

Lecture 11 – Imagination

[Question concerning assuming the wish fulfilled] . . you cannot allow any conscious fears.

Neville: The question is: having assumed the feeling of the wish fulfilled, you cannot deny that in spite of that assumption there are a few conscious doubts and fears. Well, I do not deny that, but practice will make it less and less so and you will trust God so implicitly, not as an external being who may be quite watching you when you are praying. That is what people say, "I wonder if he saw me?" because your Imagination will always...

As we started off the lecture tonight quoting from the 17th chapter of the book of Acts: "You have an unknown god...I will tell you of that unknown God and he is not far off. In him we live and move and have our being." Where could I go, departing from my Imagination? I AM all Imagination and that is God. So whatever I AM imagining, my Imagination is seeing. Eventually you have such complete confidence in Him. Imagination and faith are the stuff out of which man fashions his world. Now, faith is the subjective appropriation of the objective, hope, and faith and Imagination are the stuff out of which we fashion our world.

Good night.

Lecture 12 – The Secret of Imagining

Lecture 12

Neville Goddard 7-20-1970
The Secret of Imagining

Tonight's subject is: "The Secret of Imagining." In almost every particular is the world about us different from what we think it. Why then should we be so incredulous? Life calls on us to believe not less, but more. The secret of imaging is the greatest of all problems, to the solution of which everyone should aspire, for supreme power, supreme wisdom, supreme delight lie in the solution of this mystery.

If you have solved the mystery of imagining you have found Jesus Christ. Jesus Christ is defined for us in scripture as "The power of God and the wisdom of God". As we are told in the eighth chapter of the Book of Proverbs, and Wisdom is speaking now, personified as a little child:

> "When He laid out the foundation of the world
> I was beside Him like a little child
> I was daily His delight,
> rejoicing before Him always
> rejoicing in His inhabited world,
> delighting in the affairs of men.
> He who finds me finds life
> He who misses me injures himself;
> All who hate me love death."

So find that child that is the symbol of Jesus Christ, who is the creative power and the wisdom of God. Believe me when I tell you that this Jesus Christ of scripture is your own wonderful human Imagination. "By him all things were

Lecture 12 – The Secret of Imagining

made, and without him was not anything made that was made". He is in the world, and the world was made by Him, and the world knows Him not.

Look into the world and name one thing that wasn't first imagined. You name one thing that does not now exist in your Imagination just name it. Name anything in the world that does not now exist in your Imagination: "All things exist in the human Imagination.".

"God is man, and exists in us and we in Him". The eternal abode of man is the Imagination; and that is God Himself. Try to disprove it.

God is my pure imagining in myself. He underlies all of my faculties, including perception, but He streams into my surface mind least disguised in the form of productive fancy. I can catch Him in the act of producing these images in my mind. Just try it as you are seated here. Try to think of anything. Try to catch Him in the act of actually producing in your own mind's eye all these images. "For all things exist in the human Imagination." But how can I single out one and clothe it so that it becomes an objective fact?

That is the secret, for they all exist within me. But how can I catch one and clothe it? Well I will try to show you tonight what I know from my own personal experience. Scripture teaches it, but it tells it in a strange and wonderful way: how to clothe it.

You see this room in which we are now? It's more real now than your own home is to you; yet you know your home more intimately than you know this room. Yet this room, at the moment, while you are in it, is more real than your own

Lecture 12 – The Secret of Imagining

home. How different the cubic reality from the plane of any depiction of it. This room is now so "real" because we are in it, and we are all Imagination. We're in it; and to us, it's real. Think of your own home. Do we not have the capacity to draw it, to paint it? But in your mind's eye you have a plane depiction of it, but it's not as real now as the room is. This room is real because we're in it.

Now this is what I mean by making something that is only a thought something that is real. How do I do it? I single out, out of my own wonderful human Imagination, that which I want to make real. It's all in you. Then I must enter into it as I have entered into this room. "If the spectator would enter into any one of these images in his Imagination, approaching it on the fiery chariot of his own contemplative thought", it would become just as real to him as this room.

You may ask, "What would that do to me? Will it become real in the not-distant future?" I know from my own experience, it will. You can sit here and enter into a state. It may not take on quite the reality of this room, but it will if you persist in it; it will become just like this. When you open your eyes, it vanishes. But does it mean that I tasted that, and that's all? No. Having gone into it, may I tell you, it will follow you? It will not recede into the past as memory; it will advance into the future and you will confront it. This is the secret of imagining, which is finding out the secret of God.

You are an immortal being. You cannot die because you are all Imagination. Man is all Imagination; and God truly is man; and He exists in us, and we in Him. And that immortal body of man is the human Imagination, and that is Jesus Christ Himself, the Eternal Body of man and it cannot die. You cannot die. The body, yes, this will fade; but I am not

Lecture 12 – The Secret of Imagining

the garment that I am wearing. I am the wearer of the garment, and the wearer of this garment is all Imagination. This is the story that the Bible teaches.

When we read in the Bible: "I, even I, AM He. I kill, and I make alive; I wound, and I heal; and there is no God beside me". This is not a being outside of you speaking; this is the Being that you really are, speaking within you, trying to persuade Himself of His own wonderful power to create. It can kill, and yet it can make alive. It can resurrect from the dead. And that is your own wonderful human Imagination.

The day will come; you will taste this power that you possess. You will come into a room just like this, and you will still it not by commanding anyone in the room to be still. Leave them just as they are. But you will arrest within yourself an activity that you feel, and as you still it in you, everything that you observe becomes still perfectly still. You could go forward and examine them, and they are dead. Everything is perfectly still and dead. The life is in you. You release the activity, and they once more become animated and continue to do what they intended to do. You could, when you stilled the activity within you, change their motivation; and when you release it, they will do entirely different from what they intended to do prior to your arrestment within you of that activity.

"As the Father has life in Himself, He has granted the Son also to have life in Himself"; and you have that within you. You're not quite aware of it yet, but you will become aware. Those that I am teaching will have dreams, as you have dreams; and in their dreams they will become awake, and then arrest it in the dream and change the motivation and see the intended act change.

Lecture 12 – The Secret of Imagining

Here is one. A friend became aware that she was dreaming, and here's a man who intended to hurt her. He got out of the car and came towards her, and she became afraid; and her fright woke her; but instead of waking on the bed, she awoke in the dream. Then she realized, "This is what he teaches. Now I will simply arrest it." She didn't argue with him; she arrested, within her, the activity that animated him. And she said to him, "You are tired. You need a good hot cup of coffee and then a good sound sleep," and then she told him exactly what he needed, and released the activity within her. He shook his head as though something strange had happened within him, and he got back into the car all in her dream and drove off. You see, she changed his intention towards her.

This may seem impossible to the world. As I started this lecture, almost everything in this world is so completely unlike what it appears to be. And I am telling you from my own experience; I am not speculating. I am not theorizing. The power of which I speak is a power within you. That power is not something on the outside; it's your own wonderful human Imagination, and you will learn to control it. Your Imagination animates the world in which you live. You change your Imagination, and you change the world.

To attempt to change circumstances before I change my own imaginal activity is to struggle against the very nature of my own being, for my own imaginal activity is animating my world. If I believe that I am injured or that others are against me, I have conjured them in my world, and they have to be against me. If I fully believe that all are working towards the fulfillment of my good, they have to work towards the fulfillment of my good. I don't ask them. I don't compel them. I simply do it only within myself, and the whole vast world

Lecture 12 – The Secret of Imagining

exists within me. Therefore, it is myself "pushed out." It's objectified. I don't have to change affairs; I only change it within myself; and then everyone, though I know him or not by name, it doesn't really matter, it's myself "pushed out."

I couldn't tell you the atoms of my body, but it is my body. I couldn't tell you, if you took the hand off, that it's my hand I am looking at, any more than I could tell you your name or anything about you; yet, you are myself "pushed out," as this body is the body I wear. And so, as the body obeys my mind, you my "pushed-out" body will obey my mind too. All I have to do is to concern myself with what I want in this world, and try to keep it within the frame of the Golden Rule; doing unto others only that which I would want done unto me, nothing more than that; hurting no one, doing not a thing to anyone other than that which I would want done unto me.

"You mean, Christ is in me?" Are we not taught that in scripture?"Know ye not that Jesus Christ is in you? Do you not know that Jesus Christ is in you, unless of course you fail to meet the test?". Well then, test it. How would I test it?

A friend of mine, maybe, is unwell; or maybe he's unemployed, or maybe he is not earning enough to meet the obligations of life. All right, he is in me. As I think of him, he's in me. He need not be physically present for me to think of him; he's in me. I think of him; I conjure him. Well, can I change his entire picture in me? I assume that he is talking to me, and he's telling me that he has never had more, he has never felt better; and as I believe in what I am seeing in my own mind's eye, I believe in him. That is Christ in me, and all things are possible to Christ.

Lecture 12 – The Secret of Imagining

Well then, test it and see if it works. See if you do not see him in the not-distant future earning more, looking better; and everything in the world that you have done within you, he responds to. He need not praise you or thank you. You don't need his praise; you don't need his thanks. You don't need confirmation from him, other than he does conform to what you have done in yourself concerning him.

You ask no one to thank you. Thank nothing. You are simply exercising the power of God within you. "And the power of God and the wisdom of God is Jesus Christ". And there is nothing in the world but God. It is all God in you "pushed out," and God is your own wonderful human Imagination. He can't be closer. God is never so far off as even to be near, for nearness implies separation. He's not separated. God actually, literally became as I am, that I may be as He is.

He is not something on the outside. No matter how near He is, He can't even touch me. He actually became me, with all of my weaknesses, all of my limitations; and now I am trying to struggle within myself to find out who I AM, and that's His name. My name is in Him. What's your name?"Go and say I AM has sent you." "Is that you name?" "Yes, forever and forever it is my name." "What name? Jehovah?" "No." "The Lord?" "No, I AM." That's His name. That is His name forever and forever.

Well I cannot say, "I AM," and point elsewhere. I can't say, "I AM," and feel something is near me. It can't even be near. Something can be near to what I am, but "I AM" can't be near. And that's the name of God forever and forever. So you are the Lord Jesus Christ.

Lecture 12 – The Secret of Imagining

Now a pattern is given to us in scripture by which you will know that you are; and I promise you, from my own personal experience, that you shall have it. It is a true story. The truest story ever told is the story of the Lord Jesus Christ. When He said, "I AM the Father," may I tell you, if he's a father, he has a son, hasn't he? Or at least he has a child; but I tell you, it's a son. He said, "When you see me, you see the Father"; but if I look at you and I say, "Well then, you are the father, show me your son." He can't show me His son outside as His son, because He and I are one. He has to show me His son not of blood nor of the will of the flesh; it has to be born, not of blood nor of the will of the flesh nor of the will of man, but of God. And He tells me that He is God, and He tells me that He and I are one. Well then, it can't be born in any normal, natural way. He has to be born of God.

Well then, who is your son? He tells me in scripture that David calls Him, "Father."

"David calls you, 'Father'?"

"Yes." He said, "I inspired the prophets," and read the Prophets; and in the Prophets, David calls the Lord, "my Father."

"You mean, David, then, is my son?"

"Yes, he's my son."

"But I do not know him," you will say.

But I will tell you, from my own personal experience, you will know it because I know it; David called me, "my Father." David called me, "my Lord." David called me the Rock of his

Lecture 12 – The Secret of Imagining

salvation. Everything that is said in scripture concerning what he said of the Lord, he said of me. And so, I stood, and here is David, and I knew it beyond all doubt that here is my son, and my son is David, not a David, the David the only David the David of biblical fame. And as he called me, "Father," memory returned.

This is the story of the Christian faith; the fulfillment of all the promises made in the Old Testament. The Old Testament is only a prophetic blueprint of the life of Jesus Christ. It's an adumbration, a foreshadowing in a not-altogether conclusive or immediately evident way; but as it unfolds within you, it's nothing more than God's memory returning. But having become you, it becomes your memory returning, and you awaken as God Himself. And there is nothing in the world like God.

Now you ask, what, all the horrors of the world, the pain, the suffering? Yes. It takes all the "furnaces" to prepare you to receive the gift that He gives, and the gift is Himself. God actually became you. He gave Himself to you, that you may be God. And God in you is your own wonderful human Imagination, that's God.

Now tonight try it. I ask you to believe me. But whether you believe me or not, try it anyway. Take a friend of yours and bring him before your mind's eye, and then talk to him from the premise of your desire for him fulfilled not going to be, but already fulfilled. And having done it, believe that all things are possible to the Lord Jesus Christ; and you just saw Jesus Christ in action, for you saw the creative power of God in action, and that's Jesus Christ. That is your own wonderful human Imagination.

Lecture 12 – The Secret of Imagining

Now believe in the reality of what you've just done. Believe that this subjective appropriation of your objective hope for a friend is a fact. That is really praying. And all things are possible to God. Go within and appropriate it just completely appropriate it, and see it unfold within your own vast marvelous world.

So this wonderful secret is the secret of the Lord Jesus Christ. If you turn on the outside and turn to another, you do not know the Lord Jesus Christ. You can make all kinds of images of Him. That's not the Lord Jesus Christ. If any man should ever come and say, "Look, there he is," or "Here he is," don't believe it. Why? Because when you actually meet Him, you are going to meet your Self. The Christ of faith comes to us as one unknown; yet one who in some ineffable mystery lets us experience who He is; and when we experience Jesus Christ, we experience Him in the first-person, singular, present-tense experience. You will never see Him coming from without. Let no one tell you you're going to meet Him coming from without. You will meet Him awakening Himself within you as you. That's the Lord Jesus Christ. That's the great sacrifice. He is crucified on Humanity.

Every human form is the cross that He wears; and in that form He awakens as the one in whom He awakens. He awakens as that Being, and that Being is the Lord Jesus Christ. And because He is the father of David, David called that Being, "Father"; then you know, "I AM He."

Oh, I can tell you from now to the ends of time, and I may not persuade you to believe it; but when it happens to you, you need no further persuasion, for you are confronted

Lecture 12 – The Secret of Imagining

with the facts and there you stand in the presence of you own son, and the son is the Son of God.

"I will tell of the decree of the Lord," said David. "He said unto me, 'Thou art my son. Today I have begotten thee.'". These are the words of David in the Second Psalm. "I will tell of the decree of the Lord. He said unto me, 'Thou art my son.'" That son is going to call you, "Father"; and then, and only then, you will know you are God the Father. That is the mystery of the entire world. And so, what you accomplish in this world concerning finances is wonderful for you as an individual in the world of Caesar. What you do concerning the social world all these things it's marvelous; but you will only really fulfill your destiny as you fulfill scripture, for the purpose of life is to fulfill scripture.

"I have accomplished the work Thou gavest me to do." What work? All that the prophets spoke about me; and beginning with Moses and the prophets and the Psalms; he interpreted to them in all the scriptures the things concerning Himself. Then said he, "Scripture must be fulfilled in you," and the purpose of life is to fulfill scripture the prophecy of God to man, for He gave man Himself, or promised to give man Himself. And He promised me a son. The son He promised was His Son; and in giving me His Son, He gave me Himself, for His Son calls me, "Father." And that is the whole mystery of life.

There's nothing but God. One Being expanding Himself forever and forever and forever, each Himself. And even though he calls you, "Father," may I tell you, you will not lose your identity. You are individualized and you will tend towards ever greater and greater individualization. And yet, you are the Father of my son; and if you are the Father of my

Lecture 12 – The Secret of Imagining

son, then you and I are one. It is a great mystery, we are brothers, for you do not lose your identity and I do not lose my identity. So you and I, behind these masks are eternal brothers the Father of the One and only Begotten Son.

Well if you are the father of my son, and my own wife is the "father" of my son, then the relationship on earth of men, or friend to friend and wife to husband, is above this level, and we are eternal brothers, all forming the one Father.

So tonight, you take me seriously; and when you go home or start it here, you put into practice this greatest of all secrets; the secret of imagining. There is no greater secret in the world. Every child born of woman is alive because it was imagined. And imagining is God in action. That's the soul of man imagining; and that is the power of God. And the power of God is Christ. And that is the wisdom of God, and the wisdom of God is Christ.

A child can imagine. Well, that's Christ. That is Christ crucified on that little tiny garment, and it suffers with everything that that little child imagines, or it enjoys with everything the little child imagines. It wears all the stripes and all the blows that man in his misuse of that power will do. He doesn't criticize him. He waits upon me as indifferently and as quickly when the will in me is evil as when it is good. That way, He bears all my stripes. He bears all of my misuse of His power, knowing that in the end, I will awaken and use it only lovingly.

When I completely awaken from the dream of life, I will use this creative power of God only lovingly. But in the meantime while I am trying to awaken to the use of this power, I misuse it. And may I tell you, you will confront this

Lecture 12 – The Secret of Imagining

vision, and you will see what you did from the beginning, for you didn't begin it a few years ago in your mother's womb. You have been coming through the centuries.

One night, here I saw this monstrous creature covered in hair. It looked like a gorilla, and the hair was all dark brown from head to toe. It was a monster. And here, the most glorious, heavenly creature a female; and this was a male monster. And it called out to this heavenly creature, "Mother, mother." Well, I knew this could not be this radiant, heavenly creature; and so I struck him. And as I struck it, it gloated; it loved violence. And I pummeled it, and it gloated all the more. Well, it could speak in a guttural tone, calling this heavenly being, "Mother." And that annoyed me. Then suddenly from within me I knew. Why, this is my own creation. And so is this one. They are only the out-picturing of my two different uses of the creative power that I AM.

Here (the monster) is the complete embodiment of every misused moment of my life. Every time I was violent, I created and fed this monster. It whispered in my ear to be monstrous, to be violent, to be bad, to be evil, for it fed only on this thought. And here (the heavenly creature) was the embodiment of all my loving thoughts. Every kind, considerate, wonderful thought in my life fed this one.

As I saw this monstrous thing and realized that it was my own offspring, it was the fruit of my misspent energy, I pledged myself. There was no one to whom I could turn, I pledged myself that if it took eternity I would redeem it. It did not come into being through any power other than my own misuse of my own power. It could not have been brought into being; and that thing could not live, and it could not help itself. I didn't condemn it.

Lecture 12 – The Secret of Imagining

At that moment, I felt compassion beyond the wildest dreams of anyone for this monstrous thing that I had created. And when I made myself that pledge that I would redeem it if it took me eternity, at that very moment, the whole thing got smaller and smaller and smaller; but it didn't waste the energy that it embodied returned to me. I began to feel a power that, until that moment, I had never felt before. And this one began to grow. The beauty that she embodied and personified glowed as the energy came back from this one (the monster) to me; and the whole thing dissolved before my eyes.

So, "nothing is lost in all my holy mountain" I did not lose that energy that I misplaced, it returned to me, that was embodied in that monster. And throughout the centuries, it was it who whispered in my ear monstrous things to be done, because it could only feed on violence. It could only feed on evil.

Then I realized what it meant: that I ate of the Tree of the Knowledge of Good and Evil. And so it fed upon evil, and she fed upon the good. And then the evil that was only the energy misspent returned to me; and then the whole thing came back to me. And then I broke the spell, and I awoke in this world.

Well everyone is going to confront that gorilla on the threshold. Everyone has him, unseen by mortal eye, and he whispers into your ear to entertain the unlovely thoughts of the world. And your every reaction that is unlovely, it feeds upon it; and your every thought that is kind and wonderful and loving, she feeds upon it. And the day will come, you will be strong enough to confront this. And may I tell you, it will

Lecture 12 – The Secret of Imagining

take you the twinkling of a second to dissolve it? You don't labor upon it. All it needs is the core of integrity within you.

When you pledge yourself, and no one else, you don't swear upon your mother, you don't swear upon a friend, you don't swear upon the Bible; you pledge yourself to redeem it. At the moment you pledge yourself, and within you, you know you mean it, the whole thing dissolves. It's no time at all in dissolving. And then all the energy returns to you, and you are stronger than ever before to go forward now and eat of the Tree of the Knowledge of Good and Evil.

And if you forward and misuse it again, you start another form building; and one day you will dissolve it again. Eventually you will become completely awakened, and you will use your wonderful power only not for good, that tree will come to an end, for Life itself. For eating of the Tree of the Knowledge of Good and Evil is this world. The day will come that you will eat of the Tree of Life that bears the fruit of truth and error.

Error will embody itself here, and one day you will confront the error, and the error will dissolve before your mind's eye as truth begins to glow before you, because you are eating, then, of the Tree of Life as you formally ate of the Tree of the Knowledge of Good and Evil. And the combat of good and evil produces this monster, and the combat of truth and error produces an entirely different form of being, more glorious than that one of good and more horrible than this. The error will dissolve just as quickly when you confront error.

So if today your teaching is not true and you live by it, you are building something just as monstrous; but one day

Lecture 12 – The Secret of Imagining

you will confront error and you will discover that you lived by a false concept of God something on the outside of Self; that you formerly worshiped a little golden figure made of gold and silver. It had eyes, but could not see. It had ears, but could not hear. It had a mouth, but could not speak. It had feet, and it could not walk. It made no sound within its throat. And those who made it are just like it. And those who trusted it are just like it too.

So all the little icons in the world that people worship these are the little things called "error"; and one day you will discover the true God. And when you discover the true God, you will find that He is all within your own wonderful being as your own wonderful human Imagination. You'll walk in the consciousness of being God. You don't brag about it.

As Blake answered when they asked him, "What do you think of Jesus Christ?" Blake answered, "Jesus Christ is the only God"; but he hastened to add to it, "But so am I, and so are you."

So you don't tell anyone. You simply know that you are the Being spoken of in scripture as "God the Father." For all that is said of Him, you are going to experience; and you are going to experience it in the first-person, singular, and a present-tense experience. And then you will know.

Today is the eleventh year since it happened to me right here in this city, right across the way at the hotel with the star at the top of the roof, the Sir Francis Drake, on the 20th day of July 1959. It was then that I, at 4:00 in the morning, felt within my head the most intense vibration, and I thought, this is a brain hemorrhage, and this is it. I knew nothing of the human form, and I thought I cannot possible

Lecture 12 – The Secret of Imagining

survive what I am feeling; so this must be what they call a massive brain hemorrhage. But instead of departing this world, I awoke to find myself within my own skull; and I knew that I was entombed completely within my own skull. I was fully awake, as I've never been awake before, and here I am sealed the skull is sealed, and I am in it. The skull is not a little thing like this (indicating the head). It's the size of a huge, big sepulcher, and I knew it to be my skull. I also know intuitively that I could get out by pushing the base of my skull.

As I pushed it, a stone rolled away, and I saw the little opening, and I put my head through it and pushed; and I came out, inch by inch, just as a child is born from the mother's womb. But instead of being born from below of flesh and blood, I was "born from above" out of the skull Golgotha, where Christ was buried. But it was not another coming out, I am coming out. There was no other. I had no companion in that skull. I myself was there, and I came out. And when I looked back at the body out of which I came, it was ghastly pale, turning its head from side to side like one in recovery from a great ordeal. I stood up and looked at it, and then suddenly I heard this strange, strange wind this unearthly wind that I had heard in the tomb within my head, well now, it seemed to be divided and coming from the corner of the room.

As I looked over to see if it really came from that side, and I looked back three or four seconds later the body had been removed. There is no body; but in its place sat my three older brothers. My eldest sat where the head was, my second one sat where the right foot was, and the third one sat where the left foot was; and they heart this same unearthly wind. They couldn't see me. I not only saw them, I could read their

Lecture 12 – The Secret of Imagining

thoughts as I could read my own. Their thoughts all were objective to me. Everything was objective. They couldn't have an emotion that wasn't objective. They couldn't have a thought that wasn't objective. And yet, I heard their voices.

And then my brother Lawrence got off the bed and started towards the same direction that I thought this wind originated this peculiar wind. As he took one or two steps, he said, "Why, it's Neville's baby. This is the cause of this peculiar, unearthly wind."

My brother Victor and my brother Cecil, they said, "How can Neville have a baby?"

He didn't argue the point. He lifted from the floor a little infant wrapped in swaddling clothes and brought it and placed it on the bed; and I took that infant up into my arms, and as I looked into its face and said, "How is my sweetheart," this little heavenly face broke into the most glorious smile; and then the whole scene dissolved.

There was the resurrection from the dead, followed by the "birth from above." So we are "born from above," as told us in the Book of Peter. "We are born anew through the resurrection of Jesus Christ from the dead." There is only one Being resurrected, the Being who descended into man; and that is Jesus Christ. He descended into man, the power of God and the wisdom of God, and united with man; and when they became one and fulfilled the destiny of that Being, only He now wakes as you. And so, you awake as the Lord Jesus Christ, without loss of identity.

So eleven years ago on the 20th day of July, back in 1959 here in this city, that drama took place within me. So it

Lecture 12 – The Secret of Imagining

is my birthday today in a spiritual sense. The little body that now stands before you, that came in the year 1905. It will depart and turn into dust; but that which awoke within me is the Immortal Self that cannot die. And those who have not had the experience, that Immortal Self is still there, and it cannot die. You will be restored to life in a world just like this to continue the drama until that experience that I've just told you takes place within you.

Nothing dies. The little rose that bloomed once, blooms forever. It turns to ash as the body will turn to ash, but you the Immortal You, who is all Imagination cannot die. But it will awaken one day in the same manner that it awoke within me. It was buried in Golgotha, which means "the skull." He is buried on Calvary, which is the skull. It is in the skull of man that God is buried; and there God-in-man will awake.

So here this night you put it to the test as you are challenged in scripture to test Him. And you test, not another, you test your own wonderful human Imagination, for that is the Lord Jesus Christ.

The truest story ever told is the story of Jesus Christ. Let the world rise in opposition and say there is no Lord. As Blake brought out so beautifully in his poem "Jerusalem":

"... Babel mocks; saying there is no God or Son of God;

That Thou, O Human Imagination,

O Divine Body of the Lord Jesus Christ art all

Lecture 12 – The Secret of Imagining

A delusion; but I know Thee, O Lord, when Thou arisest upon

My weary eyes, even in this dungeon and this iron mill ...

For Thou also sufferest with me, although I behold Thee not.

... And the Divine Voice answers,

... Fear not. Lo, I AM with you always,

Only believe in me, that I have the power to raise from death

Thy Brother who sleepeth in Albion."

You can't get away from your own Imagination. You can't get away from it because that's your own being. That is the reality. But it suffers with you. He is the Lord Jesus Christ within you. Now test Him tonight. Test Him for the good. Do you want a better job when they say they are letting people out? Forget what the papers say. Forget what anything says. "All things are possible to the Lord Jesus Christ.".

If you don't have enough money, forget what the paper says, you assume that you have it. "All things are possible to God." He sets no limits whatsoever on the power of believing. Can you believe it? Well, try to believe it. Try to believe, first of all, in God. Well God is your own Imagination. Well believe in Him; that whatever you can imagine is possible.

Can you imagine that you have now the kind of a job that you want? The income that would come from it? The fun

Lecture 12 – The Secret of Imagining

in the doing of the work? Well then walk as though it were true; and to the best of your ability believe that it's true. And that assumption though denied by your senses, though the world would say it is false; if you persist in it, it will harden into fact. This is the law of your own wonderful imagining. Believe it, and it will become a reality.

Now let us go into the silence.

Lecture 13 – Control Your Inner Conversations

Lecture 13

Neville Goddard – 4-26-1971
Control Your Inner Conversations – AKA Mind & Speech

The whole manifested world goes to show us what use we have made of God's gift. Receiving a gift does not mean that we are going to use it wisely, but we have the gift. Everyone has the gift; and the world simply reflects the use of that gift.

In "The Merchant of Venice," Shakespeare puts these words into the mouth of Portia: "If to do were as easy as to know what were good to do, chapels had been churches and poor men's cottages princes' palaces. It is a good divine who follows his own instructions. I can easier teach twenty what were good to be done than to be one of the twenty to follow my own teaching."

So you and I have been given a gift. To what use have we put it? In a book written in the First Century, written at the time of our Gospel, . . it's called the Hermetica, and this is a translation by Walter Scott. It is a wonderful series of four volumes; and in this he says: "There are two gifts that God has given to man alone, and to no other mortal creature, and these two gifts are Mind and Speech. And the gifts of Mind and Speech are essential and identical with Immortality. If they are used rightly, man will not differ in any respect from the immortals; and when he quits the body, these two will be his guides and they will lead him into the troop of the gods and. to the souls that have attained to bliss."

Lecture 13 – Control Your Inner Conversations

Now he is not speaking of any outer speech, for you and I have had this experience, . . I know I have many times. You have gone to a party, and many people you do not know, you meet them and the usual greetings: "Nice to know you," "What a joy to know you," "Pleased to meet you," and the usual clichés; and then you have drinks and your little hors d'oeuvre, and then the party breaks up and they all separate. And you hear someone say, "What a creep," "What a bore"; yet they were so pleased to meet them: "What a joy to know you." The outer words did not conform whatsoever with what they were really thinking on the inside. And God sees, not the outer man; He sees the inner Man.

It's the inner speech that is frozen in the world round about us. This whole vast world is but "frozen" inner speech. What are we saying on the inside? We may think that someone really understands us. You go along believing that they understand you, and some simple little thing happens and you realize they never really heard you. Not for one moment had they really heard you. Some little disruption, and then the whole thing is over; and then they turn against you as though you were the devil, when they formerly thought you were one who was "sent." That is all in Scripture.

Read the 7th chapter of the Book of John and the 8th chapter of John: "And some said, he is a good man; and others said, no, he is leading people astray. Others said, why, he is mad, and he has a. devil."

When he fed them with the loaves and the fish, . . oh, they loved it, . . getting things in the world. As long as they could have things and things and things, it was marvelous; and then he tells them of something entirely different: that

Lecture 13 – Control Your Inner Conversations

they would go through "furnaces", but the end would justify all the "furnaces" through which they would pass. The end would be God; they would awaken in the end, and they would awaken as God the Father. He didn't tell them of the nature of the "furnaces." He told them only of the end and that they would pass through "furnaces"; and passing through, they faltered. They could tell exactly what they were really doing on the inside.

As we are told in the 50th Psalms: "If a man orders his conversations aright, I will show him the salvation of God."

If one could only control these inner conversations morning, noon and night, and carry them right into the dream world, he would know what world he is creating. Stop for one moment and ask yourself, what am I thinking now? You are carrying on a little tiny inner speech at every moment of time. You may be in the presence of someone that the world thinks important, but you don't, and inwardly you are saying, "But only God hears it." That's what you are actually saying. Outwardly you are pleased to meet him, and you are flattered with the contact; but inwardly, what are you saying?

This is what I ask everyone to observe. Observe what you are actually doing on the inside, for that is what God sees; and what you are doing on the inside, you are doing in little tiny speech movements, and they are crystallizing in the manifested world round about you.

So, "If to do were as easy as to know what were good to do," . . well, we all would be kings. We all would be everything we want to be in this world. But we find it more difficult to do it than to know what to do. So I could tell you

Lecture 13 – Control Your Inner Conversations

from now until the ends of time, but only practice will do it . . just practice.

When a man looks and sees a building that seems beyond his wildest dream of ever acquiring it, and he has reasons that he does not share with anyone but his mother, . . she is the only one he takes into his confidence; and she despairs because she knows that he could never achieve ownership of that building, . . it's too big, too far beyond her dreams, or even ambition; but he loves her and he shares only with her what he is doing, and he sees a sign implying that he does own it, . . well, as he looks at it he could not read the sign and not inwardly repeat it.

So inwardly he is saying, "It is my building," as he reads his own name on that building. And day after day, as he goes by, he "reads" his own name on the building, which implies that he has it. And then, out of the "blue," two years later they fail, and a stranger comes in and offers to put the money up to buy it. He has no collateral, but that day he was owner of the building.

He then conducted the most fantastically marvelous, successful business in that firm for many, many years; and then an offer came that offered him many, many times more than he paid for it. He paid $50,000 for it of another person's money and sold it without any capital gain for $840,000. There was no capital gain. It was all done by inner speech, for you could not read something without using your lips. No one sees it, but I read something, and inwardly I am repeating what I am reading.

I saw that here on the bus a few months ago, going to Beverly Hills, and here is a man reading a paper, and every

Lecture 13 – Control Your Inner Conversations

word he read he was forming with his lips. I could watch him. Could I have actually interpreted the motion of his lips, I could have told you exactly what he was reading, for he formed every word. Well everyone is doing that, but not as obviously as he did it.

So you read something, and actually inwardly you are repeating the words. Well now, the whole thing is in your Imagination. That is all it was in him, only his Imagination. That was God's gift. It is translated in the Hermetica as "Mind." "And God has given to man, and to man alone, two gifts, and to no other mortal creature. The gifts are Mind and Speech; and these are like the gifts of Immortality, and by these gifts he does not differ in any respect from the Immortals. If he uses them wisely," . . the whole world is his.

Are we not told that: "The world was created by the Word of God;" and "things that are seen were made out of things that are not seen?"

So here, out of the nowhere, we create by inner speech through the use of what? Call it "mind" if you will. I like the word "Imagination." To me, it inflames me. When I imagine a state . . any state, if I can only persuade myself of the reality of the state imagined, that's the important thing; to believe in the reality of the state imagined. But to know what to do is not the same as doing it.

So, "If to do were as easy as to know what were good to do," . . well then, . . "chapels had been churches and poor men's cottages princes' palaces." And how many teachers in the world follow their own instruction? And then he goes on to confess: "I can easier teach twenty what were good to be

Lecture 13 – Control Your Inner Conversations

done than to be one of the twenty to follow my own teaching."

So I tell you, I am telling you exactly what I know from experience, whether it be the Law or the Promise. But I am not telling you that everyone will apply it wisely. I am not telling you that in the end there will not be a shake-down of those who only pretended to believe it. There are many who came out of a traditional background. They will return to it, and they will genuflect before a hand-made cross or a hand-made figure that hangs on the wall, and cross themselves for good luck, and think that the speaker who taught them in the beginning has turned into a devil. They will; but rejoice, because these signs must come. It's part of Scripture.

And when they come into my world, I rejoice because the end is upon me. Just when they come, . . and they will come, . . and they get thinner and thinner as they separate moving back, because they cannot go forward into the top . . unto the high places of the mountain. And then you know exactly who understood you and who did not understand you.

Let me now make it quite clear: You have the gift. You can speak. Even if you were dumb, you still speak . . inwardly you speak, and you form these little speech movements within yourself. Make them conform to your wish fulfilled.

Do what Robert Millikan did when he was a poor boy, and had nothing but a brilliant mind; a great, great understanding of literature; but he had no money, and he was tired of his poverty. And knowing how the mind works, he constructed a sentence that if true would imply he was no longer poor. And his sentence is a beautiful sentence; "I

Lecture 13 – Control Your Inner Conversations

have," . . not "am going to have"; "I have a lavish, steady, dependable income, consistent with integrity and mutual benefit."

That was the great Robert Millikan, who was the head of Cal-Tech, who gave us his discovery of cosmic rays, who when he died could leave a fortune behind to these charities. I know that the YMCA was one of them; they got a fortune from him. He already settled on his sons and made them financially independent, but he had enough left over to give to his favorite charities, and lived a full, wonderful, marvelous life, where everyone who met him benefited by the actual meeting with that great man. And he started off from "scratch," using this simple technique . . using the simple technique . . using the gift of God that He gave to every person in this world: Mind and Speech.

Whether you be a Frenchman or an American or any other nationality, you have speech and you have a mind. Instead of accepting what you have already done with that gift, you simply ignore it. You brought it into being. All this is solidified speech . . the whole vast manifested world. And you turn from it, and then reconstruct the sentence. Change it, as this one of whom I spoke2 changed the entire pattern. He was a poor boy, . . the whole family poor, behind the 8-ball financially . . socially and in every sense of the word, behind that 8-ball; and he constructed a scene.

As he read the so-called letters that implied that the family owned the building, he was repeating within himself as he read it. And it took two years. He persisted, and at the end of two years the family owned it; and from then on, you couldn't stop them. And they are still growing and expanding and expanding and expanding, because he never forgot how

Lecture 13 – Control Your Inner Conversations

to apply the principle. So, he was among those who didn't come within it. He found it just as easy to do it as to know what to do. And others can find it easy to know what to do but difficult to do it. I've seen it time and time again.

I would say to them, "Do you not know what you are doing to yourself?"

"Yes, but just give me one little moment because I am so enjoying the feeling of getting even with them."

You "get even" with no one. There is no one else in the world.

As you are told: "I AM the Lord, and beside Me there is no god." Read it in the 45th chapter of the Book of Isaiah, "I AM the Lord, and beside Me there is no god."

"Now you want the Word?" He said, "The Word is very near unto you.. It is in your mouth and in your heart, that you can do it. See, I set before you this day life and good, blessings and curses, death and evil. Choose life, that you and your descendants may live."

The whole thing is before you. You can choose death if you want it, because the Word is on your tongue, it is in your mouth, it is in your heart. And you can do it now. You don't have to ask who will go up to Heaven and bring it down for me, or go into the depths and bring it up for me. It is now nearer than you know; in your mouth and in your heart, that you can do it now. Well what would you do now? What sentence would imply that you are now what you would like to be? You know what to do. And I say, it's not knowing what to do; it is the doing it.

Lecture 13 – Control Your Inner Conversations

Someone got the most marvelous revelation. I was there the morning that it happened. "Stop spending your thoughts, your time and your money. Everything in life must be an investment,"3 And I so loved it, I incorporated that thought in the chapter, "The Coin of Heaven," in my book, "Awakened Imagination." She would be the first to confess, although it came through her, and it was her revelation from God to her, . . shared with me, and I shared it through the written form with those who read it in the book, . . but she is the first to confess she never applied it. There it is, but she never applied it. She was thrilled beyond measure that she was the medium through which the Voice could come, and I can see her now rushing to the library and taking out the dictionary to get the true definition of the two words: "spending" and "investing." To "spend" is to put off without hope of return; to waste. To "invest" is expecting a return on your equity. There must be a return on equity when you invest.

Well, we are told: "Stop spending your thought, your time and your money." Time must produce some return. It is precious. Your thought is speech; it must be actually invested, not wasted. And your money. Everything must be invested, and not wasted. And she's the first to confess, "I knew I never really applied it. I thought, well, now it came through, and I can go on this normal, normal way"; but it doesn't work that way.

"If to do were as easy as to know what were good to do," . . what a marvelous sentence. You'll find it if you have the works of Shakespeare in the first act, and second scene4 , put on the lips of Portia. And how difficult for a man who teaches to follow his own instruction. And he himself confessed: "I can easier teach twenty what were good to be

Lecture 13 – Control Your Inner Conversations

done than to be one of the twenty to follow my own teaching,"

So I ask you to really apply it. Don't think for one second that knowing what to do is going to do anything for you. It's the doing it that matters. So, if every moment of time you know what to do, then do it. If you find yourself carrying on any negative conversation, break it, even though it gives you pleasure, as it does many people; they find such fun in being critical. They think they are alone and no one sees them; so it doesn't matter. No one sees you? The only One that matters sees you every moment of time, and that's your Father. He sees into the very depths of your Being, and He knows exactly what you are doing. And your world is built out of these inner conversations.

So, today if you are not satisfied with the world in which you live, blame no one, but turn within to these two gifts and use them wisely, for here we are told to order our life according to our conversations.

Then in Ephesians we are told, . . it's the 4th chapter: "Put off the old nature which belongs to the former conversations, and put on the new nature." The "new nature" is sometimes translated "the new man," and the "old nature" the "old man." Well, if I equate the "old nature" with the "former conversations," I must equate the "new man" with the "new conversations." So, He identifies the inner speech with man's nature. So now, what am I actually doing on the inside of myself? And I am doing it morning, noon and night; I can't stop it. If I stop for one moment, it isn't. You can't stop it. You take it into your dreams, and you are still talking. You are really talking at all moments of time.

Lecture 13 – Control Your Inner Conversations

So what are you saying at every moment of time? Watch it; be careful what you are saying, because your whole vast world is this inner conversation "pushed out." And you can change it only by changing the conversation, because the conversation is equated with your nature.

So if you walk the street or you ride the bus, or you sit alone, you are still talking; at every moment of time you are talking. And all you need to do to find out what you have been saying is to look at your world. Your world reflects this inner speech. I have seen it every moment of time. I am not going to tell you I have not faltered. I would not for one moment tell you that I am always in control of the inner conversations.

The phone rings. This happens, and you've told them over and over, and your reaction may not be quite the right one, but you reacted anyway. No one heard it, but you heard it, and your Father heard it; and you are going to build your world based on exactly what you've done, So you watch it morning, noon and night, because you are going to "play" this part.

The end of everyone's world is Christ. Everyone is moving towards the fulfillment of being God Himself . . everyone. And therefore the story of Christ as told in the Gospels, you are going to play it, And when He awakes within you and unfolds within you and you are Christ, and you know you are, you are going to find those who will eagerly take all that you have to say when you give them the loaves and the fish; and then this is going to happen in your life: "Do not think for one moment I came to bring peace upon earth. I came not to bring peace, but a sword to set a man against his father and

Lecture 13 – Control Your Inner Conversations

the daughter against her mother and a daughter-in-law against her mother-in-law."

This will happen. And then comes the conflict in the world, and he is accused of being the devil. They say, "He has a devil. Why do you listen to him? He is mad."

But then when you who have awakened from the dream of life hear these things, you rejoice, because you know your end is near. Oh it has to take place to "separate the sheep from the goats," and let them go back into their world and genuflect and cross themselves for luck. And then, those who can actually follow, they will follow, for "My own must come to me."

So I hope that everyone here, not only listens, but believes what I have said, for I've told you what I know from experience. God Himself came, and comes into human history in the person of Jesus Christ . . in you, in me, in everyone. But when He comes in you, He awakens as you. Read the story then. All that is told in that story concerning Jesus Christ, you are going to experience.

So when you tell the story to those who will readily believe it when you "feed" them with the loaves and the fish, based upon the Law, . . how to get the building, how to get money, how to become famous: and all that, . . they love it. Then you turn and you emphasize the end, the Promise and the Promise is: "Ye will be as God." You don't need buildings, because the whole world is yours and all within it. But they can't see that. They want more loaves and more fish; and then something will happen because you didn't come to bring peace upon earth, . . you came to bring a sword to separate the old from the new, and the conflict is on.

Lecture 13 – Control Your Inner Conversations

And then suddenly eruptions will take place within families, and they will turn . . completely turn against you; but you, knowing that you are the central figure of the Gospel, you rejoice.

You have nothing but pity for those who couldn't follow beyond a certain point. That's all that you have. No criticism. No condemnation. Only pity that they couldn't go a little bit further. But it's all part of the "play."

So I tell you, you watch carefully what you are saying morning, noon and night. When you go to bed at night, just watch your inner conversations, and see that the sun is not descending upon your anger. Resolve it at that very moment, and make it conform to your wish fulfilled, and make that "wish fulfilled" a thing of love. What would it be like if it were true? Just what would it be like? Then carry on a conversation from the premise of the wish fulfilled, all clothed in love, for anyone that you think of; and watch how things happen in your world.

Your night, . . may I tell you . . if that is your last thought, it will dominate the dream of the night, You are completely dominated, and your Father is speaking to you constantly through the medium of dreams and through the medium of vision, and you will see the whole thing unfolding within you; and you will know that you are the Lord Jesus Christ.

You don't go out and scream it from the housetops. You know it, and you walk in the comfort of being the Awakened Man, who is God. Let everyone say exactly what he wants to say about you, and pay no attention to it, because they have

Lecture 13 – Control Your Inner Conversations

to do it. When you come down to the end, they have to do it. The separation must take place.

And you don't justify it. Self-justification is the voice of hell. So you don't justify anything, and you don't try to always be right. Another almost incurable disease of man is the necessity of always being right. So you don't make any effort to prove that you are right. You know what you have experienced, and you can't deny the experience; so you go your way, telling it just as it comes to you. And it comes to you in the most glorious manner. It's all in Scripture; so when you come to the end, you aren't disappointed and you aren't surprised that those that you sent off alive and free will now take up arms against you and call you insane, call you a devil, and would disrupt their family life. You know exactly what you've done. You have only told the truth. And when the Truth comes into the world, it comes not to bring peace but a sword. He is going to separate you from that traditional background that enslaved you in the past, because real progress in this world, . . religious progress, . . is a gradual transition from a god of tradition to a. God of experience. You experience God: and the whole thing reflects it.

His Son calls you Father; and there is no uncertainty as to who he is and Who-You-Are. And your whole memory returns. And here you stand before your everlasting Son, and he knows it and you know it: and no person in the world could in any way dissuade you from knowing this. You have experienced it. You can't deny it.

So I am telling you what is in store for you. Use the gift wisely. Start now to use it. For if you use it, you are told: "I will show you the salvation of God." Read it in the very last

Lecture 13 – Control Your Inner Conversations

verse of the 50th Psalm. They translate the word "conversations" as "manner of life," and some the "way of life"; but in the King James version it's always translated "conversations." Thirteen times that phrase is used, and it is always "conversations."

"Put off the former conversation, and then be renewed in the spirit of your mind."

If you put it off . . it's equated with the "old man." Now, as I put it off, I have to replace it with something . . a "new conversation"; so you are told in the Book of Joel: "Let the weak say, I AM strong." You read that in the 3rd chapter, the 10th verse. "Let the weak say, I AM strong," for there is no other God. "I AM the Lord, and beside Me there is no god." So, "I set before you," . . and you make the choice. You can choose life or you can choose death. You can choose the good or choose the evil, a blessing or a curse. It's entirely up to man to choose anything. And look into this manifested world, and you'll see what we have chosen.

But every morning you see headlines . . nothing but disaster, you see what man has chosen. He seems either to want it or he is "fed" it, . . one or the other. Look at the editorials. "We need that in order to sell papers," Or else, we ourselves are demanding it from Him, but you "feed" upon it. Morning, noon and night we feast upon all this unloveliness and carry on these little internal mental conversations with ourselves; but they don't remain there. They balloon and objectify themselves and become solidified as our manifested world.

So this whole manifested world goes to show us what use or misuse we have made of God's gift. And God's gift is your

Lecture 13 – Control Your Inner Conversations

Mind and your Speech; and it's not your outer speech, for we know how deceptive that is. You see it morning, noon and night.

A salesman goes in, and he is trained to deceive the buyer. The advertiser is trained to deceive the buyer. And everything is on the outside. God sees only the inside. Man sees the outer appearance and God sees the Inner Man. So when you watch your inner conversation, you are actually watching the new nature. That is your nature. And if you don't like it, change it. You "put off the old man," and then "put on the new man"; and "He will show you the salvation of Gad." Then the whole thing will unfold within you.

I tell you from my own experience, before the Promise was realized in me, seemingly I had this conversation with my brother. Formerly I would argue mentally, . . we were five thousand miles apart, . . and I needed money at that time; and when I found myself arguing with him, I broke it . . tore that entire record up. And whether he sent me a nickel or not, I loved him and praised him and thanked him, and went about my business, not knowing where the next was coming from, for I had spent a fortune by taking off one solid year and living at the same level that I had lived in previous years, and spent money like water. Then came that moment I needed money. And inwardly I carried on a conversation with him, and I thought that's a stupid thing to do; so I broke that record, and then I carried on the most glorious conversation with him, like two lovers, because I do love him and he loves me, And. I changed that "old man" into the "new man," by changing my conversation with him, Do you know, in no time flat, . . unasked, a very large wonderful check came to me? And no request; I didn't appeal at all.

Lecture 13 – Control Your Inner Conversations

I was "taking it out" on the one I loved because I myself had spent the money like a drunken sailor. And then here inwardly I am arguing with my brother; and when I broke it and actually carried on the most loving conversation with him . . all about the family life and all these marvelous things, suddenly out of the nowhere came a very large, wonderful check. And I didn't appeal for it. So I am telling you from experience, I know it works this way. Yet, if you are in the mood to argue, you so love the argument, . . it costs you nothing; so you are having the time of your life. But it doesn't stop there; it's going to balloon and crystallize and manifest itself in your world. So, watch it. And do you know, it becomes a pleasant thing after a while to actually carry on lovely conversations? It becomes very pleasant.

But if you are honest with yourself, you would say just what this darling of mine said to me, "I never practice it. It came through, and I recorded it, and you used it, but I personally never practiced it. Still inwardly I carried on the same old conversations that I always did."

So I say to you now, as we are going up towards the end, believe me, I would not deceive you. I have told you exactly what happened to me as to the Promise. I have told you exactly what I have proven as to the Law; it will not fail you. You can take the Law and put it into practice now. Don't wait until tomorrow. Do it now, and know that if you carry on these conversations, the promise of the 50th Psalm will take form. "He will show you the salvation of God." And the "salvation of God" is simply: You awaken as God. That's how He shows it to you.

He came, and He comes into human history in the person of Jesus Christ; and there is only one Jesus Christ.

Lecture 13 – Control Your Inner Conversations

So when it happens, you are Jesus Christ. You don't change your name. You are still Mary. You are still Stan. You are still John. But when it happens, you know Who-You-Are. You don't go and ask the judge to change your name to Jesus. You walk the streets still as Stanley, still as Mary, still as Neville; but you know Who-You-Are. And then when things do happen, because you know Who-You-Are, these things have to happen.

They must accuse you of being insane. They must accuse you of being deceitful and leading people astray. It's all part of Scripture. But you are not amazed; you only have pity and mercy for those who could not go further than they are, and then they fall by the wayside. These are the four on which the seed falls; the highway, among the thorns, among the rocks, and then on good soil. And you can't help it.

You can only scatter the seed and let it fall where it will. And it will fall on those four kinds of soil. It always falls on four; and as it falls on the good, it will simply rise within them, and they will have the identical experience that you have had. When it falls on the highway, quickly other ideas devour it. When it falls among the thorns, the cares of the world encroach upon it and choke it. If it falls on the rock and the rock is not prepared to let the root go too deep, the sun scorches it, and suddenly something comes up and it's all gone. But when the soil has been prepared, it goes deep, and it bears a hundredfold.

So, I tell you, the whole story is all about you. And one day you will know . . actually know . . you are the Lord Jesus Christ. And you cannot avoid the story. It will happen to you too. Don't think for one moment that you are going to awaken knowing you are the Lord Jesus Christ and not have

Lecture 13 – Control Your Inner Conversations

those to whom you poured out your soul, who took the loaves and the fish, turn upon you and accuse you of being mad, and therefore an evil one, and not anything should be done with you, . . turn from you completely. You'll find it.

But then, being conscious of the fact that you have experienced the entire story, you can only go back to the written Word of God and know it had to happen. It just had to happen. And when these signs come, the end is not far.

Now let us go into the silence.

Lecture 14 – Secret of Imagination

Lecture 14

Neville Goddard 6-21-1971
Secret of Imagination

I thought that this last week, we should be both practical and idealistic. So we will start on the practical side. "Think not that I AM come, to abolish the law and the prophets. I AM come, not to abolish the law and the prophets, but to fulfill them."

Now, the One speaking is now present within you. When He awakes, you will hear these words. You will find them to be your words. That One, is your own wonderful human Imagination. That One is God!

Imagination is the basis of all that is. What is now proved to be true, as far as we are concerned, was once only imagined. Think of something in the world that is now to you "real" that wasn't first imagined. So, the secret of imagining, is the secret of God.

And so:

"The secret of imagining is the greatest of all problems, to the solution of which everyone should aspire, because supreme power, supreme wisdom, supreme delight lie in the far-off solution of this mystery."

I can acquaint you with it and then leave you to your choice and its risk, because everything in the world is created by this power.

Lecture 14 – Secret of Imagination

"I kill and I make alive; I wound and I heal; and none can deliver out of my hand. "

"I create the light and make darkness; I create woe and I make weal."

"I, even I, AM He, and there is no other God beside me." That's your own wonderful human Imagination.

Well, there are secrets to this power, and you and I might experiment. We try to discover the secret. As we discover the secret of imagining, we are discovering the secret of God. So, God and Imagination . . human Imagination . . are synonymous terms. They're interchangeable.

So, when we read that "If we know, that He hears us in whatever we ask, we know that we have obtained that which we requested of Him." If we know that He hears us in whatever we ask . . no restraint. Now, you may sit down and commune with what you think to be "another" than yourself, God; but because there are billions of us in the world, and there is but one God, in this fabulous universe, you might wonder if He heard you. But you have no doubt in your mind if you identify God with your own wonderful human Imagination, that He heard you!

Can you believe that your own wonderful human Imagination is God? So, when you sit down, as told us in the Fourth Psalms "Commune with your own hearts, upon your beds, and be silent."

He hears you, if you commune with Self, but can you believe that communion with Self, was communion with God? Can you, now, assume that you are, the one that you

Lecture 14 – Secret of Imagination

would like to be? Can you assume that one that you love, is as you would like her, or like him to be? Can you really believe that you are answered?

I do not expect tonight, that after a certain conception, that the child will be born tomorrow.

"The vision has its own appointed hour, it ripens, it will flower; if it be long, then wait, it is sure, it will not be late."

A little child takes nine months, a lamb five months, a chicken 21 days, an elephant . . so they tell me . . a year or more; a horse, a year anyway. So every conception has its own appointed hour; it ripens, it will flower. If it seems to you long, then wait. It is sure; it will not be late relative to its own nature. So, can I now commune and expect that my communion with Self is communion with God? Can I dare to assume, that I AM exactly what I want to be? Can I dare to assume that I AM where I want to be, even though at the moment my reason denies it, my senses deny it? Will it work? Well, it costs you nothing. Try it! It doesn't cost one penny to try it.

As you are told: "Come, buy wine, buy milk, without money, without price", come and take it. It doesn't cost you one penny to dare to assume that you are where you would like to be, though at the moment reason denies that you are.

Now, I am telling you what I know from experience. When I didn't have a nickel and desired a trip that would cost me well in excess of one thousand dollars, I dared to assume that I was where I would like to be; and I viewed the world from that assumption. Instead of thinking of it, I thought from it. Then I thought of, where physically I was,

Lecture 14 – Secret of Imagination

and I saw that place in my Imagination, two thousand miles to the northwest of me. And I slept in that assumption. And then in a way that I did not consciously devise, . . I had no way of knowing, how it would ever work; but in a way I did not know, it unfolded; and that assumption hardened into fact.

On the strength of that, I tried it again and again; and when it worked, I began to teach it. I began to tell others that their Imagination is the cause of the phenomena of life. This was long before I realized the Promise, as we call it in Scripture. This was only the Law.

So, we are told: "Blessed is the man who delights in the Law of the Lord. In all that he does, he prospers."

He didn't say if it was good for you; he left that entirely up to you, to make the decision. You could choose something that may be horrible in time. You choose it without contemplating consequences. But he tells you your imaginal act is a fact.

Now, as He awakens within you, He reinterprets the Law. He can't change the Law. He interprets the Law. Instead of abiding by the external traditions of our fathers, He tells us what the Law really is, when He awakes within us.

"You have heard it said of old, You shall not Commit adultery'; but I say to you, Any man who looks lustfully upon a woman has already committed the act in his heart with her."

He tells us that the restraint of that impulse is not enough. The act was committed at the moment of the

Lecture 14 – Secret of Imagination

imaginal act. I may contemplate the consequences and be afraid . . my reputation would be at stake, if they catch me. But at that very moment of the imaginal act, that was the fact. That's how he interprets the Law.

Well now, no one can stop you from imagining. No one can stop you from imagining that you are secure; but you may say I have no one in this world to whom I could turn who could leave me a penny, but I have no money. I am beyond the age where they would employ me. And you could give yourself a thousand reasons why, it could not be. He is not asking for any reasons. Can you imagine? Well, who can stop you from imagining? That's all that concerns the Awakened Man within you.

Can I dare imagine that I am what I want to be? Well, I can. I've done it, unnumbered times. I've done it successfully for many that I love dearly and many that I do not know. I have failed often, too; but the failure is in me, it is not in the Law.

Imagination plus faith is the stuff out of which we make the world. We are told all things were made in this manner. "He calls a thing that is not seen as though it were seen, and the unseen becomes seen." And when I come to Him, I must believe that He exists, and that He rewards those who believe in Him. I must have faith in the imaginal act.

If tonight I can stand here and simply, quietly imagine a state and really believe that I am in communion with God, when I did that, and that my imaginal act is God's act, . . it's not something other than God, . . and go unconcerned as to the result, the results will follow me. For that imaginal act was causal at the moment that I did it. The effect when it

Lecture 14 – Secret of Imagination

appears, . . I may try to trace the effect to some physical cause and give all credit to a physical cause. I tell you, every physical effect has an imaginal cause, and not a physical cause. A physical cause only seems; it is a delusion, of our fading memory. We do not remember when we imagined it.

In this audience tonight, . . and he may not even remember when he did it, . . is my dentist. I went to him in great need of a lot of work but I have had dentistry all over this country and in London and Barbados, but it all was horrible. I was always on the move. I was with the theater. Getting in town for a week, what could they do when I needed such work? They patched me up. So when I met him, he gave me a complete job because I was here . . living here then.

When one day a tooth gave way which was an anchor tooth, he said to me quite innocently, whether he remembers it or not, "When I saw your mouth and did this, I said to myself, 'This tooth will last thirteen years.'"

It was thirteen years. Had he only said 25, but he didn't think I would live that long! So, thirteen years . . out came that anchor tooth, and therefore a complete restructure of my entire mouth. He set it in motion. Whether he remembers or not, he said, "This is going to last thirteen years." He didn't tell me; he didn't have to tell me. That was his imaginal act. I was only the victim of his creative power, Now I am telling you, don't take anything lightly. You are creating morning, noon and night. Your imaginal acts are God's acts, because your Imagination is God! And there is no other God.

"God actually became as we are," . . became man, . . "that man may become God." And He has set up within

Lecture 14 – Secret of Imagination

Himself, in man, a series of events, which He will now unfold within man, which the one in whom He unfolds it, will know, He Is God. He Calls it "giving glory unto man."

"I will not give my glory to another," he said. "I have tried you in the furnace of affliction. For my own sake, I do it, for my own sake, for how should my name be profaned? My glory I will not give to another."

God's glory is God, as told us in the 33d Chapter of the Book of Exodus. "I will make my glory to pass before you." And I will cover you. And when I have passed by, So "my glory" is equated with the "I" of God, for His name is I AM. ' He cannot give His Glory, which is Himself, to another. So, in becoming man, He puts man in the furnaces. But then read the story carefully: "He took upon Himself all of my infirmities and bore my diseases." Who else suffers?

But I will say, well I suffer. Well, that's God. "But I am feeling it; He isn't." That is no "he"; His name is I AM. So, I feel the pain I feel the infirmity. I feel the diseases. That's God! So, the fool says in his heart: "There is no God, nor Son of God That Thou, O Human Imagination, art all a delusion; but I know Thee, O Lord, when Thy arisest upon My weary eyes, even in this dungeon, and this iron mill . . Thou also sufferest with me, although I behold Thee not."

I do not behold Imagination as I behold an object in space. I AM the Reality that is named "Imagination"; but I cannot actually see it as an object in space. I see the results of my imagining, but not the Being imagining, for God is invisible.

Then the Voice replied, "Fear not! I AM with you always."

Lecture 14 – Secret of Imagination

Can I ever get away from imagining? If I fall asleep now and I start dreaming, what is dreaming but imagining? When I awake, He is still with me, and I AM still imagining. " I AM with you always." Only believe in me, that I have power to raise from death Thy Brother who sleeps in Albion."

This comes, now, to the Promise that He made all of us. His Promise is to give Himself to us, as though there were no "others" in the world, . . just you, because in giving Himself to you, there is no "other." Your whole vast world is "yourself pushed out." Everything in the world is "yourself pushed out," and you manipulate it by your imaginal acts . . everything in the world.

Now, the first act begins with the Resurrection. It's not outside of you, in spite of what you've been taught. The day will come, you will rise within yourself. And that's the only God that was ever resurrected, Who will ever be resurrected. It's not another; it's you. And when you rise, there is no one on the outside. It's all you. And you are rising in the only tomb in the world where God was ever buried, and that's your own skull. God is buried in the human skull, and that's where He rises. And when He rises, as foretold by His own words in Scripture, he is "born." Resurrection begins the act.

That same night, you come out of the tomb, which is your skull, and you are "born from above," . . not from the womb of woman where the "garment" was born; you are "born from above," . . born of God. "Born not of blood, nor of the will of the flesh, nor of the will of man, but of God." In other words, you are Self-begotten!

God begets Himself, in you, as told us in the Epistle to the Hebrews: He is "bringing many sons to glory", but the

Lecture 14 – Secret of Imagination

sons are numbered. Everyone born of woman is that "son of God," as told us in the 32d Chapter of Deuteronomy: "He has set bounds to the peoples of earth, according to the number of the sons of God."

But you will say, "But look, there are three billion in the world." So, what's that?"I will make them more numerous than the stars, more numerous than the sands of the beach", We'll, count them. You can't count the stars. We estimate them to be trillions and trillions. These are the "sons of God," . . bringing each that He chooses. He didn't bring all together. He brought a certain number, and that certain number he calls the "second son." The "second son" is represented by this fabulous number. The first son is still waiting to come out. He complains, because the second son went berserk . . went amuck and spent his power unwisely, then he came to his senses and returned to his Father, and the Father embraced him and gave him the authority of Himself. He gave him the ring, the robe, the fatted calf . . everything for the one who went out and came back to the Father. For His gift is the gift of Himself to you who came out. "I chose you in me before the foundation of the world." That's what we are told.

Let the first son complain. He will complain and complain: "I served you and you gave me nothing," . . not even a kid. He said, "My son, all that I have is yours." But the most fabulous gift in the world, or possession in the world, is without meaning unless there is a knowledge of it and a readiness to use it.

Going out as we did, we become aware of our possession; then we can use it. Unless we went out into the world and

Lecture 14 – Secret of Imagination

misused it as we have done, we could not become aware of this power that is our own creative power . . our Imagination.

I saw it so clearly one night. Here I am in this fabulous field of sunflowers . . huge, lovely sunflowers. Each sunflower was a face . . the human face, but they were all anchored in the earth. And I walked up and down among the sunflowers. They moved like an orchestra moves; they all moved in unison. If one smiled, they all smiled. If one didn't smile, no one smiled. They simply followed like an orchestra. If one bent over, they all bent over. And everyone did what the whole did. They automatically did it. And I felt, though I was alone . . I could walk up and down; they were anchored, . . they couldn't do it. I felt that I was freer, limited as I was, than all of them put together, beautiful as they were . . these sunflowers of human faces, but they had not gone out.

I was once a part of that infinite garden . . not aware of what I possessed; and my Father chose me in Him "before the foundation of the world," and he went out, to go through "hell" in this world, that I may become aware that "All Thine are mine." To become aware that all that is God's belonged to me, I had to go through the furnaces of affliction. And having gone through the furnaces, then He awakes within me; and He tells me how I will know He has awakened within me.

He set up in the beginning the result of the experiences of humanity, and that result is a "son." And the son is called David." And when I find him, I will know he is my son, and I will know the 89th Psalm: "I have found David. He has cried unto me, Thou art my Father, my God, and the Rock of my Salvation." Well, I've found him, and he cried these words to me, and I knew exactly who he was; and I knew then Who I

Lecture 14 – Secret of Imagination

AM. Until then I did not know I was one with God! He is God's Son . . God's only Son. Now he's my son!

I tell you, you are going to find him, and he will be your son; and because he is my son, you and I are one. How can he be your son, and I know he's my son, and you and I not be one father? So, we are told, "There is only one body, one spirit, one lord, one God and Father of all." So, in the end, there will not be Greek and Jew, bond and free, male and female; only one . . all one in God. And you will be that God! So, this is the Promise that He made.

Now when I read the Bible, I take all the related parts of the Promise and put them all together, for all these things put together will find their fulfillment in you. All His Promises find their "Yes" in Him, as you read it in Second Corinthians: "All the promises of God find their Yes" . . their fulfillment . . "in Him". So there are 39 books; together they form one Book; but the context, which means the meaning of it, you will find related, scattered over the 39. He pulls from this, from that, from the other, written over the centuries, and pulls it into one pattern, for Christ is the Pattern Man. That pattern is buried in man. It's the only Christ in the world. When the pattern unfolds in man, it unfolds in man as the man, in whom it unfolds. And then he knows Who He Is. And he has no doubt in his mind as to who he is. He is the Lord spoken of in Scripture. And that Lord is God the Father. And the whole thing unfolds within him. But he does not abolish the law that he gave; he explains the law as a psychological law and not a physical law.

But if I long after someone at that very moment the act was committed. I state it boldly. I state it boldly, as my dentist stated it boldly. It was committed. So, I went blindly

Lecture 14 – Secret of Imagination

on, enjoying everything that he did. It was perfect. And suddenly comes a little bleeding thing which no one could stop. Out comes the tooth. He set it in motion the day he said to himself, . . not to me: "It will last thirteen years." I checked it; it was thirteen years.

So Blake said in his wonderful "Jerusalem": "Oh, what have I said? What have I done, Oh, all-powerful human words?" For the word of man is the word of God! "And the word shall not return unto me void, but it must accomplish that which I purpose and prosper in the thing for which I sent it."

But man forgets his word. Then it comes up and he looks for physical causes for it. Now he'll start searching. Do you know what?

Well, "Your system is run down." Did you have fever? Did you have so and so? And you ask a thousand questions of the one: Did you have so and so? You said, No, no, no. No one thinks of that moment when the word went out. Well, the word goes forward, and it cannot return unto us void. It must accomplish that which we purposed and prosper in the thing for which I sent it.

I can see my father now back in 1919. There were ten of us: nine boys and a girl. He was a ship chandler. He had a grocery store, a liquor store and a meat store . . a regular little grocery, and he supplied ships; and the ships were bringing the boys back from the first World War, and they would tell him all kinds of stories.

At dinner he would say to my mother, "We will have another war, in twenty years. In twenty years there will be

Lecture 14 – Secret of Imagination

another war. It is Germany; but this time, it's going to be Germany and Japan." He didn't mention Italy, but it will be Germany and Japan. "We will again have America as our ally. France will be our ally."

Mother would say, "Joseph, we have nine sons. In twenty years they all will be eligible to go to war." We were all kids in 1919. I was 14 years old.

In 1939, on the 1st day of September, war broke . . exactly twenty years. What did my father know of any prophecy concerning this? He was only repeating what he had heard from the captains and the stewards and the chief officers as he did business with them. But they were his words! And he said it with conviction, because he believed these men knew what they were talking about.

And our headlines . . day after day, they are setting the picture in motion, for tomorrow's confusion. The men are paid enormous salaries to write "scare" headlines. All right, so he writes a scare headline, thinking; It only sells the papers; it isn't going to hurt anyone. But we are going to fulfill them. We fulfill all of our words because God and man are one.

"Man is all Imagination; and God is man, and exists in us, and we in Him." "The eternal body of man is the Imagination, and that is God Himself."

And God's Word is man's word, and it cannot return unto him void. It just can't if he speaks it with conviction. So, Imagination plus faith . . these are the very stuff out of which we fashion our world.

Lecture 14 – Secret of Imagination

So, can I tonight, be alone, and commune with my Self, and be confident that He heard me? I know that I heard myself. Well, that Self is God!

"If we know that He hears us in whatever we ask, we know we have obtained," not are going to, . . "we have obtained that which we request of Him." Read it in John's Epistle . . the First Epistle, the 5th Chapter, the 15th verse.. We have obtained it! Well, it'll take a little interval. It may come tonight, but depending on what seed you planted. One seed will grow overnight; other seeds will take a little longer. But each has "its own appointed hour."

There is not a thing wrong in your noble dreams in this world. You want to be wealthy? What is wrong with it? You want to be anything, . . what's wrong with it? Everything is possible.

A friend of mine called me last week. He is now appointed, the head purchasing agent, for the City of Culver. By law he is not qualified; he does not have the educational background. The law demands you must have a college degree. He doesn't have anything outside of high school. They rearranged it to appoint him the head purchasing agent of Culver City. Why? He came here, he and his brother . . I buried the brother a few years ago; he got this job, not dreaming for one moment he could ever transcend it. I said, "Don't for one moment entertain that thought, Dwayne. The job is yours if you want it. Don't push the other one out. Let him go higher. You want to be the Purchasing Agent of the whole City of Culver? You are the Purchasing Agent. Sleep in it just as though it were true, and you hurt no one."

Lecture 14 – Secret of Imagination

Last week they rearranged the law and he was appointed Purchasing Agent, to take effect in July. Now everything was rearranged. Everything will be rearranged for you.

A friend of mine told me here that you aren't allowed to speak at any state university unless you have a college degree. Well, he confessed that he did not have one, but he was invited by a Professor at U.C.L.A. to take his class . . I think there were three or four classes . . in the use of Imagination, in advertising; so here he went in without the degree, and he was given all the freedom that the Professor enjoyed and he gave either three or four lectures, instead of the Professor who went off for those three or four lectures. So, they suspended the rules. They'll suspend every rule.

They are not supposed to do this, not supposed to do that. Ignore it. Ignore every rule. My friend used to say to me, "You can't smoke in here. Look: 'No smoking.'" And he was a very wonderful lad. He said, "They didn't say it positively." And so he would go right through the gate to the airplane, and I would say, "Mort, you cannot smoke in here. You are not supposed to smoke."

"It didn't say 'positively.'" And here's Mort going right through with his cigarette. No one stopped him. I'm not saying you should do it. He didn't do it to brag. He simply believed in himself. He wouldn't hurt anyone.

Now, you don't have to hurt anyone. I tell you, your own wonderful human Imagination is immortal! That's the Man in you that cannot die. I meet them . . those who are called "dead," and I tell you, they aren't dead. Nothing dies. Everything is restored. Everything is restored. But the day will come, you will go beyond restoration, and you will

Lecture 14 – Secret of Imagination

resurrect. And who is resurrecting? God. And God-in-you awakens, and you are God, because God is the Father of David. That is the way you know you are God.

"I will tell of the decree of the Lord. He has said unto me, Thou art my son, today I have begotten thee."

These are the words of David, what is going to happen to you. Then you'll know you are God! You have no other way of knowing that you are God unless God's only son calls you "Father," for "No one knows who the Son is except the Father, and no one knows who the Father is, except the Son, and anyone to whom the Son chooses to reveal Him."

So, "No one has seen God; but the only Son, who is in His bosom, has made Him known". He comes out of you, and calls you "Father"! And then you know Who You Are.

And I am telling you, everyone of you . . because you and I "were chosen in Him before the foundation of the world" . . chosen for the purpose of receiving the gift of God which is His Glory, for He gives me Himself. And in giving me Himself, if He is a father, He gives me His Son. You can't give me yourself in part; give it to me in totality. So, if you are a father, then where is your son? Your son must be my son; and He gives me His Son.

So, "He so loved us He gave His only-begotten Son". To whom? To you, to me, to every child born of woman. So, everyone of us will become fully aware that we are God. And yet, I will know you as Jim; I will know you as Jim, but I will also know that you are God. I will know you as Sol, and know you are God. I will know you as Bill, and know you are God. I will know everyone of you, and the unnumbered

Lecture 14 – Secret of Imagination

billions that are not known to me here, in that day I'll know them all, and still know them all as God, for there's nothing but God!

When the curtain comes down on the final act, we are all God! We are then the Glory of God. So, we will finish the work. He said, "I have finished the work Thou gavest me to do. Now, glorify Thou me with Thine own Self, with the glory that I had with Thee before that the world was." It's returning now. The whole memory returns, and every man becomes God.

But now, do not fail to apply the Law. "Blessed is the man who delights in the Law of the Lord. In all that he does he prospers." You name it, and you can be it. You just name it; and if you dare to assume that you are it and view the world from that assumption instead of thinking of it, you will crystallize it. You will actually manifest it in this world.

That definition of Imagination . . I'll go along with it to a certain point . . up to a point, that things present, are sense perceived and called "real"; things absent, are called "Imagination." But man being all Imagination, man must be wherever he is in Imagination. So, I need not be anchored to where my senses dictate. I can stand here and assume that I AM elsewhere; and then if I assume that I AM elsewhere, let me anchor myself there and view the world from it. If I view the world from it, I should see this place as I would see it were I were physically there. I can't see it surrounding me and under me, then I did not move in Imagination. If I move in Imagination, then I must think of where I was physically and see it elsewhere. I can see it where I AM in Imagination and be moved, for all motion . . well, I can tell myself, If have I moved, by a frame of reference. If I have moved relative to

Lecture 14 – Secret of Imagination

this room, let me look to see, where am I now? I must have moved, for motion can be detected only by a change of position relative to another object. Well here is the object?

I assume that I AM now . . and I name it. If I AM elsewhere, let me think of this room. Well, I can't see it as I now see it. If I see it as I now see it, then I didn't move. I can only move if I see it differently.

Well now, if I move, and now I AM standing in my home, sitting in my chair in the living room, let me think of this club. I must see it away down on Catalina, and feel myself at home on Carol Street, and then think of the club, and it can't be here. It must be way down on Catalina. Then I've moved. For man being all Imagination, he must be wherever he is in Imagination. If I practice this, it becomes easier and easier.

I just read a story of a very dear friend of mine who used to come to my . . not to my meetings, but I would say once a month she came home, for a personal appointment in New York City. She was killed last week in a car driven by her husband. And I can now see this perfectly lovely, gracious lady. She had a home in Oyster Bay, Long Island; and she had her apartment in New York City. Her name is possibly one of the most prominent names in America. The name is Roosevelt. She was of the Teddy Roosevelt branch. Her name was Grace. Her husband was Archibald. Teddy was Governor of New York; he was Vice President of our Country; he was President of our Country . . a very powerful, wonderful leader. He did not leave, as so many presidents leave, a fortune. He didn't go in there to make a fortune. He went in there to lead the country. And he said, "I don't consider public opinion. I perform what I think is best for our country.

Lecture 14 – Secret of Imagination

I feed them what they ought to know. I feed them what I think is best for our country."

But he didn't go in there to make a personal fortune, and he came out without a personal fortune. So she . . in spite of her name . . did not have a personal fortune. She had a home in Oyster Bay, Long Island, and a lovely apartment . . beautifully furnished from things that her father-in-law had given her. If she did not rent her New York apartment for the summer, she could not open her home in Long Island. She could not afford it. Being a lovely home in a very wonderful, fashionable area of New York City, she always got a wonderful price paid in advance for the three or four months. Then came the end of a season where they aren't looking for any homes, and she came to see me.

She said, "Neville, I am desperate. Unless I rent the place in New York City, we can't open our home in Long Island."

I said, "All right. It's rented, and you are living in Long Island ."

"Oh but," she said, "Neville, I can't do that."

I said, "Tonight you sleep in your home in Long Island."

"But," she said, "I can't do that.. How could I go and sleep there?" I said, "You don't do it physically. Tonight you sleep physically in New York City in your apartment; but in your Imagination, which is the only reality, you sleep in your home in Long Island, and then you think of your place in New York. The reason why you see it across the East River is because you are physically sleeping in Long Island. And the

Lecture 14 – Secret of Imagination

reason why you are sleeping there is because you rented it. Put them all together; that's why you are there."

She said to me, "If it rents, I'll call you."

I said, "There's no 'if' about it. The only 'if' is if, you do it. Then you'll call me."

I took her to the elevator. She went downstairs, went back to her place. The next day, at 9:00 in the morning, Mrs. Roosevelt is on the phone. She said, "Neville, this is Grace Roosevelt."

I said, "How are you, Mrs. Roosevelt?"

She said, "I am calling you from Long Island where I slept last night physically. When I went home, no one came at all over the period that you rent places. But as I got home, soon after I got home, an agent called and asked if I could show the apartment. A single man came in. He liked the place. Money meant nothing to him. He said I want immediate possession, but I mean immediate, I mean now!'"

"Well," she said, "I can't get out now. I have to call my husband at the office."

"I don't care what you do. I want immediate possession. And here is my check in advance. Call the bank, to see if the check is good."

She got out that day, She called her husband to meet her, and off they went to their home in Long Island.

Lecture 14 – Secret of Imagination

Well, she was just killed last week, at the age of 73, I think it was. He was driving; he wasn't injured, and the friend in the car was injured, but Grace was killed instantly. But at least, she learned the Law. She didn't come to the meetings very often because she said in her capacity, she was a pillar of the Episcopal Church in New York City . . also in Long Island; it would not be advisable to be seen in my meeting place. That would be "slumming." But she always came to my home with any problem.

One she had with her son. He came back from Egypt where he was in the State Department, and he came with a huge, big beard, and she said, "Neville, I am embarrassed." It was long before people wore beards; today it would be the thing to do, but he came back long before the young fellows wore beards. It was a huge, big beard. She said, "Neville, I am so embarrassed, I just don't want to walk down Fifth Avenue with him. I would make him walk ahead or walk behind me. I don't want to be seen with him. What must I do? Because he gets annoyed and will do nothing that his father or I suggest."

I said, "How would you feel if you kissed him and he had no beard? You would kiss your son, wouldn't you?"

"Oh, yes."

"Well then, put your hand on his face and he doesn't have any beard, and then kiss him and feel that smooth skin that is your son's face, and he has no beard."

"All right, I will do that."

Lecture 14 – Secret of Imagination

She didn't tell me. I opened the morning paper one Monday morning. There was a big fashionable social wedding, and here was Mrs. Roosevelt and her husband, and here is her son and here is the bride coming down the steps of the Episcopal Church, and he has no beard! So the next time she came to see me, I reminded her; I said, "You know, you came here the last time about the beard, and the beard is off."

She said, "Do you know why?"

I said, "Yes, I know why, but you tell me why."

"Well, the girl that he married refused to go through with it unless he shaved." She saw the physical act.

I said, "No, that wasn't it. You promised me that you would kiss him and feel his smooth skin; and if you would feel the smooth skin, it would come off."

She said, "I did do it, but the girl demanded it."

So, she goes back to a physical causation, and it wasn't so at all. There is no natural effect with a natural cause. Every natural effect has an imaginal cause, and the natural only seems. So she still is going to insist it is because the girl wanted the beard off, and that's why he took it off. Well now, she knows better. She's now in a world just like this. At least she learned the lesson of the Law. She didn't learn the Promise, because when I spoke to her, I did not have the Promise. I had not realized it.

You know the Promise because it only happened to me twelve years ago this coming month. So, those who knew me

Lecture 14 – Secret of Imagination

before, have not heard from me, the Promise. Those who have known me since, they know the Promise.

So, I ask you tonight to please take it seriously. Watch your every imaginal act. And I will say to everyone, Don't take anything lightly. Don't voice an opinion that may be embarrassing or hurtful to yourself or to another, even though reason dictates it. Because reason could dictate that this is the fact, for "I've seen so many similar cases that this is going to be so-and-so." Your words are the words of God.

"Oh, what have I said? What have I done, Oh, all-powerful human words?"

Now let us go into the silence.

Lecture 15 – I AM Reality Called Imagination

Lecture 15

Neville Goddard – Date Unknown
I AM Reality Called Imagination

We'll be here every Monday and Friday through April. Same place same time. I think you will find tonight, a very practical message. But to understand it, you must go back and see if you really believe the same thing. I make the claim that the eternal body of man, is the Imagination. And that is God himself. The one we speak of in scripture as Jesus Christ.

Now we are told in scripture to examine ourselves, to see whether we are holding to the Faith. Test yourselves said Paul; do you not realize that Jesus Christ is in you? Unless of course you fail, to meet the test. Now you just had the test and you and you alone can judge whether you failed or not for you heard the word, Jesus Christ. You heard the word God, now if it conveyed the sense, our existent something outside of man you fail the test. When you hear the word God or the word Jesus or the word Christ, the word Lord and the mind jumps to something outside of you, outside of man, you fail the test.

Now we are told by Him all things were made and without him not anything was made, that was made. And that I tell you, is your own wonderful human Imagination. What is now true in the world, was once only imagined.

But this is the greatest of all secrets, the secret of imagining. Something that you and I and everyone in the world, should strive to understand. For the secret of

Lecture 15 – I AM Reality Called Imagination

imagining, is the greatest of all problems, to the solution of which everyone should aspire, for supreme power, supreme wisdom, supreme delight, lies in the solution, of this mystery.

When you actually discover it, you discover God, your finding the creative power of the Universe, and what you're finding is your own wonderful human Imagination.

We can only barely scratch the surface of this mystery. One, Imagination it seems, will do little for our wish, until we have imagined, the wish fulfilled.

As Shakespeare said; it hath been taught us from the primal state, that which is, was wished, until it were. So you and I want something, and we define our objective, how to realize it, if this power is within us, then we are the operant power. We do not seek anyone on the outside, it's simply within us. Well how do I operate it? If I could put it in a simple little frame, the subjective appropriation, of the objective hope, is the way to success.

It's imagining as if it were true. What would the feeling be like, if it were true? So I start from the feeling of the wish fulfilled. I must begin by feeling, that I've already arrived, I've already achieved my goal, and catch the mood that would be mine, if it were true, and then wear that mood. If I wear that mood as if it were true, I will realize it in my world.

A Friend of mine was here tonight. She thought that she had failed this past November in her visit to Poughkeepsie, not Poughkeepsie, Pittsburgh. Friends of hers that she knew well and they were a little bit down because of the seeming recession. One friend had worked for 27 years at Jones &

Lecture 15 – I AM Reality Called Imagination

Laughlin, one of the great big steel firms of our country. In the months of September and October, they let out 4000 workers.

He had to put in 3 more years and 2 months to complete a 30 year service with the firm. After 30 years he could retire at a very good, I would say, retirement fund. But he also had 6 more years to go for his social security. And they let out 4000, and then it was rumored in the plant that they're going to close that plant. She reminded him of the use of Imagination, which she had used with him successfully, in her previous visit to Pittsburgh. Well he laughed it off. Those things would have happened anyway. She reminded him of 6 distinct requests on his part, that he thought he could not realize.

Every one, came to pass and she reminded him. And then she took a vision of mine and explained it to him. She said what I told you the last time. Neville had a vision, well the bible tells us, that the depth of our own being speaks to us through the medium of dreams and vision. So here in this dream of mine, call it a dream if you will, it was just as real as this. I was taken in spirit, into an enormous mansion, and here, 3 generations were present, but one was invisible and that was the grandfather. The father was explaining to his children, the secret of his own father's success.

So there was the grandfather departed from the world , leaving behind him an enormous fortune, for the benefit of his son and then his grandchildren. And so the father said to the children, grandfather used to say, while standing on an empty lot, I remember when, this was an empty lot. Then he would paint a word picture, so vividly of what he intended to do with that empty lot, that it ceased to be an empty lot

Lecture 15 – I AM Reality Called Imagination

and you saw the structure that he intended to build, but he acted as though it was already a completed act. He began with the feeling of having arrived at his ideal for that empty lot. Then I woke on my bed and I recall the dream and I knew that the depth of my own being had constructed that scene, to instruct me. Here is one purpose of the great use of this power, called Imagination, which is God.

It was too early to rise so I went back to sleep and I re-dreamed the dream, this time, I AM the grandfather. I am not the father telling the story. I am not an eavesdropper listening to the story as it was told, in the original dream. I am now the grandfather. That I would say to everyone, while standing on an empty lot, I remember when this was an empty lot.

So she reminded him of this technique, how she said, you are afraid, that you might be let out, after 27 years and two months, in Jones & Laughlin. I will now remember when, you were afraid. I will remember when you thought it all came to an end. That's one. He said two years ago I was interviewed and I thought it was a very good interview but after two years it has never appeared in the trade paper and I wondered what had been done with it, had they simply forgotten it, mislaid it or deliberately not used it? She said I will read that magazine and I'll be lifted up by it, it's humorously written as you tell me, but I will take that book right now, in my hand, that magazine and I will read it. All about you.

She went into two or three others, then she returned, now she's here tonight. She said in December, I received the magazine, it's very well written and very, very humorous, all about this man. Then she said, I heard on the radio that

Lecture 15 – I AM Reality Called Imagination

Jones & Laughlin had decided not to close the plant but instead to spend $13 million dollars on the plant, modernizing. And then beginning January 1st to recall over 4000 workers that they had let out.

Now he is walking on air, but like all of these fellows, he will still forget it. He will still turn to a God outside of himself. This to him would have happened anyway. They would have spent the $13 million, brought back the 4000. That thing that was found after 2 years and printed, oh that would have happened. And man goes blindly on, worshipping a false God. Because he does not know God.

The only God is your own wonderful human Imagination. The only name forever and forever, that is his name, is I AM. That is my name forever . So when you come to the people of Israel and they ask you what is his name. Just simply say, I AM. That is who I AM. And by this name I should be known throughout all generations. There is no other name. You cannot separate I AM from yourself. That's your essential being. And when you say I AM, you're all Imagination. You cannot stick Imagination on the outside and point to it.

So you do not observe it, as you observe the fruit of imagining. You do not observe Imagination as you do objects in space. Because you are the reality that is called Imagination. This is what we teach here, night after night. Now you can test it, what would the feeling be like, if it were true that I AM now the man I would like to be? What would the feeling be like, catch the mood, for the mood determines the fortunes of people, rather that the fortunes determine the mood. Man puts it just the opposite. If I had a million you say, of I would feel so good. Now, feel as you would, if you

Lecture 15 – I AM Reality Called Imagination

had it. Catch the mood and the mood will create that objective hope, if that is your hope.

What would the feeling be like if you were now the person you want to be? Well catch that mood. And wear that mood as you would a suit of clothes, and that mood will actually create an objective state that reflects that mood. That's what she did. She put herself into a mood, actually feeling that she was reading a story of a friend and here it came as a complete stretch, two full pages, all about this man. And then a little news bulletin on the radio and then conformation from him, a telephone call from his wife, confirming the news bulletin, that they're all back on the job, and here now, as he said for years, after 27 years, I walked through that plant and I thought I would go crazy. I wanted to climb the wall because of the noise. When I heard the hammers and the bellows and the furnaces and all these thousands of workman, that constant, constant ding, I wanted to climb the wall.

Now, after 4000 were let out, my footsteps echoes through the entire area. I would like to run and scream, running towards my office. What he does in the plant I do not know. If he goes towards his office, and he does, he has an executive position, is at place and is not working at the furnaces. But if you can't imagine when 4000 were let out, how empty the place was and everything simply echoed and my footsteps seemed like some hundred things, as I walked through that plant towards my office. And many a moment I wanted to simply jump up and start running, it seemed so empty, she said alright, that's something, I will remember when, and she applied that technique. Then, your footsteps, scares you, and you wanted to run towards the office. Now is the clacker all over again. So I tell you,

Lecture 15 – I AM Reality Called Imagination

I know from my own experience, that these moods, you catch a mood, I could tell, from the mood that possessed me through the day, that I would meet a certain character, and I met that character. It may be someone I knew or some total stranger but I could tell, from the very mood that possessed me, that I'm drawing into my world, an affinity, with that mood. You can catch a mood and create the world, that is in harmony with the mood. Anyone can do it, in fact you're doing morning, noon and night anyway. So when you turn to some external God, you're turning to a false God. There is no external God.

Examine yourselves said Paul, to see whether you are holding to your Faith. Test yourselves, do you not realize that Jesus Christ is in you? Unless indeed you failed to meet the test. You've just had the test. So if you think of something on the outside, and I use the word Jesus Christ, you have the wrong Jesus Christ. We are told by him all things are made and without him not anything was made that is made. Look into the room, all this was once only imagined, the suits you wear, the dresses you wear, the hats you wear, everything here, the building was once only conceived in the human Imagination. And then executing. And if all things were made by him or did I come to find out who he is. Well I can go beyond my own Imagination. I'm exactly what I imagined. I see the results, so I go back, all things made by him, yes, good, bad and indifferent.

He waits on me just as quickly and just as indifferently, when the will in me is evil as when it is good. Is that in scripture? You'll find it in scripture, read it in the book of Deuteronomy. I kill, I make alive, I wound, I heal and none can deliver out of my hands. I, I AM the Lord. Read it. The 32nd chapter of book of Deuteronomy. There is no other

Lecture 15 – I AM Reality Called Imagination

God. I AM the Lord your God and besides me there is no other God. I AM is that God. As we are told in the 46th Psalm, "Be still and know, that I AM God."

A man will not believe it and yet he has evidence morning, noon and night that is own wonderful creative power, which is his own wonderful human Imagination, is producing the phenomena of life. He sees it all around him but he shuns it away. It's easier for him to genuflect before some little thing made by the human hand. So he put him on the wall and he crosses himself for luck. I think if that's it, that's good. Now I done my duty for today.

So he goes to church and sings the hymns with all the others, and he thinks, I've done my duty, and gives generously to the church, perfectly alright, if you get any pleasure out of it, do it, but that's not serving the true God. If you want a social gathering, certainly go to church. Go to the coffee breaks following the service and ask 1% of those who come out of service, what was the text today? And he will look at you with some vacant look, what? What was the text? What did he say? What was the theme of his subject today? They don't know. But it's a place to go, on certain days of the year. Especially on Christmas, on Easter and days of that nature.

Others make it a point to go once a week. They think they're doing God a favor. You're walking with God morning, noon and night. You take him to bed with you because your essential being is God, and there is no other God. Were he not within you, you couldn't even breathe, your breath is God. Every child born of woman is God incarnate. If man only knew that, there could be no war in the world. Killing man is killing God. For every child born of woman, is the

Lecture 15 – I AM Reality Called Imagination

incarnation of God. Whether you be black, yellow, pink, white or any other color, there is no other being in this world but God.

So the incarnation takes place every time a little child is born and it breathes and you spank it, to get it to cry. That moment was the incarnation of God. How can you kill him? How can you hurt him? Just teach him and show him what power is latent within him. For the whole vast world aches for the awakening of the Imagination in man. And the story as told us in scripture is a true story but not as its told. The day will come you'll actually find yourself reenacting the entire drama as told us in the gospel and you will know it in the first person, singular, present tense experience. And then you'll know who he is. He comes to us as one unknown, yet one who in the most wonderful mysterious manner, let's man experience who he is. When you experience who he is, it's all about you, it's not about another. The whole vast drama is all about the individual that you see as a little child, right in this wonderful world of ours.

But here tonight let us keep it on this level. And on this level tonight, when you dream of some wonderful objective in this world that is not yet realized, realize who the dreamer is and the dreamer is God, and by dreamer I mean your own wonderful Imagination, now, a day dream, that's God, that's God in action. Now do not let your reason and your senses dictate what is possible. All things are possible to God. So suspend for a moment your reason, suspend the senses that that are dictating what you must accept, for many of you accept the facts of life, alright, if you could accept the facts of life and let reason dictate it, you'll never go beyond where you are.

Lecture 15 – I AM Reality Called Imagination

So suspend them, just for a moment, and try this technique. What would the feeling be like? How would I feel, if it were true, that I were already the man, I would like to be. And if I AM, how would I see my friends and how would they see me? It's all within us, so let my wonderful human Imagination see them as they would have to see me if it were true. Bring them into my mind's eye and let them see me and let them talk to me and let them congratulate me on my good fortune and don't duck, accept the congratulations of your friends, if they really mean it. Actually play the part all within yourself and then believe it 100%.

As we are told in Johns letter, the 5th chapter of his 1st Epistle, If we believe that he hears us, if all that we ask of him, then we know that we have obtained the request made of him. But if you get the right God you have no doubts in your mind, as to whether he heard you or not, for you know you heard it, and that's God. But if you're not quite sure that he heard it, because there are 3 billion talking to him, begging, well then you may be not quite sure that he heard you. For you don't think you're good enough but you can't deny that you hear your own mind, you hear your own inner conversation, you hear your own inner speech, well if you know that one is God, well then you are sure he heard you.

Now you are told in that 5th chapter, the 15th verse, of 1st Epistle of John, If we know that he hears us, in all that we ask of him, then we know, that we have already obtained the request made of him. Well alright there's an interval between that imaginal act and its fulfillment, as there is between the creative act of a man and the birth of that child.

Every little thing has an interval of time between the act and it fulfillment. A horse will take 12 months. a woman

Lecture 15 – I AM Reality Called Imagination

takes 9 months, the little sheep will take 5 months, a chicken will take 21 days. There are intervals of time, so the bible teaches every vision has its own appointed hour. It ripens, it will flower. If it be late, then wait, for it is sure and it will not be late. Different intervals of time. So it may take me a longer time. In this case of this man, 2 months to bring back 4000 that were unemployed.

To put his mind at rest that he doesn't have now, to feel, that he's going to be fired, he could put in now the extra time, only a little while, 3 years and two months will complete his 30 years with Jones & Laughlin and then, what's, a man of his age, 6 more years, and then social security. So he'll have both. If it happened now he wouldn't have it. He will be cut on social security and he will be let out without a good retirement fund. So she goes back and she reminds him that it happened before, he couldn't afford the roof for the house and she said I will see the roof on the house. I remember when it needed a roof and so she told him, I recall telling you, I remember when it needed it. Well soon after something happened in his work, he got the money and the roof is on.

The wife wanted an organ, couldn't afford the organ, alright she said I will remember when you didn't have one, she has the organ. And she took one after the other, of all these things, he still, with all the evidence in the world, he's still working on some outside God. He thinks he's doing the wrong thing. He feels that if perchance, that man, is simply a devil incarnate, and he's taken me from my real God, which being something external to himself, that he fashions out of his own mind, and fashions with his hand because all of these little nonsense's that you buy and stick them up as holy objects. First of all no artist really ever designed them.

Lecture 15 – I AM Reality Called Imagination

They said it fits to speak of an artist, when you see these horrible monstrosities that we buy and stick around the place and call them religious objects.

So find who he is, he is the living God, he is no dead God. You want to find . . Read the 115th Psalm, about the kind of God that men worship. The whole Psalm is devoted to the false God that the whole vast world worships. Says eyes, but he sees not, ears that he hears not, feet and he walks not, hands and he touches not. Just a dead thing made by human hands. When the living God is within man, as his own wonderful human Imagination.

So I tell you all that you behold, though it appears without, it is within, in your own wonderful human Imagination, of which this world of mortality is but a shadow. All things exist in the human Imagination and everything you see as an objective reality, was produced by imaging. Think of one thing, just think of one thing, that would simply deny it. You can't think of one thing.

So you go to the moon, you first had to imagine it. Had to imagine everything concerning the machine that took you to the moon. Everything in the world, first has to be imagined, and then executed. Alright, the intelligence to do it will come, but should take the group in first and conceive it and dwell in it as though it were true and no power on Earth can stop it from becoming so. Your visions will clarify itself, at night, it's a different kind of a night, your days are different, you see people differently, you can't walk by any man and not see God incarnated. Can't do it. Even if he had the most horrible background and he said simply, well, a murderer and it's proven that he is, you still see God incarnate, but so summed to sleep the poor thing doesn't know it.

Lecture 15 – I AM Reality Called Imagination

If he could only get to him and show him that he really is God incarnate. And the one he thought he killed, he has been restored to life. Not to the senses of man, but he is restored in a world just like this, terrestrial, just like this. About his business, he continues his work, until he too awakens from this dream of life. But all will awaken eventually, but why not start now. Start now to tell man who you really are. God and man are one. Man is all Imagination and God is man and exists in us and we in him. The eternal body of man, is the Imagination, and that is God himself.

Nothing but God in the Universe, all God and eventually you and I will awake and because God is one, not two, you and I are one. Without loss of identity, that's one of the strangest mysteries in the world. Without loss of identity, we are one. I know that from my own personal experience, we are one and yet I am individualized and you are individualized and we attain forever and forever toward ever a greater individualization and yet we are one. And I will bring that out to the best of my ability. But tonight if you're here for the first time and you want something practical, you'll apply what I told you.

First have an objective, you must have an objective. You can't say well I don't know what I want, well alright, come back the next time. Ask yourself , what would I like of life? Don't be ashamed to name it, what would I like of life? Well then try to get the objective. Now, prayer as far as I'm concerned is nothing more than the subjective appropriation of the objective hope. That is the way to success. I appropriate it subjectively. How do I appropriate a space subjectively?

Lecture 15 – I AM Reality Called Imagination

Well suppose now this very moment, I wanted a ball, an ordinary baseball. But there isn't a baseball in the room, alright, but I want one. I would actually assume that I am holding a baseball in my hand and that I could feel it. You think you can't feel it, well now try it. Try to feel what it would feel like if you held a baseball. Now to prove that you have held it, see what it feels like, the difference now, a tennis ball. Feel the difference? Alright a Golf ball. Feel the difference? A piece of silk. You feel any difference? If you can distinguish between this many objects, though they are subjective, then they must exist somewhere.

If you can actually separate them in your mind's eye and distinguish between these objects? I begin to feel, begin to sense, begin to smell a rose, well a rose doesn't smell or doesn't actually have the odor of another flower, I can detect the rose. Now a lily, an Easter lily. I can detect that. Well what does it do? Well I'm going to get them. Someone will think of Neville and send him a flower. And it's going to be the flower that I'm actually going to feel and touch and smell. Prayer works that way.

Money has an odor, it's unlike any odor in the world. It's more fragrant, to the miser, than the most marvelous perfume in the world. He can tell it. You put a money bag to his face is like putting roses to mine. He loves it, he can smell money. He can feel it, money has a distinct feel about it. Put a $20 bill in your hand and ask him to feel it and then put another piece of paper in your hand and you can tell the difference. There is a difference, there is an odor to it. All this is part of the inner man, that all things are possible to him. Try it, before you condemn it, try it. And if you have the evidence to support, my claim, then it doesn't matter what the world will tell you.

Lecture 15 – I AM Reality Called Imagination

If he laughs at you so what, for they laugh at everyone who had an idea that seemed a little bit, off center. Always laughed at them. They laughed at the idea of going to the moon, well not it's an accomplished fact. There are still those who won't believe it happened you know. Because they don't want to believe it ever happened. There are those who say you couldn't go down and actually live under water. Well we have a submarine. There are still those who won't believe it. You can present them with all the facts in the world, and they won't believe it. So I tell you, you try it first and if it proves itself in performance, it doesn't really matter what the whole vast world thinks. Go about your father's business, which is yourself and then live a full and wonderful life, in this world of Caesar, and the day will come you will actually depart this world,

I mean this age, cause those who are departing it now, unless they are awakened, they'll still find themselves in a world just like this. But those who have awakened, will experience the second birth, the birth from above, find themselves in an entirely different age, where they're all Imagination and they are perfect and wherever they go everything is perfect, they don't have to raise a finger to make anything perfect, because they are perfect. All things must conform to them, for their perfect. That's heaven. So Heaven is not an area, it's not a realm, it's a body and when that body is awaken within you, which is the wonderful human Imagination, completely awaken, then wherever you go clothed in that body that is completely awake, everything is perfect.

If you found yourself in a forest, of dead trees, they'd all burst into foliage. In the desert they would all bloom like the rose, because you are there. No blind man, deaf man, no

Lecture 15 – I AM Reality Called Imagination

handicap man, could stand in your presence. He would be instantly transformed into a perfect man because you are perfect, that's heaven, it's harmony. So it's not a place that you would go, o sleep and all that nonsense, no, it's just simply you in a world, that's perfect, because you are perfect. And the day will come you will awaken that body, working in you now. That body is in you but it's sound asleep. One day you will experience the resurrection and you'll know the mystery of the resurrection, when you rise, and you rise within yourself, for the grave in which Christ is buried, that the Lord is buried, is your own skull. That's where he is buried. And in that tomb where he is buried, one day, he will awake and he will come out of that tomb, and you will come out of the tomb and you will know who you are.

He us buried in every child in the world, this Universal being and yet one. Billions of us and yet only one Lord. And that one Lord in his fullness is buried in you, individually. And when you awaken, you are He. So tonight, take a goal, make it a lovely goal, either for yourself or another. Anytime you exercise your Imagination, lovingly, on behalf of another, you are mediating God to that person. So bring a friend before your mind's eye, represent him to yourself as the man or the woman you would like them to be. And don't tell them, ask for no praise, just assume they are talking to you and telling you the most marvelous news about themselves. And you congratulate them on that good news. And go your own way. Believe in the reality of that imaginal act. It may happen tomorrow, it may happen the day after, or a week later or a month later. It has its own appointed hour. And it is ripening and it is going to flower. But don't be concerned, leave it alone and it will come to pass. So this is what I mean by feeling is the secret.

Lecture 15 – I AM Reality Called Imagination

I catch the mood, the feeling, if I were, what I want to be. I don't have to touch something, I can if I want to. But it's the mood I'm speaking of. What would the feeling be if she were well? If she were this? And then you catch it just as though it were true. You always go to the end and the end is where you begin. You're always imagining ahead of our evidence. So go to the end, and feel the end and then live in the end, even though reason denies it and your senses deny it. You've turned your back upon the doubters, that is your senses and what reason dictates. That's the hell or the devil or Satan in the world. That's the doubter, so you turn your back upon it. And then you walk as thought things were as you want them to be. And living in that assumption, it slowly hardens into fact. Even though at the moment of the assumption it was denied by reason, an assumption, though false, if persisted in, will harden into fact. So you learn to assume and learn to persist in the assumption and it will come to pass.

Now let us go into the silence.... After which we will have questions.

Neville continues speaking after one (full) minute of silence:

Good, well I hope you caught a good mood. It'll work. Are there any questions please? Any questions?

Yes sir.

Question: (inaudible) You mentioned that you met your secretary ..... (and after that is it is hard to make out the rest of the question)

Lecture 15 – I AM Reality Called Imagination

Neville: Well to answer your question I must first go back and explain it to those that are here for the first time.

Audience member: (he interrupts Neville, but it is mostly inaudible)

Neville: No, no, no. I make the statement based upon my own experience and nothing dies. That's not only true of man, it is true of the flowers, of the animal world, of the trees, of everything, nothing dies. I AM the God of the living, not of the dead, so nothing dies, the little flower that blooms once, blooms forever. It's renewed by the seed of contemplated thought.

Well I had a wonderful friend who died suddenly at the age of 50, while I was out here. I then lived in New York City. He was born in Upstate New York. He lived in Manhattan and took care of my books and took care of all of my business affairs. Well I got a cable saying that he was dead. They found his body on the floor the next morning when they went into clean and I must come back and take care of the funeral affairs. So I went back.

I have two sister in laws, my wife is one of three girls. The other two are pillars of the Episcopal Church. The older of the two lives in Summit, New Jersey. And she's always said to me, you know, I like you personally as a brother in law because you're kind to my sister and to your child and for that, I like you. But I don't believe one word you talk about. That's not my God. I said alright. She said I don't believe in immortality. Don't believe in survival. I said you call yourself a Christian? She said what has that to do with it. I said didn't you realize that the Christian foundation is the fatherhood of God, the brotherhood of man and life

Lecture 15 – I AM Reality Called Imagination

everlasting? You realize one of these is going to collapse? No, she didn't say a word, she said I still don't believe what you teach. I said alright. Well he died in August. I went back to prepare the funeral. In the next year, I presume around January or February I found myself consciously in that world where Jack is. I do it time and time again. This does not restrain me. I can put it on a bed and find myself in another world. It is nowhere, it is right here, they're penetrating each other and yet not interfering with each other.

And here is Jack and here is my sister in law Al, I call her Al, her name is Alice. And I said, she said to me, I still don't believe what you teach you know. I said how can you say that when you see Jack. She said what is Jack to do with it? I said Jack died, Jack then spoke to me, who's dead? I said you are dead jack, but you died, I went to your funeral. I saved for it. I got you a good catholic funeral, Jack. Cause your sister insisted that you must be given a nice catholic funeral. I didn't cremate you, I put you in Holy ground Jack. I got a priest and the priest did all little things he has to do so you are very well planted. He just looked at me .....

Now let us go into the silence.

Lecture 16 – Self-Talk Creates Reality / Mental Diet

Lecture 16

Neville Goddard, (1955)
Self-Talk Creates Reality / Mental Diet

Talking to oneself is a habit everyone indulges in. We could no more stop talking to ourselves than we could stop eating and drinking. All that we can do is control the nature and the direction of our inner conversations. Most of us are totally unaware of the fact that our inner conversations are the causes of the circumstance of our life.

We are told that "as a man thinketh in his heart, so is he." But do we know that man's thinking follows the tracks laid down in his own inner conversations? To turn the tracks to which he is tied in the direction in which he wants to go, he must put off his former conversation, which is called in the Bible, the Old Man, and be renewed in the spirit of his mind. Speech is the image of mind; therefore, to change his mind, he must first change his speech. By 'speech' is meant those mental conversations we carry on with ourselves.

The world is a magic circle of infinite possible mental transformations. For there are an infinite number of possible mental conversations. When man discovers the creative power of inner talking, he will realize his function and his mission in life. Then he can act to a purpose. Without such knowledge, he acts unconsciously. Everything is a manifestation of the mental conversations which go on in us without our being aware of them. But as civilized beings, we must become aware of them and act with a purpose.

Lecture 16 – Self-Talk Creates Reality / Mental Diet

A man's mental conversations attracts his life. As long as there is no change in his inner talking, the personal history of the man remains the same. To attempt to change the world, before we change our inner talking is to struggle against the very nature of things. Man can go 'round and around in the same circle of disappointments and misfortunes, not seeing them as caused by his own negative inner talking, but as caused by others. This may seem far-fetched, but it is a matter which lends itself to research and experiment. The formula the chemist illustrates is not more certainly provable than the formula of this science by which words are clothed in objective reality.

One day a girl told me of her difficulties in working with her employer. She was convinced that he unjustly criticized and rejected her very best efforts. Upon hearing her story, I explained that if she thought him unfair, it was a sure sign that she herself was in need of a new conversation piece. There was no doubt but that she was mentally arguing with her employer, for others only echo, that which we whisper to them in secret. She confessed that she argued mentally with him all day long. When she realized what she had been doing, she agreed to change her inner conversations with her employer. She imagined that he had congratulated her on her fine work, and that she in turn had thanked him for his praise and kindness. To her great delight, she soon discovered that her own attitude was the cause of all that befell her. The behavior of her employer reversed itself. It echoed, as it had always done, her mental conversations with him.

I rarely see a person alone without wondering, "to what conversation piece is he tied? On what mysterious track is he walking?" We must begin to take life consciously. For the

Lecture 16 – Self-Talk Creates Reality / Mental Diet

solution of all problems lies just in this: the Second Man, the Lord from heaven in all of us, is trying to become self-conscious in the body, that he may be about his father's business. What are his labors? To imitate his father, to become master of the Word, master of his inner talking, that he may mold this world of ours into a likeness with the Kingdom of Love.

The prophet said, "Be ye imitators of God as dear children." How would I imitate God? Well, we are told that God calls things that are not seen as though they were seen, and the unseen becomes seen. This is the way the girl called forth praise and kindness from her employer. She carried on an imaginary conversation with her employer from the premise that he had praised her work, and he did.

Our inner conversations represent in various ways the world we live in. Our individual worlds are self-revelations of our own inner speech. We are told that every idle word that men shall speak they shall give account thereof. For by their words shall they be justified, and by their words they shall be condemned. We abandon ourselves to negative inner talking, yet expect to retain command of life. Our present mental conversations do not recede into the past as man believes. They advance into the future to confront us as wasted or invested words. "My Word," said the prophet, "shall not return unto me void, but it shall accomplish that which I please, and it shall prosper in all the things whereto I sent it."

How would I send my Word to help a friend? I would imagine that I am hearing his voice, that he is physically present, that my hand is on him. I would then congratulate him on his good fortune, tell him that I have never seen him

Lecture 16 – Self-Talk Creates Reality / Mental Diet

look better. I would listen as though I heard him; I would imagine that he is telling me he has never felt better, he has never been happier. And I would know that in this loving, knowing communion with another, a communion populous with loving thoughts and feelings, that my word was sent, and it shall not return unto me void, but it shall prosper in the thing whereto I sent it.

"Now it the accepted time, now is the day of salvation." It is only what is done now, that counts, even though its effects may not be visible until tomorrow. We call not out loud, but by an inner effort of intense attention. To listen attentively, as though you heard, is to create. The events and relationships of life are your Word made visible. Most of us rob others of their willingness and their ability to be kind and generous by our fixed attitudes towards them. Our attitudes unfold within us in the form of mental conversations. Inner talking from premises of fulfilled desire is the way to consciously create circumstances.

Our inner conversations are perpetually out-pictured all around us in happenings. Therefore, what we desire to see and hear without, we must see and hear within, for the whole manifested world goes to show us what use we have made of the Word. If you practice this art of controlled inner speaking, you too will know what a thrill it is to be able to say, "And now I have told you before it come to pass, that when it is come to pass, ye might believe." You will be able to consciously use your Imagination to transform and channel the immense creative energies of your inner speech from the mental, emotional level to the physical level. And I do not know what limits, if any, there are to such a process.

Lecture 16 – Self-Talk Creates Reality / Mental Diet

What is your aim? Does your inner talking match it? It must, you know, if you would realize your aim. For as the prophet asked, "Can two walk together, except they be agreed?" And of course the answer is, "No, they cannot." The two who must agree are your inner conversation and the state desired. That is, what you desire to see and hear without, you must see and hear within. Every stage of man's progress, is made by the conscious exercise of his Imagination matching his inner speech to his fulfilled desire. As we control our inner talking, matching it to our fulfilled desires, we can lay aside all other processes. Then we simply act by clear Imagination and intention: we imagine the wish fulfilled and carry on mental conversations from that premise. The right inner speech is the speech that would be yours were you to realize your ideal. In other words, it is the speech of fulfilled desire.

Now you will understand how wise the ancient was, when he told us in the Hermetica, "There are two gifts which God has bestowed upon man alone and on no other mortal creature. These two are Mind and Speech, and the gift of Mind and Speech is equivalent to that of immortality. If a man uses these two gifts rightly, he will differ in nothing from the Immortals. And when he quits his body, Mind and Speech will be his guides, and by them he will be brought into the troop of the gods and the souls that have attained to bliss."

With the gift of Mind and Speech you create the conditions and circumstances of life. "In the beginning was the Word, and the Word was with God, and the Word was God." The Word, said Hermes, is Son, and Mind is Father of the Word. They are not separate one from the other, for life is the union of Word and Mind. You and your inner talking, or

Lecture 16 – Self-Talk Creates Reality / Mental Diet

Word, are one. If your mind is one with your inner conversations, then to be transformed in mind is to be transformed in conversation. It was a flash of the deepest insight that taught Paul to write, "Put off the former conversation, the Old Man which is corrupt, and be renewed in the spirit of your mind. Put on the New Man." "Put on the New Man," and "be renewed in the spirit of your mind," is to change your inner conversation, for speech and mind are one .. a change of speech is a change of mind.

The prophet Samuel said, "The Lord spake by me, and his Word was in my tongue." If the Lord's Word was in the prophet's tongue, then the Lord's mouth that uttered the Word must be the prophet's mind, for inner conversations originate in the mind and produce little tiny speech movements in the tongue. The prophet is telling us that the mouth of God is the mind of man, that our inner conversations are the Word of God creating life about us, as we create it within ourselves.

In the Bible you are told that the Word is very near to you, in your mouth and in your heart, that you may do it. "See, I have set before you this day life and good, death and evil, blessings and cursings. Choose life." The conditions and circumstances of life are not created by some power external to yourself; they are the conditions which result from the exercise of your freedom of choice, your freedom to choose the ideas to which you will respond.

Now is the accepted time. This is the day of salvation. Whatsoever things are of good report, think on these things. For your future will be formed by the Word of God which is your present inner talking. You create your future by your

Lecture 16 – Self-Talk Creates Reality / Mental Diet

inner conversations. The worlds were framed by the Word of God, that is, your inner talking.

See yonder fields? The sesamum was sesamum, the corn was corn. The silence and the darkness knew! So is a man's fate born.

For ends run true to origins. If you would reap success, you must plant success. The idea in your mind which starts the whole process going is the idea which you accept as truth. This is a very important point to grasp, for truth depends upon the intensity of Imagination, not upon "facts." When the girl imagined that her employer was unfair, his behavior confirmed her Imagination. When she changed her assumption of him, his behavior reflected the change, proving that an assumption, though false, if persisted in, will harden into fact.

The mind always behaves according to the assumption with which it starts. Therefore, to experience success, we must assume that we are successful. We must live wholly on the level of the Imagination itself, and it must be consciously and deliberately undertaken. It does not matter if at the present moment external facts deny the truth of your assumption, if you persist in your assumption it will become a fact. Signs follow, they do not precede.

To assume a new concept of yourself, is to that extent, to change your inner talking or Word of God, and is therefore, putting on the New Man. Our inner talking, though unheard by others, is more productive of future conditions than all the audible promises and threats of men. Your ideal is waiting to be incarnated, but unless you yourself offer it human parentage it is incapable of birth. You must define

Lecture 16 – Self-Talk Creates Reality / Mental Diet

the person you wish to be and then assume the feeling of your wish fulfilled, in faith that that assumption will find expression through you.

The true test of religion is in its use, but men have made it a thing to defend. It is to you that the words are spoken, "Blessed is she that believed, for there shall be an accomplishment of those things which were spoken unto her from the Lord." Test it. Try it. Conceive yourself to be one that you want to be and remain faithful to that conception, for life here is only a training ground for image making. Try it and see if life will not shape itself on the model of your Imagination.

Everything in the world bears witness of the use or misuse of man's inner talking. Negative inner talking, particularly evil and envious inner talking, are the breeding ground of the future battlefields and penitentiaries of the world. Through habit man has developed the secret affection for these negative inner conversations. Through them he justifies failure, criticizes his neighbors, gloats over the distress of others, and in general pours out his venom on all. Such misuse of the Word perpetuates the violence of the world.

The transformation of self requires that we meditate on a given phrase, a phrase which implies that our ideal is realized, and inwardly affirm it over and over and over again until we are inwardly affected by its implication, until we are possessed by it. Hold fast to your noble inner convictions or "conversations." Nothing can take them from you but yourself. Nothing can stop them from becoming objective facts. All things are generated out of your Imagination by the Word of God, which is your own inner conversation. And

Lecture 16 – Self-Talk Creates Reality / Mental Diet

every Imagination reaps its own Words which it has inwardly spoken.

The great secret of success is a controlled inner conversation from premises of fulfilled desire. The only price you pay for success is the giving up of your former conversation which belongs to the Old Man, the unsuccessful man. The time is ripe for many of us to take conscious charge in creating heaven on earth. To consciously and voluntarily use our Imagination, to inwardly hear and say only that which is in harmony with our ideal, is actively bringing heaven to earth.

Every time we exercise our Imagination lovingly on behalf of another, we are literally mediating God to that one. Always use your Imagination masterfully, as a participant, not an onlooker. In using your Imagination to transform energy, from the mental, emotional level to physical level, extend your senses . . look and imagine that you are seeing what you want to see, that you are hearing what you want to hear, and touching what you want to touch. Become intensely aware of doing so. Give your imaginary state all the tones and feeling of reality. Keep on doing so until you arouse within yourself the mood of accomplishment and the feeling of relief.

This is the active, voluntary use of the Imagination as distinguished from the passive, involuntary acceptance of appearances. It is by this active, voluntary use of the Imagination that the Second Man, the Lord from heaven, is awakened in man. Men call Imagination a plaything, the "dream faculty." But actually it is the very gateway of reality. Imagination is the way to the state desired, it is the truth of the state desired, and the life of that state desired.

Lecture 16 – Self-Talk Creates Reality / Mental Diet

Could you realize this fully, there would you know that what you do in your Imagination is the only important thing. Within the circle of our Imagination the whole drama of life is being enacted over and over again. Through the bold and active use of the Imagination we can stretch out our hand and touch a friend ten thousand miles away and bring health and wealth to the parched lips of his being. It is the way to everything in the world. How else could we function beyond our fleshly limitations? But Imagination demands of us, a fuller living of our dreams in the present.

Through the portals of the present the whole of time must pass. Imagine elsewhere as here, and then as now. Try it and see. You can always tell if you have succeeded in making the future dream a present fact by observing your inner talking. If you are inwardly saying what you would audibly say were you physically present and physically moving about in that place, then you have succeeded. And you could prophesy it from these inner conversations, and from the moods which they awaken within you, what your future will be. For one power alone makes a prophet . . Imagination, the divine vision.

All that we meet is our Word made visible. And what we do not now comprehend, is related by affinity, to the unrecognized forces of our own inner conversations and the moods which they arouse within us. If we do not like what is happening to us, it is a sure sign that we are in need of a change of mental diet. For man, we are told, lives not by bread alone but by every Word that proceeds from the mouth of God. And having discovered the mouth of God to be the mind of man, a mind which lives on Words or inner talking, we should feed into our minds only loving, noble thoughts. For with Words or inner talking, we build our world.

Lecture 16 – Self-Talk Creates Reality / Mental Diet

Let love's lordly hand raise your hunger and thirst to all that is noble and of good report, and let your mind starve e'er you raise your hand to a cup love did not fill or a bowl love did not bless. That you may never again have to say, "What have I said? What have I done, O all powerful human Word?"

Now let us go into the silence.

Neville Goddard

1948 Lessons Series
With
Questions and Answers

Lesson 1 – Consciousness is the Only Reality
Lesson 2 – Assumptions Harden into Fact
Lesson 3 – Thinking Fourth-Dimensionally
Lesson 4 – No One to Change But Self
Lesson 5 – Remain Faithful to Your Idea
Questions and Answers

Lesson 1 – Consciousness is the Only Reality

This is going to be a very practical Course. Therefore, I hope that everyone in this class has a very clear picture of what he desires, for I am convinced that you can realize your desires by the technique you will receive here this week in these five lessons.

That you may receive the full benefit of these instructions, let me state now that the Bible has no reference at all to any persons who ever existed or to any event that ever occurred upon earth.

The ancient story tellers were not writing history but an allegorical picture lesson of certain basic principles which they clothed in the garb of history, and they adapted these stories to the limited capacity of a most uncritical and credulous people.

Throughout the centuries we have mistakenly taken personifications for persons, allegory for history, the vehicle that conveyed the instruction, for the instruction, and the gross first sense for the ultimate sense intended.

The difference between the form of the Bible and its substance is as great as the difference between a grain of corn and the life germ within that grain. As our assimilative organs discriminate between food that can be built into our system and food that must be discarded, so do our awakened intuitive faculties discover beneath allegory and parable, the psychological life-germ of the Bible; and, feeding on this, we, too, cast off the form which conveyed the message.

1948 Lessons – Lesson 1 – Consciousness is the Only Reality

The argument against the historicity of the Bible is too lengthy; consequently, it is not suitable for inclusion in this practical psychological interpretation of its stories. Therefore, I will waste no time in trying to convince you that the Bible is not an historical fact.

Tonight I will take four stories and show you what the ancient story-tellers intended that you and I should see in these stories.

The ancient teachers attached psychological truths to phallic and solar allegories. They did not know as much of the physical structure of man as do modern scientists, neither did they know as much about the heavens as do our modern astronomers. But the little they did know they used wisely and they built phallic and solar frames to which they tied the great psychological truths that they had discovered.

In the Old Testament you will find much of the Phallic worship. Because it is not helpful, I am not going to emphasize it. I shall only show you how to interpret it.

Before we come to the first of the psychological dramas, that you and I may use in a practical sense, let me state the two outstanding names of the Bible: the one you and I translate as GOD or JEHOVAH, and the one we call his son, which we have as JESUS.

The ancients spelled these names by using little symbols. The ancient tongue, called the Hebraic language, was not a tongue that you exploded with the breath. It was a mystical language never uttered by man. Those who understood it, understood it as mathematicians understand symbols of higher mathematics. It is not something people used to convey thought, as I now use the English language.

They said that God's name was spelled, JOD HE VAU HE. I shall take these symbols and in our normal, down to earth language, explain them in this manner.

The first letter, JOD in the name GOD is a hand or a seed, not just a hand, but the hand of the director. If there is one organ of man that discriminates and sets him apart from the entire world of creation, it is his hand. What we call a hand in the anthropoid ape is not a hand. It is used only for the purpose of conveying food to the mouth, or to swing from branch to branch. Man's hand fashions, it molds. You cannot really express yourself without the hand. This is the builder's hand, the hand of the director; it directs, and molds, and builds within your world.

The ancient story-tellers called the first letter JOD, the hand, or the absolute seed out of which the whole of creation will come.

To the second letter, HE, they gave the symbol of a window. A window is an eye . . the window is to the house what the eye is to the body.

The third letter, VAU, they called a nail. A nail is used for the purpose of binding things together. The conjunction "and" in the Hebraic tongue is simply the third letter, or VAU. If I want to say 'man and woman', I put the VAU in the middle, it binds them together.

The fourth and last letter, HE, is another window or eye.

1948 Lessons – Lesson 1 – Consciousness is the Only Reality

In this modern, down to earth language of ours, you can forget eyes and windows and hands and look at it in this manner. You are seated here now. This first letter, JOD, is your I AM-ness, your awareness. You are aware of being aware . . that is the first letter. Out of this awareness all states of awareness come.

The second letter, HE, called an eye, is your Imagination, your ability to perceive. You imagine or perceive something which seems to be other than Self. As though you were lost in reverie and contemplated mental states in a detached manner, making the thinker and his thoughts separate entities.

The third letter, VAU, is your ability to feel you are that which you desire to be. As you feel you are it, you become aware of being it. To walk as though you were what you want to be is to take your desire out of the imaginary world and put the VAU upon it.

You have completed the drama of creation. I AM aware of something. Then I become aware of actually being, that of which I was aware.

The fourth and last letter in the name of God is another HE, another eye, meaning the visible objective world which constantly bears witness of that which I AM conscious of being.

You do nothing about the objective world; it always molds itself in harmony with that which you are conscious of being.

1948 Lessons – Lesson 1 – Consciousness is the Only Reality

You are told this is the name by which all things are made, and without it there is nothing made that is made. The name is simply what you have now as you are seated here. You are conscious of being, aren't you? Certainly you are. You are also conscious of something that is other than yourself: the room, the furniture, the people.

You may become selective now. Maybe you do not want to be other than what you are, or to own what you see. But you have the capacity to feel what it would be like were you now other than what you are. As you assume that you are that which you want to be, you have completed the name of God or the JOD HE VAU HE.

The final result, the objectification of your assumption, is not your concern. It will come into view automatically, as you assume the consciousness of being it.

Now let us turn to the Son's name, for he gives the Son dominion over the world.

You are that Son, you are the great Joshua, or Jesus, of the Bible. You know the name Joshua or Jehoshua we have Anglicized as Jesus.

The Son's name is almost like the Father's name. The first three letters of the Father's name are the first three letters of the Son's name, JOD HE VAU, then you add a SHIN and an AYIN, making the Son's name read, JOD HE VAU SHIN AYIN'.

You have heard what the first three are: JOD HE VAU. JOD means that you are aware; HE means that you are aware of something; and VAU means that you became aware of being that of which you were aware.

You have dominion because you have the ability to conceive and to become that which you conceive. That is the power of creation.

But why is a SHIN put in the name of the Son?

Because of the infinite mercy of our Father. Mind you, the Father and the Son are one. But when the Father becomes conscious of being man he puts within the condition called man that which he did not give unto himself. He puts a SHIN for this purpose; a SHIN is symbolized as a tooth.

A tooth is that which consumes, that which devours. I must have within me the power to consume that which I now dislike. I, in my ignorance, brought to birth certain things I now dislike and would like to leave behind me. Were there not within me the flames that would consume it, I would be condemned forever to live in a world of all my mistakes. But there is a SHIN, or flame, within the name of the Son, which allows that Son to become detached from states He formerly expressed within the world.

Man is incapable of seeing other than the contents of his own consciousness.

If I now become detached in consciousness from this room by turning my attention away from it, then, I am no longer conscious of it. There is something in me that devours it within me. It can only live within my objective world if I keep it alive within my consciousness.

1948 Lessons – Lesson 1 – Consciousness is the Only Reality

It is the SHIN, or a tooth, in the Son's name that gives him absolute dominion. Why could it not have been in the Father's name? For this simple reason: Nothing can cease to be in the Father. Even the unlovely things cannot cease to be.

If I once give it expression, forever and ever it remains locked within the dimensionally greater Self which is the Father. But I would not like to keep alive within my world all of my mistakes. So I, in my infinite mercy gave to myself, when I became man, the power to become detached from these things that I, in my ignorance, brought to birth in my world.

These are the two names which give you dominion.

You have dominion if, as you walk the earth, you know that your consciousness is God, the one and only reality. You become aware of something you would like to express or possess. You have the ability to feel that you are and possess that which but a moment before was imaginary.

The final result, the embodying of your assumption, is completely outside of the offices of a three-dimensional mind. It comes to birth in a way that no man knows.

If these two names are clear in your mind's eye, you will see that they are your eternal names. As you sit here, you are this JOD HE VAU HE; you are the JOD HE VAU SHIN AYIN.

The stories of the Bible concern themselves exclusively with the power of Imagination. They are really dramatizations of the technique of prayer, for prayer is the secret of changing the future.

The Bible reveals the key by which man enters a dimensionally larger world for the purpose of changing the conditions of the lesser world in which he lives.

A prayer granted implies that something is done in consequence of the prayer, which otherwise would not have been done. Therefore, man is the spring of action, the directing mind, and the one who grants the prayer.

The stories of the Bible contain a powerful challenge to the thinking capacity of man. The underlying truth . . that they are psychological dramas and not historical facts . . demands reiteration, inasmuch as it is the only justification for the stories. With a little Imagination we may easily trace the psychological sense in all the stories of the Bible.

"And God said, Let us make man in our image, and after our likeness: and let them have dominion over the fish of the sea, and over the fowl of the air, and over the cattle, and over all the earth, and over every creeping thing that creepeth upon the earth. So God created man in his own image, in the image of God created he him"

Here in the first chapter of the Bible the ancient teachers laid the foundation that God and man are one, and that man has dominion over all the earth. If God and man are one, then God can never be so far off as even to be near, for nearness implies separation.

The question arises: What is God? God is man's consciousness, his awareness, his I AM-ness.

1948 Lessons – Lesson 1 – Consciousness is the Only Reality

The drama of life is a psychological one in which we bring circumstances to pass by our attitudes rather than by our acts.

The corner-stone on which all things are based is mans concept of himself. He acts as he does, and has the experiences that he does, because his concept of himself is what it is, and for no other reason. Had he a different concept of himself, he would act differently and have different experiences.

Man, by assuming the feeling of his wish fulfilled, alters his future in harmony with his assumption, for, assumptions though false, if sustained, will harden into fact.

The undisciplined mind finds it difficult to assume a state which is denied by the senses.

But the ancient teachers discovered that sleep, or a state akin to sleep, aided man in making his assumption. Therefore, they dramatized the first creative act of man as one in which man was in a profound sleep. This not only sets the pattern for all future creative acts, but shows us that man has but one substance that is truly his to use in creating his world and that is himself.

"And the Lord God (man) caused a deep sleep to fall upon Adam and he slept: and he took one of his ribs, and closed up the flesh instead thereof; and the rib, which the Lord God had taken from man, made he a woman."

Before God fashions this woman for man he brings unto Adam the beasts of the field, and the fowls of the air and has Adam name them.

1948 Lessons – Lesson 1 – Consciousness is the Only Reality

"Whatsoever Adam called every living creature, that was the name thereof."

If you will take a concordance or a Bible dictionary and look up the word thigh as used in this story you will see that it has nothing to do with the thigh. It is defined as the soft parts that are creative in a man, that hang upon the thigh of a man.

The ancient story-tellers used this phallic frame to reveal a great psychological truth.

An angel is a messenger of God. You are God, as you have just discovered for your consciousness is God, and you have an idea, a message.

You are wrestling with an idea, for you do not know that you are already that which you contemplate, neither do you believe you could become it. You would like to, but you do not believe you could.

Who wrestles with the angel? Jacob? And the word Jacob, by definition, means the supplanter.

You would like to transform yourself and become that which reason and your senses deny. As you wrestle with your ideal, trying to feel that you are it, this is what happens. When you actually feel that you are it, something goes out of you. You may use the words, "Who has touched me, for I perceive virtue has gone out of me?"

You become for a moment, after a successful meditation, incapable of continuing in the act, as though it were a physical creative act. You are just as impotent after you have

1948 Lessons – Lesson 1 – Consciousness is the Only Reality

prayed successfully as you are after the physical creative act. When satisfaction is yours, you no longer hunger for it. If the hunger persists you did not explode the idea within you, you did not actually succeed in becoming conscious of being that which you wanted to be. There was still that thirst when you came out of the deep.

If I can feel that I AM That which but a few seconds ago I knew I was not, but desired to be, then I AM no longer hungry to be it. I AM no longer thirsty because I feel satisfied in that state. Then something shrinks within me, not physically but in my feeling, in my consciousness, for that is the creativeness of man. He so shrinks in desire, he loses the desire to continue in this meditation. He does not halt physically, he simply has no desire to continue the meditative act.

"When you pray believe that you have received, and you shall receive."

When the physical creative act is completed, the sinew which is upon the hollow of man's thigh shrinks, and man finds himself impotent or is halted. In like manner when a man prays successfully he believes that he is already that which he desired to be, therefore he cannot continue desiring to be that which he is already conscious of being. At the moment of satisfaction, physical and psychological, something goes out which in time bears witness to man's creative power.

Our next story is in the 38th chapter of the book of Genesis. Here is a King whose name is Judah, the first three letters of whose name also begins JOD HE VAU. Tamar is his daughter-in-law.

The word Tamar means a palm tree or the most beautiful, the most comely. She is gracious and beautiful to look on and is called a palm tree. A tall, stately palm tree blossoms even in the desert -- wherever it is there is an oasis. When you see the palm tree in the desert, there will be found what you seek most in that parched land. There is nothing more desirable to a man moving across a desert than the sight of a palm tree.

In our case, to be practical, our objective is the palm tree. That is the stately, beautiful one that we seek. Whatever it is that you and I want, what we truly desire, is personified in the story as Tamar the beautiful.

We are told she dresses herself in the veils of a harlot and sits in the public place. Her father-in-law, King Judah, comes by; and he is so in love with this one who is veiled that he offers her a kid to be intimate with her.

She said, "What will you give me as a pledge that you will give me a kid?"

Looking around he said, "What do you want me to give as a pledge?"

She answered, "Give me your ring, give me your bracelets, and give me your staff."

Whereupon, he took from his hand the ring, and the bracelet, and gave them to her along with his sceptre. And he went in unto her and knew her, and she bore him a son.

1948 Lessons – Lesson 1 – Consciousness is the Only Reality

That is the story; now for the interpretation. Man has one gift that is truly his to give, and that is himself. He has no other gift, as told you in the very first creative act of Adam begetting the woman out of himself. There was no other substance in the world but himself with which he could fashion the object of his desire.

In like manner Judah had but one gift that was truly his to give . . himself, as the ring, the bracelets and the staff symbolized, for these were the symbols of his kingship.

Man offers that which is not himself, but life demands that he give the one thing that symbolizes himself. "Give me your ring, give me your bracelet, give me your sceptre." These make the King. When he gives them he gives of himself.

You are the great King Judah. Before you can know your Tamar and make her bear your likeness in the world, you must go in unto her and give of self. Suppose I want security. I cannot get it by knowing people who have it. I cannot get it by pulling strings. I must become conscious of being secure.

Let us say I want to be healthy. Pills will not do it. Diet or climate will not do it. I must become conscious of being healthy by assuming the feeling of being healthy.

Perhaps I want to be lifted up in this world. Merely looking at kings and presidents and noble people and living in their reflection will not make me dignified. I must become conscious of being noble and dignified and walk as though I were that which I now want to be.

When I walk in that light I give of myself to the image that haunted my mind, and in time she bears me a child;

which means I objectify a world in harmony with that which I AM conscious of being.

You are King Judah and you are also Tamar. When you become conscious of being that which you want to be you are Tamar. Then you crystallize your desire within the world round about you.

No matter what stories you read in the Bible, no matter how many characters these ancient story-tellers introduced into the drama, there is one thing you and I must always bear in mind . . they all take place within the mind of the individual man. All the characters live in the mind of the individual man.

As you read the story, make it fit the pattern of self.

Know that your consciousness is the only reality. Then know what you want to be. Then assume the feeling of being that which you want to be, and remain faithful to your assumption, living and acting on your conviction. Always make it fit that pattern.

Our third interpretation is the story of Isaac and his two sons: Esau and Jacob. The picture is drawn of a blind man being deceived by his second son into giving him the blessing which belonged to his first son. The story stresses the point that the deception was accomplished through the sense of touch.

"And Isaac said unto Jacob, Come near, I pray thee that I may feel thee, my son, whether thou be my very son Esau or

1948 Lessons – Lesson 1 – Consciousness is the Only Reality

not. And Jacob went near unto Isaac his father; and he felt him.... And it came to pass, as soon as Isaac had made an end of blessing Jacob, and Jacob was yet scarce gone out from the presence of Isaac his father, that Esau his brother came in from his hunting."

This story can be very helpful if you will re-enact it now. Again bear in mind that all the characters of the Bible are personifications of abstract ideas and must be fulfilled in the individual man. You are the blind father and both sons.

Isaac is old and blind, and sensing the approach of death, calls his first son Esau a rough hairy boy, and sends him into the woods that he may bring in some venison.

The second son, Jacob, a smooth skin boy, overheard the request of his father. Desiring the birthright of his brother, Jacob, the smooth skinned son, slaughtered one of his father's flock and skinned it. Then, dressed in the hairy skins of the kid he had slaughtered, he came through subtlety and betrayed his father into believing that he was Esau.

The father said, "Come close my son that I may feel you. I cannot see, but come that I may feel." Note the stress that is placed upon feeling in this story.

He came close and the father said to him, "The voice is Jacob's voice, but the hands are the hands of Esau." And feeling this roughness, the reality of the son Esau, he pronounced the blessing and gave it to Jacob.

1948 Lessons – Lesson 1 – Consciousness is the Only Reality

You are told in the story that as Isaac pronounced the blessing and Jacob had scarcely gone out from his presence, that his brother Esau came in from his hunting.

This is an important verse. Do not become distressed in our practical approach to it, for as you sit here you, too, are Isaac. This room in which you are seated is your present Esau. This is the rough or sensibly known world, known by reason of your bodily organs. All of your senses bear witness to the fact that you are here in this room. Everything tells you that you are here, but perhaps you do not want to be here.

You can apply this toward any objective. The room in which you are seated at any time . . the environment in which you are placed, this is your rough or sensibly known world or son which is personified in the story as Esau. What you would like in place of what you have or are is your smooth skinned state or Jacob, the supplanter.

You do not send your visible world hunting, as so many people do, by denial. By saying it does not exist you make it all the more real.

Instead, you simply remove your attention from the region of sensation which at this moment is the room round about you, and you concentrate your attention on that which you want to put in its place, that which you want to make real.

In concentrating on your objective, the secret is to bring it here. You must make elsewhere here and then now imagine that your objective is so close that you can feel it.

1948 Lessons – Lesson 1 – Consciousness is the Only Reality

Suppose at this very moment I want a piano here in this room. To see a piano in my mind's eye existing elsewhere does not do it.

But to visualize it in this room as though it were here and to put my mental hand upon the piano and to feel it solidly real, is to take that subjective state personified as my second son Jacob and bring it so close that I can feel it.

Isaac is called a blind man. You are blind because you do not see your objective with your bodily organs, you cannot see it with your objective senses.

You only perceive it with your mind, but you bring it so close that you can feel it as though it were solidly real now. When this is done and you lose yourself in its reality and feel it to be real, open your eyes.

When you open your eyes what happens? The room that you had shut out but a moment ago returns from the hunt.

You no sooner gave the blessing . . felt the imaginary state to be real . . than the objective world, which seemingly was unreal, returns. It does not speak to you with words as recorded of Esau, but the very room round about you tells you by its presence that you have been self-deceived.

It tells you that when you lost yourself in contemplation, feeling that you were now what you wanted to be, feeling that you now possess what you desire to possess, that you were simply deceiving self. Look at this room. It denies that you are elsewhere.

1948 Lessons – Lesson 1 – Consciousness is the Only Reality

If you know the law, you now say: "Even though your brother came through subtlety and betrayed me and took your birthright, I gave him your blessing and I cannot retract."

In other words, you remain faithful to this subjective reality and you do not take back from it the power of birth. You gave it the right of birth and it is going to become objective within this world of yours. There is no room in this limited space of yours for two things to occupy the same space at the same time. By making the subjective real it resurrects itself within your world.

Take the idea that you want to embody, and assume that you are already it. Lose yourself in feeling this assumption is solidly real. As you give it this sense of reality, you have given it the blessing which belongs to the objective world, and you do not have to aid its birth any more than you have to aid the birth of a child or a seed you plant in the ground.

The seed you plant grows unaided by a man, for it contains within itself all the power and all the plans necessary for self-expression.

You can this night re-enact the drama of Isaac blessing his second son and see what happens in the immediate future in your world.

Your present environment vanishes, all the circumstances of life change and make way for the coming of that to which you have given your life. As you walk, knowing that you are what you wanted to be, you objectify it without the assistance of another.

1948 Lessons – Lesson 1 – Consciousness is the Only Reality

The fourth story for tonight is taken from the last of the books attributed to Moses. If you need proof that Moses did not write it, read the story carefully. It is found in the 34th chapter of the book of Deuteronomy. Ask any priest or rabbi, 'who is the author of this book?', and they will tell you that Moses wrote it.

In the 34th chapter of Deuteronomy you will read of a man writing his own obituary , that is, Moses wrote this chapter. A man may sit down and write what he would like to have placed upon his tombstone, but here is a man who writes his own obituary. And then he dies and so completely rubs himself out that he defies posterity to find where he has buried himself.

"So Moses the servant of the Lord died there in the land of Moab, according to the word of the Lord. And he buried him in a valley in the land of Moab, over against Beth-poer: but no man knoweth of his sepulcher unto this day. And Moses was an hundred and twenty years old when he died: his eye was not dim, nor his natural force abated."

You must this night . . not tomorrow . . learn the technique of writing your own obituary and so completely die to what you are that no man in this world can tell you where you buried the old man. If you are now ill and you become well, and I know you by reason of the fact that you are ill, where can you point and tell me you buried the sick one?

If you are impoverished and borrow from every friend you have, and then suddenly you roll in wealth, where did you bury the poor man? You so completely rub out poverty in your mind's eye that there is nothing in this world you can point to and claim, that is where I left it. A complete transformation of consciousness rubs out all evidence that anything other than this ever existed in the world.

The most beautiful technique for the realizing of man's objective is given in the first verse of the 34th chapter of Deuteronomy:

"And Moses went up from the Plains of Moab unto the mountain of Nebo, to the top of Pisgah, that is over against Jericho. And the Lord shewed him all the land of Gilead, unto Dan.

You read that verse and say, "So what?" But take a concordance and look up the words.

The first word, Moses, means to draw out, to rescue, to lift out, to fetch. In other words, Moses is the personification of the power in man that can draw out of man that which he seeks, for everything comes from within, not from without. You draw from within yourself that which you now want to express as something objective to yourself.

You are Moses coming out of the plains of Moab. The word Moab is a contraction of two Hebraic words, Mem and Ab, meaning mother-father.

Your consciousness is the mother-father, there is no other cause in the world. Your I AMness, your awareness, is this Moab or mother-father. You are always drawing something out of it.

The next word is Nebo. In your concordance Nebo is defined as a prophecy.

1948 Lessons – Lesson 1 – Consciousness is the Only Reality

A prophecy is something subjective. If I say, "So-and-so will be," it is an image in the mind; it is not yet a fact. We must wait and either prove or disprove this prophecy.

In our language Nebo is your wish, your desire. It is called a mountain because it is something that appears difficult to ascend and is therefore seemingly impossible of realization. A mountain is something bigger than you are, it towers over you. Nebo personifies that which you want to be in contrast to that which you are.

The word Pisgah, by definition, is to contemplate. Jericho is a fragrant odor. And Gilead means the hills of witnesses. The last word is Dan the Prophet.

Now put them all together in a practical sense and see what the ancients tried to tell us.

As I stand here, having discovered that my consciousness is God, and that I can by simply feeling that I AM what I want to be transform myself into the likeness of that which I AM assuming I AM; I know now that I AM all that it takes to scale this mountain.

I define my objective. I do not call it Nebo, I call it my desire.

Whatever I want, that is my Nebo, that is my great mountain that I AM going to scale. I now begin to contemplate it, for I shall climb to the peak of Pisgah.

I must contemplate my objective in such a manner that I get the reaction that satisfies. If I do not get the reaction that pleases then Jericho is not seen, for Jericho is a fragrant

1948 Lessons – Lesson 1 – Consciousness is the Only Reality

odor. When I feel that I AM what I want to be I cannot suppress the joy that comes with that feeling.

I must always contemplate my objective until I get the feeling of satisfaction personified as Jericho. Then I do nothing to make it visible in my world; for the hills of Gilead, meaning men, women, children, the whole vast world round about me, come bearing witness. They come to testify that I AM what I have assumed myself to be, and am sustaining within myself.

When my world conforms to my assumption the prophecy is fulfilled.

If I now know what I want to be, and assume that I AM it, and walk as though I were, I become it and becoming it I so completely die to my former concept of self that I cannot point to any place in this world and say: that is where my former self is buried. I so completely died that I defy posterity to ever find where I buried my old self.

There must be someone in this room who will so completely transform himself in this world that his close immediate circle of friends will not recognize him.

For ten years I was a dancer, dancing in Broadway shows, in vaudeville, night clubs, and in Europe. There was a time in my life when I thought I could not live without certain friends in my world. I would spread a table every night after the theatre and we would all dine well. I thought I could never live without them. Now I confess I could not live with them.

1948 Lessons – Lesson 1 – Consciousness is the Only Reality

We have nothing in common today. When we meet we do not purposely walk on the opposite side of the street, but it is almost a cold meeting because we have nothing to discuss. I so died to that life that as I meet these people they cannot even talk of the old times.

But there are people living today who are still living in that state, getting poorer and poorer. They always like to talk about the old times. They never buried that man at all, he is very much alive within their world.

Moses was 120 years, a full, wonderful age as 120 indicates. One plus two plus zero equals three, the numerical symbol of expression. I AM fully conscious of my expression. My eyes are undimmed and the natural functions of my body are not abated. I AM fully conscious of being what I do not want to be.

But knowing this law by which a man transforms himself, I assume that I AM what I want to be and walk in the assumption that it is done. In becoming it, the old man dies and all that was related to that former concept of self dies with it. You cannot take any part of the old man into the new man. You cannot put new wine in old bottles or new patches on old garments. You must be a new being completely.

As you assume that you are what you want to be, you do not need the assistance of another to make it so. Neither do you need the assistance of anyone to bury the old man for you. Let the dead bury the dead. Do not even look back, for no man having put his hand to the plow and then looking back is fit for the kingdom of heaven.

1948 Lessons – Lesson 1 – Consciousness is the Only Reality

Do not ask yourself how this thing is going to be. It does not matter if your reason denies it. It does not matter if all the world round about you denies it. You do not have to bury the old. "Let the dead bury the dead." You will so bury the past by remaining faithful to your new concept of Self that you will defy the whole vast future to find where you buried it. To this day no man in all of Israel has discovered the sepulcher of Moses.

These are the four stories I promised you tonight. You must apply them every day of your life.

Even though the chair on which you are now seated seems hard and does not lend itself to meditation you can, by Imagination, make it the most comfortable chair in the world.

Let me now define the technique as I want you to employ it. I trust each one of you came here tonight with a clear picture of your desire. Do not say it is impossible. Do you want it? You do not have to use your moral code to realize it. It is altogether outside the reach of your code.

Consciousness is the one and only reality. Therefore, we must form the object of our desire out of our own consciousness.

People have a habit of slighting the importance of simple things, and the suggestion to create a state akin to sleep in order to aid you in assuming that which reason and your senses deny, is one of the simple things you might slight.

1948 Lessons – Lesson 1 – Consciousness is the Only Reality

However, this simple formula for changing the future, which was discovered by the ancient teachers and given to us in the Bible, can be proved by all.

The first step in changing the future is Desire, that is, define your objective . . know definitely what you want.

Second: construct an event which you believe you would encounter FOLLOWING the fulfillment of your desire . . an event which implies fulfillment of your desire . . something which will have the action of Self predominant.

The third step is to immobilize the physical body and induce a state akin to sleep. Then mentally feel yourself right into the proposed action, imagine all the while that you are actually performing the action HERE AND NOW. You must participate in the imaginary action, not merely stand back and look on, but FEEL that you are actually performing the action, so that the imaginary sensation is real to you.

It is important always to remember that the proposed action must be one which FOLLOWS the fulfillment of your desire, one which implies fulfillment.

For example, suppose you desired promotion in office. Then being congratulated would be an event you would encounter following the fulfillment of your desire.

Having selected this action as the one you will experience in Imagination to imply promotion in office, immobilize your physical body and induce a state bordering on sleep, a drowsy state, but one in which you are still able to control the direction of your thoughts, a state in which you are attentive without effort.

Then visualize a friend standing before you.

Put your imaginary hand into his. Feel it to be solid and real, and carry on an imaginary conversation with him in harmony with the FEELING OF HAVING BEEN PROMOTED.

You do not visualize yourself at a distance in point of space and at a distance in point of time being congratulated on your good fortune. Instead, you MAKE elsewhere HERE and the future NOW. The difference between FEELING yourself in action, here and now , and visualizing yourself in action, as though you were on a motion-picture screen, is the difference between success and failure.

The difference will be appreciated if you will now visualize yourself climbing a ladder. Then, with eyelids closed imagine that a ladder is right in front of you and FEEL YOURSELF ACTUALLY CLIMBING IT.

Experience has taught me to restrict the imaginary action which implies fulfillment of the desire, to condense the idea into a single act, and to re-enact it over and over again until it has the feeling of reality. Otherwise, your attention will wander off along an associational track, and hosts of associated images will be presented to your attention, and in a few seconds they will lead you hundreds of miles away from your objective in point of space and years away in point of time.

If you decide to climb a particular flight of stairs, because that is the likely event to follow the fulfillment of your desire, then you must restrict the action to climbing that particular flight of stairs. Should your attention wander off, bring it back to its task of climbing that flight of stairs,

1948 Lessons – Lesson 1 – Consciousness is the Only Reality

and keep on doing so until the imaginary action has all the solidity and distinctness of reality.

The idea must be maintained in the mind without any sensible effort on your part. You must, with the minimum of effort permeate the mind with the feeling of the wish fulfilled.

Drowsiness facilitates change because it favors attention without effort, but it must not be pushed to the state of sleep in which you no longer are able to control the movements of your attention. But a moderate degree of drowsiness in which you are still able to direct your thoughts.

A most effective way to embody a desire is to assume the feeling of the wish fulfilled and then, in a relaxed and drowsy state, repeat over and over again like a lullaby, any short phrase which implies fulfillment of your desire, such as, "Thank you, thank you, thank you" as though you addressed a higher power for having given you that which you desired.

I know that when this course comes to an end on Friday many of you here will be able to tell me you have realized your objectives. Two weeks ago I left the platform and went to the door to shake hands with the audience. I am safe in saying that at least 35 out of a class of 135 told me that which they desired when they joined this class they had already realized.

This happened only two weeks ago. I did nothing to bring it to pass save to give them this technique of prayer. You need do nothing to bring it to pass . . save apply this technique of prayer.

1948 Lessons – Lesson 1 – Consciousness is the Only Reality

With your eyes closed and your physical body immobilized induce a state akin to sleep and enter into the action as though you were an actor playing the part.

Experience in Imagination what you would experience in the flesh were you now in possession of your objective. Make elsewhere HERE and then NOW. And the greater you, using a larger focus will use all means, and call them good, which tend toward the production of that which you have assumed.

You are relieved of all responsibility to make it so, because as you imagine and feel that it is so your dimensionally larger self determines the means. Do not think for one moment that someone is going to be injured in order to make it so, or that someone is going to be disappointed. It is still not your concern. I must drive this home. Too many of us, schooled in different walks of life, are so concerned about the other.

You ask, 'If I get what I want will it not imply injury to another?' There are ways you know not of, so do not be concerned.

Close your eyes now because we are going to be in a long silence. Soon you will become so lost in contemplation, feeling that you are what you want to be, that you will be totally unconscious of the fact that you are in this room with others.

You will receive a shock when you open your eyes and discover we are here. It should be a shock when you open your eyes and discover that you are not actually that which, a moment before, you felt you were, or felt you possessed. Now we will go into the deep.

1948 Lessons – Lesson 1 – Consciousness is the Only Reality

SILENCE PERIOD.........

I need not remind you that you are now that which you have assumed that you are. Do not discuss it with anyone, not even self.

You cannot take thought as to the HOW, when you know that you ARE already.

Your three-dimensional reasoning, which is a very limited reasoning indeed should not be brought into this drama. It does not know. What you have just felt to be true is true.

Let no man tell you that you should not have it. What you feel that you have, you will have. And I promise you this much, after you have realized your objective, on reflection you will have to admit that this conscious reasoning mind of yours could never have devised the way.

You are that and have that which this very moment you appropriated. Do not discuss it. Do not look to someone for encouragement because the thing might not come. It has come. Go about your Father's business doing everything normally and let these things happen in your world.

Lesson 2 – Assumptions Harden Into Fact

This Bible of ours has nothing to do with history. Some of you may yet be inclined tonight to believe that, although we can give it a psychological interpretation, it still could be left in its present form and be interpreted literally. You cannot do it. The Bible has no reference at all to people or to events as you have been taught to believe. The sooner you begin to rub out that picture the better.

We are going to take a few stories tonight, and again I am going to remind you that you must re-enact all of these stories within your own mind.

Bear in mind that although they seem to be stories of people fully awake, the drama is really between you, the sleeping one, the deeper you, and the conscious waking you. They are personified as people, but when you come to the point of application you must remember the importance of the drowsy state.

All creation, as we told you last night, takes place in the state of sleep, or that state which is akin to sleep . . the, sleepy drowsy state.

We told you last night the first man is not yet awakened. You are Adam, the first man, still in the profound sleep.

The creative you, is the fourth-dimensional you, whose home is simply the state you enter, when men call you asleep.

1948 Lessons – Lesson 2 – Assumptions Harden Into Fact

Our first story for tonight is found in the Gospel of John. As you hear it unfold before you, I want you to compare it in your mind's eye to the story you heard last night from the book of Genesis.

The first book of the Bible, the book of Genesis, historians claim is the record of events which occurred on earth some 3,000 years before the events recorded in the book of John. I ask you to be rational about it and see if you do not think the same writer could have written both stories. You be the judge as to whether the same inspired man could not have told the same story and told it differently.

This is a very familiar story, the story of the trial of Jesus. In this Gospel of John it is recorded that Jesus was brought before Pontius Pilate, and the crowd clamored for his life, they wanted Jesus. Pilate turned to them and said:

"But ye have a custom, that I should release unto you one at the Passover; will ye therefore that I release unto you the King of the Jews? Then cried they all again, saying, Not this man, but Barabbas. Now Barabbas was a robber."

You are told that Pilate had no choice in the matter, he was only a judge interpreting law, and this was the law. The people had to be given that which they requested. Pilate could not release Jesus against the wishes of the crowd, and so he released Barabbas and gave unto them Jesus to be crucified.

Now bear in mind that your consciousness is God. There is no other God. And you are told that God has a son whose name is Jesus. If you will take the trouble to look up the word Barabbas in your concordance, you will see that it is a

1948 Lessons – Lesson 2 – Assumptions Harden Into Fact

contraction of two Hebraic words: BAR, which means a daughter or son- or child, and ABBA, which means father. Barabbas is the son of the great father. And Jesus in the story is called the Savior, the Son of the Father.

We have two sons in this story. And we have two sons in the story of Esau and Jacob. Bear in mind that Isaac was blind, and justice to be true must be blind folded. Although in this case Pilate is not physically blind, the part given to Pilate implies that he is blind because he is a judge. On all the great law buildings of the world we see the lady or the man who represents justice as being blindfolded.

"Judge not according to the appearance, but judge righteous judgment. "

Here we find Pilate is playing the same part as Isaac. There are two sons. All the characters as they appear in this story can apply to your own life. You have a son that is robbing you this very moment of that which you could be.

If you came to this meeting tonight conscious of wanting something, desiring something, you walked in the company of Barabbas.

For to desire is to confess that you do not now possess what you desire, and because all things are yours, you rob yourself by living in the state of desire.

My savior is my desire.

As I want something I am looking into the eyes of my savior.

1948 Lessons – Lesson 2 – Assumptions Harden Into Fact

But if I continue wanting it, I deny my Jesus, my savior, for as I want I confess I am not and "except ye believe that I AM He, ye die in your sins."

I cannot have and still continue to desire what I have. I may enjoy it, but I cannot continue wanting it.

Here is the story. This is the feast of the Passover. Something is going to change right now, something is going to Passover. Man is incapable of passing over from one state of consciousness into another unless he releases from consciousness that which he now entertains, for it anchors him where he is.

You and I may go to physical feasts year after year as the sun enters the great sign of Aries, but it means nothing to the true mystical Passover.

To keep the feast of the Passover, the psychological feast, I pass from one state of consciousness into another.

I do it by releasing Barabbas, the thief and robber that robs me of that state which I could embody within my world.

The state I seek to embody is personified in the story as Jesus the Savior . If I become what I want to be then I AM saved from what I was. If I do not become it, I continue to keep locked within me a thief who robs me of being that which I could be.

These stories have no reference to any persons who lived nor to any event that ever occurred upon earth. These characters are everlasting characters in the mind of every man in the world.

1948 Lessons – Lesson 2 – Assumptions Harden Into Fact

You and I perpetually keep alive either Barabbas or Jesus. You know at every moment of time who you are entertaining.

Do not condemn a crowd for clamoring that they should release Barabbas and crucify Jesus. It is not a crowd of people called Jews. They had nothing to do with it.

If we are wise, we too should clamor for the release of that state of mind that limits us from being what we want to be, that restricts us, that does not permit us to become the ideal that we seek and strive to attain in this world.

I am not saying that you are not tonight embodying Jesus. I only remind you, that if at this very moment you have an unfulfilled ambition, then you are entertaining that which denies the fulfillment of the ambition, and that which denies it is Barabbas.

To explain the mystical, psychological transformation known as the Passover, or the crossing over, you must now become identified with the ideal that you would serve, and you must remain faithful to the ideal. If you remain faithful to it, you not only crucify it by your faithfulness, but you resurrect it unaided by a man.

As the story goes, no man could rise early enough to roll away the stone. Unaided by a man the stone was removed, and what seemingly was dead and buried was resurrected unassisted by a man.

You walk in the consciousness of being that which you want to be, no one sees it as yet, but you do not need a man

1948 Lessons – Lesson 2 – Assumptions Harden Into Fact

to roll away the problems and the obstacles of life in order to express that which you are conscious of being.

That state has its own unique way of becoming embodied in this world, of becoming flesh that the whole world may touch it.

Now you can see the relationship between the story of Jesus and the story of Isaac and his two sons, where one transplanted the other, where one was called the Supplanter of the other. Why do you think those who compiled the sixty odd books of our Bible made Jacob the forefather of Jesus?

They took Jacob, who was called the Supplanter, and made him father of twelve, then they took Judah or praise, the fifth son and made him the forefather of Joseph, who is supposed to have fathered in some strange way this one called Jesus. Jesus must supplant Barabbas as Jacob must supplant and take the place of Esau.

Tonight you can sit right here and conduct the trial of your two sons, one of whom you want released. You can become the crowd who clamors for the release of the thief, and the judge who willingly releases Barabbas, and sentences Jesus to fill his place. He was crucified on Golgotha, the place of the skull, the seat of the Imagination.

To experience the Passover or passage from the old to the new concept of self, you must release Barabbas, your present concept of self, which robs you of being that which you could be, and you must assume the new concept which you desire to express.

1948 Lessons – Lesson 2 – Assumptions Harden Into Fact

The best way to do this is to concentrate your attention upon the idea of identifying yourself with your ideal. Assume you are already that which you seek and your assumption, though false, if sustained, will harden into fact.

You will know when you have succeeded in releasing Barabbas, your old concept of self, and when you have successfully crucified Jesus, or fixed the new concept of self, by simply looking MENTALLY at the people you know.

If you see them as you formerly saw them, you have not changed your concept of self, for all changes of concepts of self result in a changed relationship to your world.

We always seem to others an embodiment of the ideal we inspire. Therefore, in meditation, we must imagine that others see us as they would see us were we what we desire to be.

You can release Barabbas and crucify and resurrect Jesus if you will first define your ideal. Then relax in a comfortable arm chair, induce a state of consciousness akin to sleep and experience in Imagination what you would experience in reality were you already that which you desire to be.

By this simple method of experiencing in Imagination what you would experience in the flesh were you the embodiment of the ideal you serve, you release Barabbas who robbed you of your greatness, and you crucify and resurrect your savior, or the ideal you desired to express.

1948 Lessons – Lesson 2 – Assumptions Harden Into Fact

Now let us turn to the story of Jesus in the garden of Gethsemane. Bear in mind that a garden is a properly prepared plot of ground, it is not a wasteland.

You are preparing this ground called Gethsemane by coming here and studying and doing something about your mind. Spend some time daily in preparing your mind by reading good literature, listening to good music and entering into conversations that ennoble.

We are told in the Epistles, "Whatsoever things are true, whatsoever things are honest, whatsoever things are just, whatsoever things are pure, whatsoever things are lovely, whatsoever things are of good report; if there be any virtue, and if there be any praise, think on these things."

Continuing with our story, as told in the 18th chapter of John, Jesus is in the garden and suddenly a crowd begins to seek him. He is standing there in the dark and he says, "Whom seek ye?"

The spokesman called Judas answers and says, "We seek Jesus of Nazareth."

A voice answers, "I AM He."

At this instant they all fall to the ground, thousands of them tumbled. That in itself should stop you right there and let you know it could not be a physical drama, because no one could be so bold in his claim that he is the one sought, that he could cause thousands who seek him to fall to the ground.

1948 Lessons – Lesson 2 – Assumptions Harden Into Fact

But the story tells us they all fell to the ground. Then when they regained their composure they asked the same question.

"Jesus answered, I have told you that I AM He: if therefore ye seek me, let these go their way."

"Then said Jesus unto him, That thou doest, do quickly."

Judas, who has to do it quickly, goes out and commits suicide.

Now to the drama.

You are in your garden of Gethsemane or prepared mind, if you can, while you are in a state akin to sleep, control your attention and not let it wander away from its purpose. If you can do that, you are definitely in the garden.

Very few people can sit quietly and not enter a reverie or a state of uncontrolled thinking. When you can restrict the mental action and remain faithful to your watch, not permitting your attention to wander all over the place, but hold it without effort within a limited field of presentation to the state you are contemplating, then you are definitely this disciplined presence in the garden of Gethsemane.

The suicide of Judas is nothing more than changing your concept of yourself.

When you know what you want to be you have found your Jesus or savior.

1948 Lessons – Lesson 2 – Assumptions Harden Into Fact

When you assume that you are what you want to be you have died to your former concept of self (Judas committed suicide) and are now living as Jesus.

You can become at will detached from the world round about you, and attached to that which you want to embody within your world.

Now that you have found me, now that you have found that which would save you from what you are, let go of that which you are and all that it represents in the world. Become completely detached from it. In other words, go out and commit suicide.

You completely die to what you formerly expressed in this world, and you now completely live to that which no one saw as true of you before. You are as though you had died by your own hand, as though you had committed suicide. You took your own life by becoming detached in consciousness from what you formerly kept alive, and you begin to live to that which you have discovered in your garden. You have found your savior.

It is not men falling, not a man betraying another, but you detaching your attention, and refocusing your attention in an entirely new direction.

From this moment on, you walk as though you were that, which you formerly wanted to be.

Remaining faithful to your new concept of yourself you die or commit suicide. No one took your life, you laid it down yourself.

1948 Lessons – Lesson 2 – Assumptions Harden Into Fact

You must be able to see the relation of this to the death of Moses, where he so completely died that no one could find where he was buried. You must see the relationship of the death of Judas. He is not a man who betrayed a man called Jesus.

The word Judas is praise; it is Judah, to praise, to give thanks, to explode with joy. You do not explode with joy unless you are identified with the ideal you seek and want to embody in this world. When you become identified with the state you contemplate you cannot suppress your joy. It rises like the fragrant odor described as Jericho in the Old Testament.

I am trying to show you that the ancients told the same story in all the stories of the Bible. All that they are trying to tell us is how to become that which we want to be. And they imply in every story that we do not need the assistance of another. You do not need another to become now what you really want to be.

Now we turn to a strange story in the Old Testament; one that very few priests and rabbis will be bold enough to mention from their pulpits.

Here is one who is going to receive the promise as you now receive it. His name is Jesus, only the ancients called him Joshua, Jehoshua Ben Nun, or savior, son of the fish, the Savior of the great deep. Nun means fish, and fish is the element of the deep, the profound ocean. Jehoshua means Jehovah saves, and Ben means the offspring or son of. So he was called the one who brought the fish age.

1948 Lessons – Lesson 2 – Assumptions Harden Into Fact

This story is in the 6th book of the Bible, the book of Joshua. A promise is made to Joshua as it is made to Jesus in the Anglicized form in the gospels of Matthew, Mark, Luke and John.

In the gospel of John, Jesus says, "All things whatsoever thou hast given me are of thee.". "And all mine are thine, and thine are mine."

In the Old Testament in the book of Joshua it is said in these words: "Every place that the sole of your foot shall tread upon, that have I given unto you."

It does not matter where it is; analyze the promise and see if you can accept it literally. It is not physically true but it is psychologically true. Wherever you can stand in this world mentally that you can realize.

Joshua is haunted by this promise that wherever he can place his foot (the foot is understanding), wherever the sole of his foot shall tread, that will be given unto him. He wants the most desirable state in the world, the fragrant city, the delightful state called Jericho.

He finds himself barred by the impassable walls of Jericho. He is on the outside, as you are now on the outside.

You are functioning three-dimensionally and you cannot seem to reach the fourth-dimensional world where your present desire is already a concrete objective reality. You cannot seem to reach it because your senses bar you from it. Reason tells you it is impossible, all things round about you tell you it is not true.

1948 Lessons – Lesson 2 – Assumptions Harden Into Fact

Now you employ the services of a harlot and a spy, and her name is Rahab. The word Rahab simply means the spirit of the father. RACE means the breath or spirit, and AB the father. Hence we find that this harlot is the spirit of the father and the father is man's awareness of being aware, man's I AMness, man's consciousness.

Your capacity to feel is the great spirit of the father, and that capacity is Rahab in this story. She has two professions that of a spy and that of a harlot.

The profession of a spy is this: to travel secretly, to travel so quietly that you may not be detected. There is not a single physical spy in this world who can travel so quietly that he will be altogether unseen by others. He may be very wise in concealing his ways, and he may never be truly apprehended, but at every moment of time he runs the risk of being detected.

When you are sitting quietly with your thoughts, there is no man in the world so wise that he can look at you and tell you where you are mentally dwelling.

I can stand here and place myself in London. Knowing London quite well, I can close my eyes and assume that I am actually standing in London. If I remain within this state long enough, I will be able to surround myself with the environment of London as though it were a solid concrete objective fact.

Physically I am still here, but mentally I am thousands of miles away and I have made elsewhere here. I do not go there as a spy, I mentally make elsewhere here, and then now.

1948 Lessons – Lesson 2 – Assumptions Harden Into Fact

You cannot see me dwelling there, so you think I have just gone to sleep and that I am still here in this world, this three-dimensional world that is now San Francisco. As far as I am physically concerned, I am here but no one can tell me where I am when I enter the moment of meditation.

Rahab's next profession was that of a harlot, which is to grant unto men what they ask of her without asking man's right to ask. If she be an absolute harlot, as her name implies, then she possesses all and can grant all that man asks of her. She is there to serve, and not to question man's right to seek what he seeks of her.

You have within you the capacity to appropriate a state without knowing the means that will be employed to realize that end and you assume the feeling of the wish fulfilled without having any of the talents that men claim you must possess in order to do so.

When you appropriate it in consciousness you have employed the spy, and because you can embody that state within yourself by actually giving it to yourself, you are the harlot, for the harlot satisfies the man who seeks her.

You can satisfy self by appropriating the feeling that you are what you want to be. And this assumption though false, that is, although reason and the senses deny it, if persisted in will harden into fact. By actually embodying that which you have assumed you are, you have the capacity to become completely satisfied. Unless it becomes a tangible, concrete reality you will not be satisfied; you will be frustrated.

You are told in this story that when Rahab went into the city to conquer it, the command given to her was to enter the

1948 Lessons – Lesson 2 – Assumptions Harden Into Fact

heart of the city, the heart of the matter, the very center of it, and there remain until I come. Do not go from house to house, do not leave the upper room of the house into which you enter. If you leave the house and there be blood upon your head, it is upon your head. But if you do not leave the house and there be blood, it shall be upon my head.

Rahab goes into the house, rises to the upper floor, and there she remains while the walls crumble. That is, we must keep a high mood if we would walk with the highest. In a very veiled manner, the story tells you that when the walls crumbled and Joshua entered, the only one who was saved in the city was the spy and the harlot whose name was Rahab.

This story tells what you can do in this world. You will never lose the capacity to place yourself elsewhere and make it here. You will never lose the ability to give unto yourself what you are bold enough to appropriate as true of self. It has nothing to do with the woman who played that part.

The explanation of the crumbling of the walls is simple. You are told that he blew upon the trumpet seven times and at the seventh blast the walls crumbled and he entered victoriously into the state that he sought.

Seven is a stillness, a rest, the Sabbath. It is the state when man is completely unmoved in his conviction that the thing is. When I can assume the feeling of my wish fulfilled and go to sleep, unconcerned, undisturbed, I am at rest mentally, and am keeping the Sabbath or am blowing the trumpet seven times.

1948 Lessons – Lesson 2 – Assumptions Harden Into Fact

And when I reach that point the walls crumble. Circumstances alter then remold themselves in harmony with my assumption. As they crumble I resurrect that which I have appropriated within. The walls, the obstacles, the problems, crumble of their own weight if I can reach the point of stillness within me.

The man Who can fix within his own mind's eye an idea, even though the world would deny it, if he remains faithful to that idea he will see it manifested. There is all the difference in the world between holding the idea, and being held by the idea. Become so dominated by an idea that it haunts the mind as though you were it. Then, regardless of what others may say, you are walking in the direction of your fixed attitude of mind. You are walking in the direction of the idea that dominates the mind.

As we told you last night, you have but one gift that is truly yours to give, and that is yourself. There is no other gift; you must press it out of yourself by an appropriation. It is there within you now for creation is finished. There is nothing to be that is not now. There is nothing to be created for all things are already yours, they are all finished.

Although man may not be able to stand physically upon a state, he can always stand mentally upon any desired state. By standing mentally I mean that you can now, this very moment, close your eyes and visualize a place other than your present one, and assume that you are actually there. You can FEEL this to be so real that upon opening your eyes you are amazed to find that you are not physically there.

1948 Lessons – Lesson 2 – Assumptions Harden Into Fact

This mental journey into the desired state, with its subsequent feeling of reality, is all that is necessary to bring about its fulfillment.

Your dimensionally greater Self has ways that the lesser, or three-dimensional you, know not of. Furthermore, to the greater you, all means are good which promote the fulfillment of your assumption.

Remain in the mental state defined as your objective until it has the feeling of reality , and all the forces of heaven and earth will rush to aid its embodiment. Your greater Self will influence the actions and words of all who can be used to aid the production of your fixed mental attitude.

Now we turn to the book of Numbers and here we find a strange story. I trust that some of you have had this experience as described in the bock of Numbers. They speak of the building of a tabernacle at the command of God; that God commanded Israel to build him a place of worship.

He gave them all the specifications of the tabernacle. It had to be an elongated, movable place of worship, and it had to be covered with skin. Need you be told anything more? Isn't that man?

"Know ye not that ye are the temple of God, and that the Spirit of God dwelleth in you?"

There is no other temple. Not a temple made with hands, but a temple eternal in the heavens. This temple is elongated, and it is covered with skin, and it moves across the desert.

"And on the day that the tabernacle was reared up the cloud covered the tabernacle, namely, the tent of the testimony: and at even there was upon the tabernacle as it were the appearance of fire, until the morning. So it was always: the cloud covered it by day, and the appearance of fire by night."

The command given to Israel was to tarry until the cloud ascended by day and the fire by night. "Whether it were two days, or a month, or a year, that the cloud tarried upon the tabernacle, remaining thereon, the children of Israel abode in their tents, and journeyed not: but when it was taken up, they journeyed."

You know that you are the tabernacle, but you may wonder, what is the cloud. In meditation many of you must have seen it. In meditation, this cloud, like the sub-soil waters of an artesian well, springs spontaneously to your head and forms itself into pulsating, golden rings. Then, like a gentle river they flow from your head in a stream of living rings of gold.

In a meditative mood bordering on sleep the cloud ascends. It is in this drowsy state that you should assume that you are that which you desire to be, and that you have that which you seek, for the cloud will assume the form of your assumption and fashion a world in harmony with itself. The cloud is simply the garment of your consciousness, and where your consciousness is placed, there you will be in the flesh also.

1948 Lessons – Lesson 2 – Assumptions Harden Into Fact

This golden cloud comes in meditation. There is a certain point when you are approaching sleep that it is very, very thick, very liquid, and very much alive and pulsing. It begins to ascend as you reach the drowsy, meditative state, bordering on sleep. You do not strike the tabernacle; neither do you move it until the cloud begins to ascend.

The cloud always ascends when man approaches the drowsiness of sleep. For when a man goes to sleep, whether he knows it or not, he slips from a three-dimensional world into a fourth-dimensional world and that which is ascending is the consciousness of that man in a greater focus; it is a fourth-dimensional focus.

What you now see ascending is your greater self. When that begins to ascend you enter into the actual state of feeling you are what you want to be. That is the time you lull yourself into the mood of being what you want to be, by either experiencing in Imagination what you would experience in reality were you already that which you want to be, or by repeating over and over again the phrase that implies you have already done what you want to do. A phrase such as, "Isn't it wonderful, isn't it wonderful," as though some wonderful thing had happened to you.

"In a dream, in a vision of the night, when deep sleep falleth upon men, in slumberings upon the bed. Then he openeth the ears of men, and sealeth their instruction. "

Use wisely the interval preceding sleep.

Assume the feeling of the wish fulfilled and go to sleep in this mood.

1948 Lessons – Lesson 2 – Assumptions Harden Into Fact

At night, in a dimensionally larger world, when deep sleep falleth upon men, they see and play the parts that they will later on play on earth.

And the drama is always in harmony with that which their dimensionally greater selves read and play through them. Our illusion of free will is but ignorance of the causes which make us act.

The sensation which dominates the mind of man as he falls asleep, though false, will harden into fact. Assuming the feeling of the wish fulfilled as we fall asleep, is the command to this embodying process saying to our mood, "Be thou actual." In this way we become through a natural process what we desire to be.

I can tell you dozens of personal experiences where it seemed impossible to go elsewhere, but by placing myself elsewhere mentally as I was about to go to sleep, circumstances changed quickly which compelled me to make the journey.

I have done it across water by placing myself at night on my bed as though I slept where I wanted to be. As the days unfolded things began to mold themselves in harmony with that assumption and all things that must happen to compel my journey did happen. And I, in spite of myself, must make ready to go toward that place which I assumed I was in when I approached the deep of sleep.

As my cloud ascends I assume that I AM now the man I want to be, or that I AM already in the place where I want to visit. I sleep in that place now. Then life strikes the tabernacle, strikes my environment and reassembles my environment across seas or over land and reassembles it in the likeness of my assumption. It has nothing to do with men walking across a physical desert. The whole vast world round about you is a desert.

From the cradle to the grave you and I walk as though we walk the desert.

But we have a living tabernacle wherein God dwells, and it is covered with a cloud which can and does ascend when we go to sleep or are in a state akin to sleep. Not necessarily in two days, it can ascend in two minutes. Why did they give you two days? If I now become the man I want to be, I may become dissatisfied tomorrow. I should at least give it a day before I decide to move on.

The Bible says in two days, a month, or a year: whenever you decide to move on with this tabernacle let the cloud ascend. As it ascends you start moving where the cloud is.

The cloud is simply the garment of your consciousness, your assumption.

Where the consciousness is placed you do not have to take the physical body; it gravitates there in spite of you.

Things happen to compel you to move in the direction where you are consciously dwelling.

"In my Father's house are many mansions: if it were not so, I would have told you. I go to prepare a place for you. And if I go and prepare a place for you, I will come again, and receive you unto myself; that where I am, there ye may be also."

1948 Lessons – Lesson 2 – Assumptions Harden Into Fact

The many mansions are the unnumbered states within your mind, for you are the house of God.

In my Father's house are unnumbered concepts of self.
You could not in eternity exhaust what you are capable of being.

If I sit quietly here and assume that I am elsewhere, I have gone and prepared a place.

But if I open my eyes, the bilocation which I created vanishes and I am back here in the physical form that I left behind me as I went to prepare a place. But I prepared the place nevertheless and will in time dwell there physically.

You do not have to concern yourself with the ways and the means that will be employed to move you across space into that place where you have gone and mentally prepared it. Simply sit quietly, no matter where you are, and mentally actualize it.

But I give you warning, do not treat it lightly, for I AM conscious of what it will do to people who treat it lightly. I treated it lightly once because I just wanted to get away, based only upon the temperature of the day. It was in the deep of winter in New York, and I so desired to be in the warm climate of the Indies, that I slept that night as though I slept under palm trees. Next morning when I awoke it was still very much winter.

I had no intentions of going to the Indies that year, but distressing news came which compelled me to make the journey. It was in the midst of war when ships were being sunk right and left, but I sailed out of New York on a ship 48

1948 Lessons – Lesson 2 – Assumptions Harden Into Fact

hours after I received this news. It was the only way I could get to Barbados, and I arrived just in time to see my mother and say a three-dimensional "Good-bye" to her.

In spite of the fact that I had no intentions of going, the deeper Self watched where the great cloud descended. I placed it in Barbados and this tabernacle (my body) had to go and make the journey to fulfill the command, "Wherever the sole of your foot shall tread that have I given unto you." Wherever the cloud descends in the desert, there you reassemble that tabernacle.

I sailed from New York at midnight on a ship without taking thought of submarines or anything else. I had to go. Things happened in a way that I could not have devised.

I warn you, do not treat it lightly. Do not say, "I will experiment and put myself in Labrador, just to see if it will work." You will go to your Labrador and then you will wonder why you ever came to this class. It will work if you dare assume the feeling of your wish fulfilled as you go to sleep.

Control your moods as you go to sleep.

I cannot find any better way to describe this technique than to call it a "controlled waking dream." In a dream you lose control, but try preceding your sleep with a complete controlled waking dream, entering into it as you do in dream, for in a dream you are always very dominant, you always play the part.

You are always an actor in a dream, and never the audience. When you have a controlled waking dream you are an actor and you enter into the act of the controlled dream.

1948 Lessons – Lesson 2 – Assumptions Harden Into Fact

But do not do it lightly, for you must then reenact it physically in a three-dimensional world.

Now before we go into our moment of silence there is something I must make very clear, and that is this effort we discussed last night.

If there is one reason in this whole vast world why people fail it is because they are unaware of a law known to psychologists today as the law of reverse effort.

When you assume the feeling of your wish fulfilled it is with a minimum of effort. You must control the direction of the movements of your attention. But you must do it with the least effort. If there is effort in the control, and you are compelling it in a certain way you are not going to get the results. You will get the opposite results, whatever they might be.

That is why we insist on establishing the basis of the Bible as Adam slept. That is the first creative act, and there is no record where he was ever awakened from this profound sleep. While he sleeps creation stops.

You change your future best when you are in control of your thoughts while in a state akin to sleep, for then effort is reduced to its minimum.

Your attention seems to completely relax, and then you must practice holding your attention within that feeling, without using force, and without using effort.

Do not think for a moment that it is will power that does it.

1948 Lessons – Lesson 2 – Assumptions Harden Into Fact

When you release Barabbas and become identified with Jesus, you do not will yourself to be it, you imagine that you are it. That is all you do.

Now as we come to the vital part of the evening, the interval devoted to prayer, let me again clarify the technique.

Know what you want. Then construct a single event, an event which implies fulfillment of your wish. Restrict the event to a single act.

For instance, if I single out as an event, shaking a man's hand, then that is the only thing I do. I do not shake it, then light a cigarette and do a thousand other things. I simply imagine that I am actually shaking hands and keep the act going over and over and over again until the imaginary act has all the feeling of reality.

The event must always imply fulfillment of the wish.

Always construct an event which you believe you would naturally encounter following the fulfillment of your desire.

You are the judge of what event you really want to realize.

There is another technique I gave you last night. If you cannot concentrate on an act, if you cannot snuggle into your chair and believe the chair is elsewhere, just as though elsewhere were here, then do this: Reduce the idea, condense it to a single, simple phrase like, "Isn't it wonderful." or, "Thank you." or, "It's done." or, "It's finished."

There should not be more than three words.

1948 Lessons – Lesson 2 – Assumptions Harden Into Fact

Something that implies the desire is already realized. "Isn't it wonderful", or "Thank you," certainly imply that.

These are not all the phrases you could use. Make up out of your own vocabulary the phrase which best suits you. But make it very, very short and always use a phrase that implies fulfillment of the idea.

When you have your phrase in mind, lift the cloud. Let the cloud ascend by simply inducing the state that borders on sleep. Simply begin to imagine and feel you are sleepy, and in this state assume the feeling of the wish fulfilled. Then repeat the phrase over and over like a lullaby. Whatever the phrase is, let it imply that the assumption is true, that it is concrete, that it is already a fact and you know it.

Just relax and enter into the feeling of actually being what you want to be. As you do it you are entering Jericho with your spy who has the power to give it. You are releasing Barabbas and sentencing Jesus to be crucified and resurrected. All these stories you are re-enacting if now you begin to let go and enter into the feeling of actually being what you want to be. Now we can go.....

SILENCE PERIOD ....

If your hands are dry , and if your mouth is dry at the end of this meditation, that is positive proof that you did succeed in lifting the cloud. What you were doing when the cloud was lifted is entirely your business. But you did lift the cloud if your hands are dry.

1948 Lessons – Lesson 2 – Assumptions Harden Into Fact

I will give you another phenomena which is very strange and one I cannot analyze. It happens if you really go into the deep. You will find on waking that you have the most active pair of kidneys in the world. I have discussed it with doctors and they cannot explain it.

Another thing you may observe in meditation is a lovely liquid blue light. The nearest thing on earth to which I can compare it is burning alcohol. You know when you put alcohol on the plum pudding at Christmas time and set it a flame, the lovely liquid blue flame that envelopes the pudding until you blow it out. That flame is the nearest thing to the blue light which comes on the forehead of a man in meditation.

Do not be distressed. You will know it when you see it. It is like two shades of blue, a darker and a lighter blue in constant motion, just like burning alcohol, which is unlike the constant flame of a gas jet. This flame is alive, just as spirit would be alive.

Another thing that may come to you as it did to me. You will see spots before your eyes. They are not liver spots as some people will tell you who know nothing about it. These are little things that float in space like a mesh, little circles all tied together. They start with a single cell and come in groups in different geometrical patterns, like worms, like trailers, and they float all over your face. When you close your eyes you still see them, proving that they are not from without, they are from within.

When you begin to expand in consciousness all these things come. They may be your blood stream objectified by some strange trick of man that man does not quite

1948 Lessons – Lesson 2 – Assumptions Harden Into Fact

understand. I am not denying that it is your blood stream made visible, but do not be distressed by thinking it is liver spots or some other silly thing that people will tell you.

If these various phenomena come to you, do not think you are doing something wrong. It is the normal, natural expansion that comes to all men who take themselves in tow and try to develop the garden of Gethsemane.

The minute you begin to discipline your mind by observing your thoughts and watching your thoughts throughout the day, you become the policeman of your thoughts. Refuse to enter into conversations that are unlovely, refuse to listen attentively to anything that tears down.

Begin to build within your own mind's eye the vision of the perfect virgin rather than the vision of the foolish virgin. Listen only to the things that bring joy when you hear them.

Do not give a willing ear to that which is unlovely, which when you heard it you wish you had not.

That is listening and seeing things Without oil in your lamp, or joy in your mind.

There are two kinds of virgins in the Bible: five foolish and five wise virgins.

The minute you become the wise virgin, or try to make an attempt to do it, you will find all these things happen.

You will see these things, and they interest you so that you have not time to develop the foolish sight, as many

1948 Lessons – Lesson 2 – Assumptions Harden Into Fact

people do. I hope that no one here does. Because no one should be identified with this great work who can still find great joy in a discussion of another that is unlovely.

Lesson 3 – Thinking Fourth-Dimensionally

There are two actual outlooks on the world possessed by every man, and the ancient story tellers were fully conscious of these two outlooks.

They called the one "the carnal mind," and the other "the mind of Christ."

We recognize these two centers of thought in the statement: "The natural man receiveth not the things of the Spirit of God: for they are foolishness unto him: neither can he know them, because they are spiritually discerned."

To the natural mind, reality is confined to the instant called now; this very moment seems to contain the whole of reality, everything else is unreal.

To the natural mind, the past and the future are purely imaginary.

In other words my past, when I use the natural mind, is only a memory image of things that were. And to the limited focus of the carnal or natural mind the future does not exist.

The natural-mind does not believe that it could revisit the past and see it as something that is present, something that is objective and concrete to itself, neither does it believe that the future exists.

To the Christ mind, the spiritual mind, which in our language we will call the fourth-dimensional focus, the past, the present, and the future of the natural mind are a present

1948 Lessons – Lesson 3 – Thinking Fourth-Dimensionally

whole. It takes in the entire array of sensory impressions that man has encountered, is encountering, and will encounter.

The only reason you and I are functioning as we are today, and are not aware of the greater outlook, is simply because we are creatures of habit, and habit renders us totally blind to what otherwise we should see; but habit is not law. It acts as though it were the most compelling force in the world, yet it is not law.

We can create a new approach to life. If you and I would spend a few minutes every day in withdrawing our attention from the region of sensation and concentrating it on an invisible state and remain faithful to this contemplation, feeling and sensing the reality of an invisible state, we would in time become aware of this greater world, this dimensionally larger world.

The state contemplated is now a concrete reality, displaced in time.

Tonight as we turn to our Bible you be the judge as to where you stand in your present unfoldment.

Our first story for tonight is from the 5th chapter of the Gospel of Mark. In this chapter there are three stories told as though they were separate experiences of the dominant characters.

In the first story we are told that Jesus came upon an insane man, a naked man who lived in the cemetery and hid himself behind the tombs. This man appealed to Jesus not to cast out the devils that bedeviled him.

But Jesus said unto him, "Come out of the man, thou unclean spirit."

Thus Jesus cast out the devils that they may now destroy themselves, and we find this man, for the first time, clothed and in his right mind and seated at the feet of the Master. We will get the psychological sense of this chapter by changing the name Jesus to that of enlightened reason or fourth-dimensional thinking.

As we progress in this chapter we are told that Jesus now comes upon the High Priest whose name is Jairus, and Jairus the High Priest of the Synagogue has a child who is dying. She is 12 years old, and he appeals to Jesus to come and heal the child.

Jesus consents, and as he starts toward the home of the High Priest a woman in the market place touched his garment. "And Jesus, immediately knowing in himself that virtue had gone out of him, turned him about in the press, and said, Who touched my clothes?"

The woman who was healed of an issue of blood that she had had for 12 years confessed that she had touched him. " And he said unto her, Daughter, Thy faith hath made thee whole; go in peace."

As he continues toward the home the High Priest he is told that the child is dead and there is no need to go to resurrect her. She is no longer asleep, but is now dead.

1948 Lessons – Lesson 3 – Thinking Fourth-Dimensionally

"As soon as Jesus heard the word that was spoken, he saith unto the ruler of the synagogue, Be not afraid, only believe."

"And when he was come in, he saith unto them, Why make ye this ado, and weep? The damsel is not dead, but sleepeth."

With this the entire crowd mocked and laughed, but Jesus, closing the doors against the mocking crowd, took with him into the household of Jairus, his disciples and the father and mother of the dead child. They entered into the room where the damsel was lying. "And he took the damsel by the hand, and said unto her, Damsel, I say unto thee, arise."

"From this deep sleep she awoke and arose and walked, and the High Priest and all the others were astonished. And he changed them straightly that no man should know it; and he commanded that something should be given her to eat."

You are this very night, as you are seated here, pictured in this 5th chapter of Mark.

A cemetery is for one purpose: it is simply a record of the dead. Are you living in the dead past?

If you are living among the dead, your prejudices, your superstitions, and your false beliefs that you keep alive are the tombstones behind which you hide. If you refuse to let them go you are just as mad as the mad man of the Bible who pleaded with enlightened reason not to cast them out. There is no difference. But enlightened reason is incapable of

1948 Lessons – Lesson 3 – Thinking Fourth-Dimensionally

protecting prejudice and superstition against the inroads of reason.

There is not a man in this world who has a prejudice, regardless of the nature of the prejudice, who can hold it up to the light of reason. Tell me you are against a certain nation, a certain race, a certain "ism," a certain anything . . I do not care what it is . . you cannot expose that belief of yours to the light of reason and have it live. In order that it may be kept alive in your world you must hide it from reason. You cannot analyze it in the light of reason and have it live.

When this fourth-dimensional focus comes and shows you a new approach to life and casts out of your own mind all these things that bedeviled you, you are then cleansed and clothed in your right mind. And you sit at the foot of understanding, called the feet of the Master.

Now clothed and in your right mind you can resurrect the dead. What died? The child in the story is not a child. The child is your ambition, your desire, the unfulfilled dreams of your heart. This is the child housed within the mind of man.

For as I have stated before, the entire drama of the Bible is a psychological one.

The Bible has no reference at all to any person who ever existed, or any event that ever occurred upon earth. All the stories of the Bible unfold in the minds of the individual man.

In this story Jesus is the awakened intellect of man.

1948 Lessons – Lesson 3 – Thinking Fourth-Dimensionally

When your mind functions outside of the range of your present senses, when your mind is healed of all the former limitations, then you are no longer the insane man; but you are this presence personified as Jesus, the power that can resurrect the longings of the heart of man.

You are now the woman with the issue of blood. What is this issue of blood? A running womb is not a productive womb. She held it for 12 years, she was incapable of conceiving. She could not give form to her longing because of the running of the issue of blood. You are told her faith closed it. As the womb closes it can give form to the seed or idea.

As your mind is cleansed of your former concept of Self, you assume you are what you want to be, and remaining faithful to this assumption, you give form to your assumption or resurrect your child. You are the woman cleansed of the issue of blood, and you move towards the house of the dead child.

The child or state you desired is now your fixed concept of yourself. But now having assumed that I AM what formerly I desired to be, I cannot continue desiring what I AM conscious of being. So I do not discuss it. I talk to no one concerning what I AM. It is so obvious to me that I AM what I wanted to be that I walk as though I were.

Walking as though I AM what formerly I wanted to be, my world of limited focus does not see it and thinks I no longer desire it. The child is dead within their world; but I, who know the law, say, "The child is not dead." The damsel is not dead, she but sleepeth. I now awaken her. I, by my assumption, awaken and make visible in my world what I assume, for assumptions if sustained invariably awaken what they affirm.

I close the door. What door? The door of my senses. I simply shut out completely all that my senses reveal. I deny the evidence of my senses. I suspend the limited reason of the natural man and walk in this bold assertion that I AM what my senses deny.

With the door of my senses closed, what do I take into that disciplined state?

I take no one into that state but the parents of the child and my disciples. I close the door against the mocking, laughing crowd. I no longer look for confirmation. I completely deny the evidence of my senses, which mock my assumption and do not discuss with others whether my assumption is possible or not.

Who are the parents? We have discovered that the father-mother of all creation is man's I AMness.

Man's consciousness is God. I AM conscious of the state. I AM the father-mother of all my ideas and my mind remains faithful to this new concept of self. My mind is disciplined. I take into that state the disciples, and I shut out of that state everything that would deny it.

Now the child, unaided by a man, is resurrected.

The condition which I desired and assumed that I had, becomes objectified within my world and bears witness to the power of my assumption.

1948 Lessons – Lesson 3 – Thinking Fourth-Dimensionally

You be the judge, I cannot judge you. You are either living now in the dead past, or you are living as the woman whose issue of blood has been stanched.

Could you actually answer me if I asked you the question:

"Do you believe now that you, without the assistance of another, need only assume that you are what you want to be, to make that assumption real within your world?

Or do you believe that you must first fulfill a certain condition imposed upon you by the past, that you must be of a certain order, or a certain something?'

I am not being critical of certain churches or groups, but there are those who believe that anyone outside of their church or group is not yet saved.

I was born a Protestant. You talk to a Protestant, there is only one Christian, a Protestant. You talk to a Catholic, why there is nothing in the world that is a Christian but a Catholic. You talk to a Jew, and the Christians are heathens, and the Jews are the chosen. You talk to a Mohammedan, Jews and Christians are the infidels. You talk to someone else and all these are the untouchables. It does not matter to whom you talk, they are always the chosen ones.

If you believe that you must be one of these in order to be saved, you are still an insane man hiding behind these superstitions and these prejudices of the past, and you are begging not to be cleansed.

1948 Lessons – Lesson 3 – Thinking Fourth-Dimensionally

Some of you say to me, "Do not ask me to give up my belief in Jesus the man, or in Moses the man, or in Peter the man. When you ask me to give up my belief in these characters you are asking too much. Leave me these beliefs because they comfort me. I can believe that they lived upon earth and still follow your psychological interpretation of their stories."

I say, Come out of the dead past. Come out of that cemetery and walk, knowing that you and your Father are one, and your Father, who men call GOD, is your own consciousness. That is the only creative law in the world.

Of what are you conscious of being?

Although you cannot see your objective with the limited focus of your three-dimensional mind, you are now that which you have assumed you are. Walk in that assumption and remain faithful to it.

Time in this dimension of your being, beats slowly and you may not, even after you objectify your assumption, remember there was a time when this present reality was but an attitude of mind. Because of the slowness of the beat of time here you often fail to see the relationship between your inner nature and the outer world that bears witness to it.

You be the judge of the position you now occupy in this 5th chapter of Mark. Are you resurrecting the dead child? Are you still in need of having that womb of your mind closed? Is it still running and therefore cannot be fertile? Are you now the insane man living in the dead past? Only you can be the judge and answer these questions.

1948 Lessons – Lesson 3 – Thinking Fourth-Dimensionally

Now we turn to a story in the 5th chapter of the Gospel of John.

This will show you how beautifully the ancient story tellers told of the two distinct outlooks on this world- one, the limited three-dimensional focus, and the other, the fourth-dimensional focus.

This story tells of an impotent man who is quickly healed. Jesus comes to a place called Bethesda, which by definition means the House of Five Porches. On these Five Porches are unnumbered impotent folk . . lame, blind, halt, withered, and others. Tradition had it that at certain seasons of the year an angel would descend and disturb the pool which was near these Five Porches. As the Angel disturbed the pool, the first one in was always healed. But only the first one, not the second.

Jesus, seeing a man who was lame from his mother's womb, said to him, "Wilt thou be made whole?"

"The impotent man answered him, Sir, I have no man, when the water is troubled, to put me into the pool . . but while I am coming, another steppeth down before me."

"Jesus saith unto him, Rise, take up thy bed, and walk."

"And immediately the man was made whole, and took up his bed, and walked, and on the same day was the Sabbath."

You read this story and you think some strange man who possessed miraculous power suddenly said to the lame man, "Rise and walk." I cannot repeat too often that the story, even when it introduces numberless individualities, takes place within the mind of the individual man.

The pool is your consciousness.

The angel is an idea, called the messenger of GOD.

Consciousness being God, when you have an idea you are entertaining an angel.

The minute you are conscious of a desire your pool has been disturbed. Desire disturbs the mind of man. To want something is to be disturbed.

The very moment you have an ambition, or a clearly defined objective, the pool has been disturbed by the angel, which was the desire. You are told that the first one into the disturbed pool is always healed.

My closest companions in this world, my wife and my little girl, are to me when I address them, second. I must speak to my wife as, "you are." I must speak to anyone, no matter how close they are, as "You are." And after that the third person, "He is." There is only one person in this world with whom I can use the first person present and that is self. "I AM," can be said only of myself, it cannot be said of another.

Therefore, when I AM conscious of some desire that I want to be, but seemingly am not, the pool being disturbed, who can get into that pool before me?

I alone possess the power of the first person.

1948 Lessons – Lesson 3 – Thinking Fourth-Dimensionally

I AM That which I want to be. Except I believe I AM what I want to be, I remain as I formerly was and die in that limitation.

In this story you need no man to put you into the pool as your consciousness is disturbed by desire. All you need do is to assume you are already that which formerly you wanted to be and you are in it, and no man can get in before you.

What man can get in before you when you become conscious of being that which you want to be? No one can be before you when you alone possess the power to say I AM.

These are the two outlooks. You are now what your senses would deny. Are you bold enough to assume that you are already that which you want to be? If you dare assume you are already that which your reason and your senses now deny, then you are in the pool and, unaided by a man, you, too, will rise and take your couch and walk.

You are told it happened on the Sabbath. The Sabbath is only the mystical sense of stillness, when you are unconcerned, when you are not anxious, when you are not looking for results, knowing that signs follow and do not precede.

The Sabbath is the day of stillness wherein there is no working.

When you are not working to make it so you are in the Sabbath.

1948 Lessons – Lesson 3 – Thinking Fourth-Dimensionally

When you are not at all concerned about the opinion of others, when you walk as though you were, you cannot raise one finger to make it so, you are in the Sabbath.

I cannot be concerned as to how it will be, and still say I AM conscious of being it.

If I AM conscious of being free, secure, healthy, and happy, I sustain these states of consciousness without effort or labor on my part.

Therefore, I AM in the Sabbath; and because it was the Sabbath he rose and walked.

Our next story is from the 4th chapter of the Gospel of John, and it is one you have heard time and time again. Jesus comes to the well and there is a woman called the woman of Samaria, and he said to her, "Give me to drink." John 4:7

"Then saith the woman of Samaria unto him, How is it that thou, being a Jew, asketh drink of me, which am a woman of Samaria? For the Jews have no dealings with the Samaritans."

"Jesus answered and said unto her, If thou knewest the gift of God, and who it is that saith to thee, Give me to drink; thou wouldest have asked of him, and he would have given thee living water."

The woman seeing that he has nothing with which to draw the water, and knowing the well is deep, says: Art thou greater than our father Jacob, which gave us the well, and drank thereof himself, and his children, and his cattle?"

"Jesus answered and said unto her, Whosoever drinketh of this water shall thirst again- But whosoever drinketh of the water that I shall give him shall never thirst; but the water that I shall give him shall be in him a well of water springing up into everlasting life."

Then he tells her all concerning herself and asks her to go and call her husband. She answered and said, "I have no husband."

"Jesus said unto her, Thou hast well said, I have no husband: For thou hast had five husbands; and he whom thou now hast is not thy husband."

The woman, knowing this to be true, goes into the market-place and tells the other, "I have met the Messiah."

They ask her, "How do you know you have met the Messiah?"

"Because he told me all things that I have ever done." she replies. Here is a focus that takes in the entire past at least, and tells her now concerning the future.

Continuing with the story, the disciples come to Jesus and say, "Master, eat."

"But he said unto them, I have meat to eat that ye know not of."

1948 Lessons – Lesson 3 – Thinking Fourth-Dimensionally

When they speak of a harvest in four months, Jesus replies, "Say not ye, There are yet four months, and then cometh harvest? Behold, I say unto you, lift up your eyes, and look on the fields; for they are white already to harvest."

He sees things that people wait four months for, or wait four years for; he sees them as now in a dimensionally larger world, existing now, taking place now.

Let us go back to the first part of the story. The woman of Samaria is the three-dimensional you, and Jesus at the well is the fourth-dimensional you. The argument starts between what you want to be, and what reason tells you that you are. The greater you tells you that if you would dare assume you are already what you want to be, you would become it.

The lesser you, with its limited focus, tells you, "Why you haven't a bucket, you haven't a rope and the well is deep. How could you ever reach the depth of this state without the means to that end?"

You answer and say, "If you only knew who asks of you to drink you would ask of him." If you only knew what in yourself is urging upon you the embodiment of the state you now seek, you would suspend your little sight and let him do it for you.

Then he tells you that you have five husbands, and you deny it. But he knows far better than you that your five senses impregnate you morning, noon, and night with their limitations.

1948 Lessons – Lesson 3 – Thinking Fourth-Dimensionally

They tell you what children you will bear tonight, tomorrow, and the days to come. For your five senses act like five husbands who constantly impregnate your consciousness, which is the great womb of GOD; and morning, noon, and night they suggest to you, and dictate to you that which you must accept as true.

He tells you the one you would like to have for your husband is not your husband. In other words the sixth has not yet impregnated you. What you would like to be is denied by these five, and they hold the power, they dictate what you will accept as true.

What you would like to accept has not yet penetrated your mind and impregnated your mind with its reality.

He whom you call husband is really not your husband. You are not bearing his likeness. To bear his likeness is proof that you are his wife, at least you have known him intimately. You are not bearing the likeness of the sixth; you are only bearing the likeness of the five.

Then one turns to me and tells me all that I have ever known. I go back in my mind's eye and reason tells me that all through my life I have always accepted the limitations of my senses, I have always looked upon them as fact; and morning, noon, and night I have born witness to this acceptance.

Reason tells me I have only known these five from the time I was born.

Now I would like to step outside the limitation of my senses but I have not yet found within myself the courage to

1948 Lessons – Lesson 3 – Thinking Fourth-Dimensionally

assume I am what these five would deny that I am. So here I remain, conscious of my task, but without the courage to step beyond the limitations of my senses, and that which my reason denies.

He tells these, "I have meat ye know not of. I AM the bread that droppeth down from heaven. I AM the wine." I know what I want to be, and because I AM That bread I feast upon it. I assume that I AM, and instead of feasting upon the fact that I AM in this room talking to you and you are listening to me, and that I AM in Los Angeles, I feast upon the fact that I AM elsewhere and I walk here as though I were elsewhere. And gradually I become what I feast upon.

Let me give you two personal stories. When I was a boy I lived in a very limited environment, in a little island called Barbados. Feed for animals was very, very scarce and very expensive because we had to import it. I am one of a family of 10 children and my grandmother lived with us making 13 at the table.

Time and again I can remember my mother saying to the cook in the early part of the week, "I want you to put away three ducks for Sunday's dinner. "This meant that she would take from the flock in the yard three ducks and coop them up in a very small cage and feed them, stuff them morning, noon, and night with corn and all the things she wanted the ducks to feast upon.

This was an entirely different diet from what we regularly fed the ducks, because we kept those birds alive by feeding them fish. We kept them alive and fat on fish because fish were very cheap and plentiful; but you could not eat a bird that fed upon fish, not as you and I like a bird.

The cook would take three ducks, put them in a cage and for seven days stuff them with corn, sour milk and all the things we wanted to taste in the birds. Then when they were killed and served for dinner seven days later they were luscious, milk fed, corn fed birds.

But occasionally the cook forgot to put away the birds, and my father, knowing we were having ducks, and believing that she had carried out the command, did not send anything else for dinner, and three fish came to the table. You could not touch those birds for they were so much the embodiment of what they fed upon.

Man is a psychological being, a thinker. It is not what he feeds upon physically, but what he feeds upon mentally that he becomes. We become the embodiment of that which we mentally feed upon.

Now those ducks could not be fed corn in the morning and fish in the afternoon and something else at night. It had to be a complete change of diet. In our case we cannot have a little bit of meditation in the morning, curse at noon, and do something else in the evening. We have to go on a mental diet, for a week we must completely change our mental food.

"Whatsoever things are true, whatsoever things are honest, whatsoever things are just, whatsoever things are pure, whatsoever things are of good report; if there be any virtue, and if there be any praise, think on these things." Phil. 4:8

1948 Lessons – Lesson 3 – Thinking Fourth-Dimensionally

As a man thinketh in his heart so is he. If I could now single out the kind of mental food I want to express within my world and feast upon it, I would become it.

Let me tell you why I am doing what I am doing today. It was back in 1933 in the city of New York, and my old friend Abdullah, with whom I studied Hebrew for five years, was really the beginning of the eating of all my superstitions.

When I went to him I was filled with superstitions. I could not eat meat, I could not eat fish, I could not eat chicken, I could not eat any of these things that were living in the world. I did not drink, I did not smoke, and I was making a tremendous effort to live a celibate life.

Abdullah said to me, "I am not going to tell you 'you are crazy' Neville, but you are you know. All these things are stupid." But I could not believe they were stupid.

In November, 1933, I bade goodbye to my parents in the city of New York as they sailed for Barbados. I had been in this country 12 years with no desire to see Barbados. I was not successful and I was ashamed to go home to successful members of my family. After 12 years in America I was a failure in my own eyes. I was in the theatre and made money one year and spent it the next month.

I was not what I would call by their standards nor by mine a successful person.

Mind you when I said goodbye to my parents in November I had no desire to go to Barbados. The ship pulled out, and as I came up the street, something possessed me with a desire to go to Barbados.

1948 Lessons – Lesson 3 – Thinking Fourth-Dimensionally

It was the year 1933, I was unemployed and had no place to go except a little room on 75th Street. I went straight to my old friend Abdullah and said to him "Ab, the strangest feeling is possessing me.

For the first time in 12 years I want to go to Barbados."

If you want to go Neville, you have gone." he replied.

That was very strange language to me. I am in New York City on 72nd Street and he tells me I have gone to Barbados. I said to him, "What do you mean, I have gone, Abdullah?"

He said, "Do you really want to go?"

I answered "yes."

He then said to me, "As you walk through this door now you are not walking on 72nd Street, you are walking on palm lined streets, coconut lined streets; this is Barbados. Do not ask me how you are going to go. You are in Barbados. You do not say 'how' when you 'are there'. You are there. Now you walk as though you were there."

I went out of his place in a daze. I AM in Barbados. I have no money, I have no job, I am not even well clothed, and yet I AM in Barbados.

He was not the kind of a person with whom you would argue, not Abdullah. Two weeks later I was no nearer my goal than on the day I first told him I wanted to go to Barbados. I said to him, "Ab, I trust you implicitly but here is one time I cannot see how it is going to work. I have not one penny towards my journey, I began to explain."

1948 Lessons – Lesson 3 – Thinking Fourth-Dimensionally

You know what he did. He was as black as the ace of spades, my old friend Abdullah, with his turbaned head. As I sat in his living room he rose from his chair and went towards his study and slammed the door, which was not an invitation to follow him. As he went through the door he said to me, "I have said all that I have to say."

On the 3rd of December I stood before Abdullah and told him again I was no nearer my trip. He repeated his statement, "You are in Barbados."

The very last ship sailing for Barbados that would take me there for the reason I wanted to go, which was to be there for Christmas, sailed at noon on December 6th, the old Nerissa.

On the morning of December 4th, having no job, having no place to go, I slept late. When I got up there was an air mail letter from Barbados under my door. As I opened the letter a little piece of paper flickered to the floor. I picked it up and it was a draft for $50.00.

The letter was from my brother Victor and it read, "I am not asking you to come, Neville, this is a command. We have never had a Christmas when all the members of our family were present at the same time. This Christmas it could be done if you would come. "

My oldest brother Cecil left home before the youngest was born and then we started to move away from home at different times so never in the history of our family were we ever all together at the same time.

1948 Lessons – Lesson 3 – Thinking Fourth-Dimensionally

The letter continued, "You are not working, I know there is no reason why you cannot come, so you must be here before Christmas. The enclosed $50.00 is to buy a few shirts or a pair of shoes you may need for the trip. You will not need tips; use the bar if you are drinking. I will meet the ship and pay all your tips and your incurred expenses. I have cabled Furness, Withy & Co. in New York City and told them to issue you a ticket when you appear at their office. The $50.00 is simply to buy some little essentials. You may sign as you want aboard the ship. I will meet it and take care of all obligations."

I went down to Furness, Withy & Co. with my letter and let them read it. They said, "We received the cable Mr. Goddard, but unfortunately we have not any space left on the December 6th sailing. The only thing available is 3rd Class between New York and St. Thomas. When we get to St. Thomas we have a few passengers who are getting off. You may then ride 1st Class from St. Thomas to Barbados. But between New York and St. Thomas you must go 3rd Class, although you may have the privileges of the 1st Class dining room and walk the decks of the 1st Class."

I said, "I will take it."

I went back to my friend Abdullah on the afternoon of December 4th and said, "It worked like a dream." I told him what I had done, thinking he would be happy.

Do you know what he said to me? He said, "Who told you that you are going 3rd Class? Did I see you in Barbados, the man you are, going 3rd Class? You are in Barbados and you went there 1st Class."

1948 Lessons – Lesson 3 – Thinking Fourth-Dimensionally

I did not have one moment to see him again before I sailed on the noon of December 6th. When I reached the dock with my passport and my papers to get aboard that ship the agent said to me, "We have good news for you, Mr. Goddard. There has been a cancellation and you are going 1st Class."

Abdullah taught me the importance of remaining faithful to an idea and not compromising. I wavered, but he remained faithful to the assumption that I was in Barbados and had traveled 1st Class.

Now back to the significance of our two Bible stories. The well is deep and you have no bucket, you have no rope. It is four months to the harvest and Jesus says, "I have meat to eat ye know not of. I AM the bread of heaven."

Feast on the idea, become identified with the idea as though you were already that embodied state. Walk in the assumption that you are what you want to be. If you feast on that and remain faithful to that mental diet, you will crystallize it. You will become it in this world.

When I came back to New York in 1934, after three heavenly months in Barbados, I drank, I smoked, and did everything I had not done in years.

I remembered what Abdullah had said to me, "After you have proven this law you will become normal, Neville.

You will come out of that graveyard, you will come out of that dead past where you think you are being holy. For all you are really doing you know, you are being so good, Neville, you are good for nothing"

I came back walking this earth a completely transformed person. From that day, which was in February 1934, I began to live more and more. I cannot honestly tell you I have always succeeded. My many mistakes in this world, my many failures would convict me if I told you that I have so completely mastered the movements of my attention that I can at all times remain faithful to the idea I want to embody.

But I can say with the ancient teacher, although I seem to have failed in the past, I move on and strive day after day to become that which I want to embody in this world. Suspend judgment, refuse to accept what reason and the senses now dictate, and if you remain faithful to the new diet, you will become the embodiment of the ideal to which you remain faithful.

If there is one place in the world that is unlike my little island of Barbados, it is New York City. In Barbados the tallest building is three stories, and the streets are lined with palm trees and coconut trees and all sorts of tropical things. In New York City you must go to a park to find a tree.

Yet I had to walk the streets of New York as though I walked the streets of Barbados. To one's Imagination all things are possible. I walked, feeling that I was actually walking the streets of Barbados, and in that assumption I could almost smell the odor of the coconut lined lanes. I began to create within my mind's eye the atmosphere I would physically encounter were I in Barbados.

1948 Lessons – Lesson 3 – Thinking Fourth-Dimensionally

As I remained faithful to this assumption, somebody canceled passage and I received it. My brother in Barbados, who never thought of my coming home, has the commanding urge to write me a strange letter. He had never dictated to me, but this time he dictated, and thought that he originated the idea of my visit.

I went home and had three heavenly months, returned 1st Class, and brought back quite a sum of cash in my pocket, a gift. My trip, had I paid for it, would have been $3,000, yet I did it without a nickel in my pocket.

"I have ways ye know not of. My ways are past finding out." The dimensionally greater self took my assumption as the command and influenced the behavior of my brother to write that letter, influenced the behavior of someone to cancel that 1st Class passage, and did all the things necessary that would tend toward the production of the idea with which I was identified.

I was identified with the feeling of being there. I slept as though I were there, and the entire behavior of man was molded in harmony with my assumption.

I did not need to go down to Furness, Withy & Co. and beg them for a passage, asking them to cancel someone who was booked 1st Class. I did not need to write my brother and beg him to send me some money or buy me a passage. He thought he originated the act. Actually, to this day, he believes that be initiated the desire to bring me home.

My old friend Abdullah simply said to me, "You are in Barbados, Neville. You want to be there; wherever you want

1948 Lessons – Lesson 3 – Thinking Fourth-Dimensionally

to be, there you are. Live as though you are and that you shall be."

These are the two outlooks. on the world possessed by every man. I do not care who you are. Every child born of woman, regardless of race, nation, or creed, possesses two distinct outlooks on the world.

You are either the natural man who receiveth not the things of the Spirit of God, because to you in the natural focus they are foolishness unto you. Or you are the spiritual man who perceiveth things outside of the limitations of your senses because all things are now realities in a dimensionally larger world.

There is no need to wait four months to harvest.

You are either the woman of Samaria or Jesus at the well. You are the man waiting on the Five Porches for the disturbance and someone to push him in; or you are the one who can command yourself to rise and walk in spite of others who wait.

Are you the man behind the tombstones in the cemetery waiting and begging not to be clean, because you do not want to be cleansed of your prejudices? One of the most difficult things for man to give up is his superstitions, his prejudice. He holds on to these as though they were the treasure of treasures.

When you do become cleansed and you are free, then the womb, your own mind is automatically healed. It becomes the prepared ground where seeds, your desires, can take root and grow into manifestation.

1948 Lessons – Lesson 3 – Thinking Fourth-Dimensionally

The child you now bear in your heart is your present objective.

Your present longing is a child that is as though it were sick.

If you assume you are now what you would like to be, the child for a moment becomes dead because there is no disturbance any more.

You cannot be disturbed when you feel you are what you want to be because if you feel you are what you wanted to be, you are satisfied in that assumption.

To others who judge superficially you seem no longer to desire, so to them the desire or damsel is dead. They think you have lost your ambition because you no longer discuss your secret ambition. You have completely adjusted yourself to the idea. You have assumed that you are what you want to be. You know, "She is not dead, she but sleepth." "I go to awaken her."

I walk in the assumption that I AM, and as I walk, I quietly awaken her.

Then when she awakens I will do the normal, natural thing, I will give her to eat. I will not brag about it and tell others I simply go and tell no man. I feed this state I now like with my attention. I keep it alive within my world by becoming attentive to it.

Things that I am not attentive to fade and wither within my world, regardless of what they are.

1948 Lessons – Lesson 3 – Thinking Fourth-Dimensionally

They are not just born and then remain unfed. I gave them birth by reason of the fact that I became conscious of being them. When I embody them within my world that is not the end. That is the beginning. Now I am a mother who must keep alive this state by being attentive to it.

The day that I am not attentive, I have withdrawn my milk from it, and it fades from my world, as I become attentive to something else in my world.

You can either be attentive to the limitations and feed these and make them mountains, or you can be attentive to your desires; but to become attentive you must assume you are already that which you wanted to be.

Although today we speak of a third-dimensional and a fourth-dimensional focus, do not think for one moment these ancient teachers were not fully conscious of these two distinct centers of thought within the minds of all men.

They personified these two, and they tried to show man that the only thing which robs him of the man he could be, is habit.

Although it is not law, every psychologist will tell you that habit is the most inhibiting force in the world.

It completely restricts man and binds him and makes him totally blind to what otherwise he should be.

Begin now to mentally see and feel yourself as that which you want to be, and feast upon that sensation morning, noon, and night. I have scoured the Bible for a time interval that is longer than three days and I have not found it.

1948 Lessons – Lesson 3 – Thinking Fourth-Dimensionally

"Jesus answered and said unto them, Destroy this temple, and in three days I will raise it Up."

"Prepare you victuals; for within three days ye shall pass over this Jordan, to go in to possess the land, which the Lord your God giveth you to possess it."

If I could completely saturate my mind with one sensation and walk as though it were already a fact, I am promised (and I cannot find any denial of it in this great book) that I do not need more than a three day diet if I remain faithful to it.

But I must be honest about it. If I Change my diet in the course of the day, I extend the time interval.

You ask me, "But how do I know about the interval?" You, yourself determine the interval.

We have today in our modern world a little word which confuses most of us. I know it confused me until I dug deeper. The word is "action." Action is supposed to be the most fundamental thing in the world. It is not an atom, it is more fundamental. It is not a part of an atom like an electron, it is more fundamental than that. They call it the fourth-dimensional unit. The most fundamental thing in the world is action.

You ask, "What is action?" Our physicists tell us that it is energy multiplied by time. We become more confused and say, "Energy multiplied by time, what does that mean?', They answer, "There is no response to a stimulus, no matter how intense the stimulus, unless it endures for a certain length of time." There must be a minimum endurance to the stimulus

1948 Lessons – Lesson 3 – Thinking Fourth-Dimensionally

or there is no response. On the other hand there is no response to time unless there is a minimum degree of intensity. Today the most fundamental thing in the world is called action, or simply energy multiplied by time.

The Bible gives it as three days; the duration is three days for response in this world.

If I would now assume I AM what I want to be, and if I AM faithful to it and walk as though I were, the very longest stretch given for its realization is three days.

If there is something tonight that you really want in this world, then experience in Imagination what you would experience in the flesh were you to realize your goal and deafen your ears, and blind your eyes to all that denies the reality of your assumption.

If you do this you would be able to tell me before I leave this city of Los Angeles that you have realized what was only a wish when you came here. It will be my joy to rejoice with you in the knowledge that the child which was seemingly dead is now alive.

This damsel really was not dead, she was only asleep. You fed her in this silence because you have meat no one else knows of. You gave her food and she became a resurrected living reality within your world. Then you can share your joy with me and I can rejoice in your joy.

The purpose of these lessons is to remind you of the law of your own being, the law of consciousness; you are that law. You were only unconscious of its operation. You fed and

1948 Lessons – Lesson 3 – Thinking Fourth-Dimensionally

kept alive the things you did not wish to express within this world.

Take my challenge and put this philosophy to the test. If it does not work you should not use it as a comforter. If it is not true, you must completely discard it. I know it is true. You will not know it until you try either to prove or disprove it.

Too many of us have joined "isms" and we are afraid to put them to the test because we feel we might fail; and, then, where are we? Not really wanting to know the truth concerning it, we hesitate to be bold enough to put it to the test. You say, "I know it would work in some other way. I do not want to really test it. While I have not yet disproved it, I can still be comforted by it.

Now do not fool yourself, do not think for one second be that you are wise.

Prove or disprove this law. I know that if you attempt to disprove it, you will prove it, and I will be the richer for your proving it, not in dollars, not in things, but because you become the living fruit of what I believe I am teaching in this world. It is far better to have you a successful, satisfied person after five days of instruction than to have you go out dissatisfied. I hope you will be bold enough to challenge this instruction and either prove or disprove it.

Now before we go into the silence period I shall briefly explain the technique again. We have two techniques in applying this law. Everyone here must now know exactly what he wants. You must know that if you do not get it

1948 Lessons – Lesson 3 – Thinking Fourth-Dimensionally

tonight you will still be as desirous tomorrow concerning this objective.

When you know exactly what you want, construct in your mind s eye a single, simple event which implies fulfillment of your desire, an event where in self predominates. Instead of sitting back and looking at yourself as though you were on the screen, you be the actor in the drama.

Restrict the event to one single action. If you are going to shake a hand because that implies fulfillment of your desire then do that and that only. Do not shake hands and then wander off in your Imagination to a dinner party or to some other place. Restrict your action to simply shaking hands and do it over and over again, until that handshake takes on the solidity and the distinctness of reality.

If you feel you cannot remain faithful to an action, I want you now to define your objective, and then condense the idea, which is your desire, into a single phrase, a phrase which implies fulfillment of your desire, some phrase such as, "Isn't it wonderful?"

Or if I felt thankful because I thought someone was instrumental in bringing my desire to pass, I could say, "Thank you," and repeat it with feeling over and over again like a lullaby until my mind was dominated by the single sensation of thankfulness.

We will now sit quietly in these chairs with the idea which implies fulfillment of our desire condensed to a single phrase, or to a single act.

1948 Lessons – Lesson 3 – Thinking Fourth-Dimensionally

We will relax and immobilize our physical bodies. Then let us experience in Imagination the sensation which our condensed phrase or action affirms.

If you imagine yourself shaking another person's hand, do not use your physical hand, let it remain immobilized. But imagine that housed within your hand is a more subtle, more real hand, which can be extracted in your Imagination. Put your imaginary hand into the imaginary hand of your friend who stands before you and feel the handshake. Keep your physical body immobilized even though you become mentally active in what you are now about to do.

Now we will go into the silence.

1948 Lessons – Lesson 4 – No One To Change But Self

Lesson 4 – No One To Change But Self

May I take just a minute to clarify what was said last night. A lady felt from what I said last night that I am anti one nation. I do hope that I am not anti any nation, race or belief. If perchance I used a nation, it was only to illustrate a point.

What I tried to tell you was this . . we become what we contemplate.

For it is the nature of love, as it is the nature of hate, to change us into the likeness of that which we contemplate.

Last night I simply read a news item to show you that when we think we can destroy our image by breaking the mirror, we are only fooling ourselves.

When, through war or revolution, we destroy titles which to us represent arrogance and greed, we become in time the embodiment of that which we thought we had destroyed. So today the people who thought they destroyed the tyrants are themselves that which they thought they had destroyed.

That I may not be misunderstood, let me again lay the foundation of this principle.

Consciousness is the one and only reality. We are incapable of seeing other than the contents of our own consciousness

Therefore, hate betrays us in the hour of victory and condemns us to be that which we condemn. All conquest results in an exchange of characteristics, so that conquerors become like the conquered foe. We hate others for the evil which is in ourselves. Races, nations, and religious groups have lived for centuries in intimate hostility, and it is the nature of hatred, as it is the nature of love, to change us into the likeness of that which we contemplate.

Nations act toward other nations as their own citizen's act toward each other. When slavery exists in a state and that nation attacks another it is with intent to enslave. When there is a fierce economic competition between citizen and citizen, then in war with another nation the object of the war is to destroy the trade of the enemy. Wars of domination are brought about by the will of those who within a state are dominant over the fortunes of the rest.

We radiate the world that surrounds us by the intensity of our Imagination and feeling. But in this third-dimensional world of ours time beats slowly. And so we do not always observe the relationship of the visible world to our inner nature.

Now that is really what I meant. I thought I had said it. That I may not be misunderstood, that is my principle. You and I can contemplate an ideal, and become it by falling in love with it.

On the other hand we can contemplate something we heartily dislike and by condemning it we will become it. But because of the slowness of time in this three-dimensional world, when we do become what we contemplated we have forgotten that formerly we set out to worship or destroy it.

1948 Lessons – Lesson 4 – No One To Change But Self

Tonight's lesson is the capstone of the Bible, so do give me your attention. The most important question asked in the Bible will be found in the 16th chapter of the Gospel of St. Matthew.

As you know, all of the Bible stories are your stories; its characters live only in the mind of man. They have no reference at all to any person, who lived in time and space, or to any event that ever occurred upon earth.

The drama related in Matthew takes place in this manner Jesus turns to his disciples and asks them, "Whom do men say that I the Son of man am?"

"And they said, Some say that thou art John the Baptist: some, Elias; and others, Jeremiah, or one of the prophets."

"He saith unto them, But whom say ye that I AM?"

"And Simon Peter answered and said, Thou are the Christ, the Son of the living God."

"And Jesus answered and said unto him, Blessed art thou, Simon Bar-Jonah: for flesh and blood hath not revealed it unto thee, but my Father which is in heaven."

"And I say also unto thee that thou art Peter, and upon this rock I will build my church."

Jesus turning to his disciples is man turning to his disciplined mind in self-contemplation.

1948 Lessons – Lesson 4 – No One To Change But Self

You ask yourself the question, "Whom do men say that I AM?"

In our language, "I wonder what men think of me?"

You answer, "Some say John come again, Some say Elias, others say Jeremiah, and still others a Prophet of old come again."

It is very flattering to be told that you are, or that you resemble, the great men of the past, but enlightened reason is not enslaved by public opinion.

It is only concerned with the truth so it asks itself another question, "But whom say ye that I AM?" In other words, "Who am I?"

If I AM bold enough to assume that I AM Christ Jesus, the answer will come back, "Thou are Christ Jesus."

When I can assume it and feel it and boldly live it, I will say to myself, "Flesh and blood could not have told me this. But my Father which is in Heaven revealed it unto me." Then I make this concept of Self the rock on which I establish my church, my world.

"If ye believe not that I AM He, ye shall die in your sins."

Because consciousness is the only reality I must assume that I AM already that which I desire to be. If I do not believe that I am already what I want to be, then I remain as I am and die in this limitation.

1948 Lessons – Lesson 4 – No One To Change But Self

Man is always looking for some prop on which to lean. He is always looking for some excuse to justify failure. This revelation gives man no excuse for failure.

His concept of himself is the cause of all the circumstances of his life.

All changes must first come from within himself; and if he does not change on the outside it is because he has not changed within.

But man does not like to feel that he is solely responsible for the conditions of his life.

"From that time many of his disciples went back, and walked no more with him."

"Then said Jesus unto the twelve, Will ye also go away?"

"Then Simon Peter answered him, Lord, to whom shall we go? Thou hast the words of eternal life." John 6:66-68

I may not like what I have just heard, that I must turn to my own consciousness as to the only reality, the only foundation on which all phenomena can be explained. It was easier living when I could blame another. It was much easier living when I could blame society for my ills, or point a finger across the sea. and blame another nation. It was easier living when I could blame the weather for the way I feel.

But to tell me that I am the cause of all that happens to me that I am forever molding my world in harmony with my inner nature, that is more than man is willing to accept. If this is true, to whom would I go? If these are the words of

1948 Lessons – Lesson 4 – No One To Change But Self

eternal life, I must return to them, even though they seem so difficult to digest.

When man fully understands this, he knows that public opinion does not matter, for men only tell him who he is. The behavior of men constantly tells me who I have conceived myself to be.

If I accept this challenge and begin to live by it, I finally reach the point that is called the great prayer of the Bible. It is related in the 17th chapter of the Gospel of St. John, "I have finished the work which thou gavest me to do."

"And now, O Father, glorify thou me with thine own self with the glory which I had with thee before the world was."

"While I was with them in the world, I kept them in thy name: those that thou gavest me I have kept, and none of them is lost, but the son of perdition."

It is impossible for anything to be lost. In this divine economy nothing can be lost, it cannot even pass away. The little flower which has bloomed once, blooms forever. It is invisible to you here with your limited focus, but it blooms forever in the larger dimension of your being, and tomorrow you will encounter it.

All that thou gavest me I have kept in thy name, and none have I lost save the son of perdition.

The son of perdition means simply the belief in loss.

Son is a concept, an idea. Perdido is loss.

1948 Lessons – Lesson 4 – No One To Change But Self

I have only truly lost the concept of loss, for nothing can be lost.

I can descend from the sphere where the thing itself now lives, and as I descend in consciousness to a lower level within myself it passes from my world. I say, "I have lost my health. I have lost my wealth. I have lost my standing in the community. I have lost faith. I have lost a thousand things." But the things in themselves, having once been real in my world, can never cease to be. They never become unreal with the passage of time.

I, by my descent in consciousness to a lower level, cause these things to disappear from my sight and I say, "They have gone; they are finished as far as my world goes."

All I need do is to ascend to the level where they are eternal, and they once more objectify themselves and appear as realities within my world.

The crux of the whole 17th chapter of the Gospel of St. John is found in the 19th verse, "And for their sake I sanctify myself, that they also might be sanctified through the truth."

Heretofore I thought I could change others through effort. Now I know I cannot change another unless I first change myself.

To change another within my world I must first change my concept of that other; and to do it best I change my concept of self. For it was the concept I held of self that made me see others as I did.

1948 Lessons – Lesson 4 – No One To Change But Self

Had I a noble, dignified concept of myself, I never could have seen the unlovely in others.

Instead of trying to change others through argument and force, let me but ascend in consciousness to a higher level and I will automatically change others by changing self.

"There is no one to change but self; that self is simply your awareness, your consciousness and the world in which it lives is determined by the concept you hold of self.

It is to consciousness that we must turn as to the only reality. For there is no clear conception of the origin of phenomena except that consciousness is all and all is consciousness.

You need no helper to bring you what you seek. Do not for one second believe that I am advocating escape from reality when I ask you to simply assume you are now the man or the lady that you want to be.

If you and I could feel what it would be like were we now that which we want to be, and live in this mental atmosphere as though it were real, then, in a way we do not know, our assumption would harden into fact.

This is all we need do in order to ascend to the level where our assumption is already an objective, concrete reality.

I need change no man, I sanctify myself and in so doing I sanctify others. To the pure all things are pure. "There is nothing unclean of itself: but to him that esteemeth anything to be unclean, to him it is unclean."

1948 Lessons – Lesson 4 – No One To Change But Self

There is nothing in itself unclean, but you, by your concept of self, see things either clean or unclean.

"I and my Father are one."

"If I do not the works of my Father, believe me not."

"But if I do, though ye believe not me, believe the works: that ye may know, and believe, that the Father is in me, and I in him.'

He made himself one with God and thought it not strange or robbery to do the works of God.

You always bear fruit in harmony with what you are. It is the most natural thing in the world for a pear tree to bear pears, an apple tree to bear apples, and for man to mold the circumstances of his life in harmony with his inner nature.

"I AM the vine, ye are the branches."

A branch has no life save it be rooted in the vine. All I need do to change the fruit is to change the vine.

You have no life in my world save that I AM conscious of you.

You are rooted in me and, like fruit, you bear witness of the vine that I AM.

There is no reality in the world other than your consciousness.

1948 Lessons – Lesson 4 – No One To Change But Self

Although you may now seem to be what you do not want to be, all you need do to change it, and to prove the change by circumstances in your world, is to quietly assume that you are that which you now want to be, and in a way you do not know you will become it.

There is no other way to change this world. "I AM the way." My I AMness, my consciousness is the way by which I change my world.

As I change my concept of self, I change my world. When men and women help or hinder us, they only play the part that we, by our concept of self, wrote for them, and they play it automatically. They must play the parts they are playing because we are what we are.

You will change the world only when you become the embodiment of that which you want the world to be.

You have but one gift in this world that is truly yours to give and that is yourself. Unless you yourself are that which you want the world to be, you will never see it in this world.

"Except ye believe not that I AM He, ye shall die in your sins."

Do you know that no two in this room live in the same world. We are going home to different worlds tonight. We close our doors on entirely different worlds. We rise tomorrow and go to work, where we meet each other and meet others, but we live in different mental worlds, different physical worlds.

1948 Lessons – Lesson 4 – No One To Change But Self

I can only give what I AM, I have no other gift to give. If I want the world to be perfect, and who does not, I have failed only because I did not know that I could never see it perfect until I myself become perfect.

If I am not perfect I cannot see perfection, but the day that I become it, I beautify my world because I see it through my own eyes. "Unto the pure all things are pure."

No two here can tell me that you have heard the same message any one night. The one thing that you must do is hear what I say through that which you are. It must be filtered through your prejudices, your superstitions, and your concept of self. Whatever you are, it must come through that, and be colored by what you are.

If you are disturbed and you would like me to be something other than what I appear to be, then you must be that which you want me to be. We must become the thing that we want others to be or we will never see them be it.

Your consciousness, my consciousness, is the only true foundation in the world.

This is that which is called Peter in the Bible, not a man, this faithfulness that cannot turn to anyone, that cannot be flattered when you are told by men you are John come again.

That is very flattering to be told you are John the Baptist come again, or the great Prophet Elias, or Jeremiah.

Then I deafen my ears to this very flattering little bit of news men would give me and I ask myself, "But honestly who am I?"

1948 Lessons – Lesson 4 – No One To Change But Self

If I can deny the limitations of my birth, my environment, and the belief that I am but an extension of my family tree, and feel within myself that I AM Christ, and sustain this assumption until it takes a central place and forms the habitual center of my energy, I will do the works attributed to Jesus.

Without thought or effort I will mold a world in harmony with that perfection which I have assumed and feel springing within me.

When I open the eyes of the blind, unstop the ears of the deaf, give joy for mourning and beauty for ashes, then and only then, have I truly established this vine deep within. That is what I would automatically do were I truly conscious of being Christ. It is said of this presence, He proved that He was Christ by His works.

Our ordinary alterations of consciousness, as we pass from one state to another, are not transformations, because each of them is so rapidly succeeded by another in the reverse direction; but whenever our assumption grows so stable as to definitely expel its rivals, then that central habitual concept defines our character and is a true transformation.

Jesus, or enlightened reason, saw nothing unclean in the woman taken in adultery. He said to her, "Hath no man condemned thee?"

"She said, No man, Lord. And Jesus said unto her, neither do I condemn thee; go, and sin no more."

1948 Lessons – Lesson 4 – No One To Change But Self

No matter what is brought before the presence of beauty, it sees only beauty. Jesus was so completely identified with the lovely that He was incapable of seeing the unlovely.

When you and I really become conscious of being Christ, we too will straighten the arms of the withered, and resurrect the dead hopes of men.

We will do all the things that we could not do when we felt ourselves limited by our family tree.

It is a bold step and should not be taken lightly, because to do it is to die. John, the man of three dimensions is beheaded, or loses his three-dimensional focus that Jesus, the fourth-dimensional Self may live.

Any enlargement of our concept of Self involves a somewhat painful parting with strongly rooted hereditary conceptions.

The ligaments are strong that hold us in the womb of conventional limitations.

All that you formerly believed, you no longer believe.

You know now that there is no power outside of your own consciousness.

Therefore you cannot turn to anyone outside of self.

You have no ears for the suggestion that something else has power in it.

1948 Lessons – Lesson 4 – No One To Change But Self

You know the only reality is God, and God is your own consciousness. There is no other God. Therefore on this rock you build the everlasting church and boldly assume you are this Divine Being, self-begotten because you dared to appropriate that which was not given to you in your cradle, a concept of Self not formed in your mother's womb, a concept of self conceived outside of the offices of man.

The story is beautifully told us in the Bible using the two sons of Abraham: one the blessed, Isaac, born outside of the offices of man and the other, Ishmael, born in bondage.

Sarah was much too old to beget a child, so her husband Abraham went in unto the bondservant Hagar, the pilgrim, and she conceived of the old man and bore him a son called Ishmael. Ishmael's hand was against every man and every man's hand against him.

Every child born of woman is born into bondage, born into all that his environment represents, regardless of whether it be the throne of England, the White House, or any great place in the world. Every child born of woman is personified as this Ishmael, the child of Hagar.

But asleep in every child is the blessed Isaac, who is born outside of the offices of man, and is born through faith alone. This second child has no earthly father. He is Self-begotten.

What is the second birth?

I find myself man, I cannot go back into my mother's womb, and yet I must be born a second time. "Except a man be born again he cannot enter the kingdom of God."

1948 Lessons – Lesson 4 – No One To Change But Self

I quietly appropriate that which no man can give me, no woman can give me. I dare to assume that I AM God.

This must be of faith, this must be of promise. Then I become the blessed, I become Isaac.

As I begin to do the things that only this presence could do, I know that I AM born out of the limitations of Ishmael, and I have become heir to the kingdom.

Ishmael could not inherit anything, although his father was Abraham, or God.

Ishmael did not have both parents of the godly; his mother was Hagar the bond-woman, and so he could not partake of his father's estate.

You are Abraham and Sarah, and contained within your own consciousness there is one waiting for recognition.

In the Old Testament it is called Isaac, and in the New Testament it is called Jesus, and it is born without the aid of man.

No man can tell you that you are Christ Jesus, no man can tell you and convince you that you are God. You must toy with the idea and wonder what it would be like to be God.

No clear conception of the origin of phenomena is possible except that consciousness is all and all is consciousness. Nothing can be evolved from man that was not potentially involved in his nature. The ideal we serve and hope to attain could never be evolved from us were it not potentially involved in our nature.

1948 Lessons – Lesson 4 – No One To Change But Self

Let me now retell and emphasize an experience of mine printed by me two years ago under the title, THE SEARCH. I think it will help you to understand this law of consciousness, and show you that you have no one to change but self, for you are incapable of seeing other than the contents of your own consciousness.

Once in an idle interval at sea, I meditated on "the perfect state," and wondered what I would be, were I of too pure eyes to behold iniquity, if to me all things were pure and were I without condemnation. As I became lost in this fiery brooding, I found myself lifted above the dark environment of the senses. So intense was feeling I felt myself a being of fire dwelling in a body of air. Voices, as from a heavenly chorus, with the exaltation of those who had been conquerors in a conflict with death, were singing, "He is risen . . He is risen," and intuitively I knew they meant me.

Then I seemed to be walking in the night. I soon came upon a scene that might have been the ancient Pool of Bethesda for in this place lay a great multitude of impotent folk . . blind, halt, withered . . waiting not for the moving of the water as of tradition, but waiting for me.

As I came near, without thought or effort on my part, they were one after the other, molded as by the Magician of the Beautiful. Eyes, hands, feet . . all missing members . . were drawn from some invisible reservoir and molded in harmony with that perfection which I felt springing within me. When all were made perfect the chorus exulted, "It is finished."

1948 Lessons – Lesson 4 – No One To Change But Self

I know this vision was the result of my intense meditation upon the idea of perfection, for my meditations invariably bring about union with the state contemplated.

I had been so completely absorbed within the idea that for awhile I had become what I contemplated, and the high purpose with which I had for that moment identified myself drew the companionship of high things and fashioned the vision in harmony with my inner nature.

The ideal with which we are united works by association of ideas to awaken a thousand moods to create a drama in keeping with the central idea.

My mystical experiences have convinced me that there is no way to bring about the perfection we seek other than by the transformation of ourselves.

As soon as we succeed in transforming ourselves, the world will melt magically before our eyes and reshape itself in harmony with that which our transformation affirms.

We fashion the world that surrounds us by the intensity of our Imagination and feeling, and we illuminate or darken our lives by the concepts we hold of ourselves.

Nothing is more important to us than our conception of ourselves, and especially is true of our concept of the deep, dimensionally greater One within us.

Those that help or hinder us, whether they know it or not, are the servants of that law which shapes outward circumstances in harmony with our inner nature.

1948 Lessons – Lesson 4 – No One To Change But Self

It is our conception of ourselves which frees or constrains us, though it may use material agencies to achieve its purpose.

Because life molds the outer world to reflect the inner arrangement of our minds, there is no way of bringing about the outer perfection we seek other than by the transformation of ourselves.

No help cometh from without: the hills to which we lift our eyes are those of an inner range.

It is thus to our own consciousness that we must turn as to the only reality, the only foundation on which all phenomena can be explained. We can rely absolutely on the justice of this law to give us only that which is of the nature of ourselves.

To attempt to change the world before we change our concept of ourselves is to struggle against the nature of things. There can be no outer change until there is first an inner change.

As within, so without.

I am not advocating philosophical indifference when I suggest that we should imagine ourselves as already that which we want to be, living in a mental atmosphere of greatness, rather than using physical means and arguments to bring about the desired changes.

Everything we do, unaccompanied by a change of consciousness, is but futile readjustment of surfaces. However we toil or struggle, we can receive no more than our

1948 Lessons – Lesson 4 – No One To Change But Self

concepts of Self affirm. To protest against anything which happens to us is to protest against the law of our being and our ruler ship over our own destiny.

The circumstances of my life are too closely related to my conception of myself not to have been formed by my own spirit from some dimensionally larger storehouse of my being. If there is pain to me in these happenings, I should look within myself for the cause, for I am moved here and there and made to live in a world in harmony with my concept of myself.

If we would become as emotionally aroused over our ideas as we become over our dislikes, we would ascend to the plane of our ideal as easily as we now descend to the level of our hates.

Love and hate have a magical transforming power, and we grow through their exercise into the likeness of what we contemplate. By intensity of hatred we create in ourselves the character we imagine in our enemies. Qualities die for want of attention, so the unlovely states might best be rubbed out by imagining "'beauty for ashes and joy for mourning" rather than by direct attacks on the state from which we would be free.

"Whatsoever things are lovely and of good report, think on these things," for we become that with which we are en rapport.

There is nothing to change but our concept of self. As soon as we succeed in transforming self, our world will dissolve and reshape itself in harmony with that which our change affirms.

1948 Lessons – Lesson 4 – No One To Change But Self

I, by descent in consciousness, have brought about the imperfection that I see. In the divine economy nothing is lost. We cannot lose anything save by descent in consciousness from the sphere where the thing has its natural life.

And now, O Father, glorify thou me with thine own self with the glory which I had with thee before the world was."

As I ascend in consciousness the power and the glory that was mine return to me and I too will say "I have finished the work thou gavest me to do." The work is to return from my descent in consciousness, from the level wherein I believed that I was a son of man, to the sphere where I know that I am one with my Father and my Father is God.

I know beyond all doubt that there is nothing for man to do but to change his own concept of himself to assume greatness and sustain this assumption.

If we walk as though we were already the ideal we serve, we will rise to the level of our assumption, and find a world in harmony with our assumption. We will not have to lift a finger to make it so, for it is already so. It was always so.

You and I have descended in consciousness to the level where we now find ourselves and we see imperfection because we have descended!

When we begin to ascend while here in this three-dimensional world, we find that we move in an entirely different environment, we have entirely different circles of friends, and an entirely different world while still living here. We know the great mystery of the statement, "I am in the world but not of it."

1948 Lessons – Lesson 4 – No One To Change But Self

Instead of changing things I would suggest to all to identify themselves with the ideal they contemplate.

What would the feeling be like were you of too pure eyes to behold iniquity if to you all things were pure and you were without condemnation? Contemplate the ideal state and identify yourself with it and you will ascend to the sphere where you as Christ have your natural life.

You are still in that state where you were before the world was. The only thing that has fallen is your concept of self.

You see the broken parts which really are not broken. You are seeing them through distorted eyes, as though you were in one of those peculiar amusement gallery's where a man walks before a mirror and he is elongated, yet he is the same man. Or he looks into another mirror and he is all big and fat. These things are seen today because man is what he is.

Toy with the idea of perfection. Ask no man to help you, but let the prayer of the 17th chapter of the Gospel of St. John be your prayer. Appropriate the state that was yours before the world was.

Know the truth of the statement, "None have I lost save the son of perdition." Nothing is lost in all my holy mountain.

The only thing that you lose is the belief in loss or the son of perdition.

"And for their sake I sanctify myself, that they also might be sanctified through the truth."

1948 Lessons – Lesson 4 – No One To Change But Self

There is no one to change but self. All you need do to make men and women holy in this world is to make yourself holy. You are incapable of seeing anything that is unlovely when you establish within your own mind's eye the fact that you are lovely.

It is far better to know this than to know anything else in the world.

It takes courage, boundless courage, because many this night, after having heard this truth will still be inclined to blame others for their predicament.

Man finds it so difficult to turn to himself, to his own consciousness as to the only reality. Listen to these words:

"No man can come to me, except the Father which hath sent me draw him."

"I and my Father are one."

"A man can receive nothing, except it be given him from heaven."

"Therefore doth my Father love me, because I lay down my life, that I might take it again."

"No man taketh it from me, but I lay it down of myself." John

"You did not choose me, I have chosen you." My concept of myself molds a world in harmony with itself and draws men to tell me constantly by their behavior who I AM.

1948 Lessons – Lesson 4 – No One To Change But Self

The most important thing in this world to you is your concept of self.

When you dislike your environment, the circumstances of life and the behavior of men, ask yourself, " Who am I?" It is your answer to this question that is the cause of your dislikes.

If you do not condemn self there will be no man in your world to condemn you.

If you are living in the consciousness of your ideal you will see nothing to condemn. "To the pure all things are pure."

Now I would like to spend a little time making as clear as I can what I personally do when I pray, what I do when I want to bring about changes in my world. You will find it interesting, and you will find that it works. No one here can tell me they cannot do it. It is so very simple all can do it. We are what we imagine we are.

This technique is not difficult to follow, but you must want to do it. You cannot approach it with the attitude of mind "Oh well I'll try it." You must want to do it, because the mainspring of action is desire.

Desire is the mainspring of all action. Now what do I want? I must define my objective. For example, suppose I wanted now to be elsewhere. This very moment I really desire to be elsewhere. I need not go through the door, I need not sit down. I need do nothing but stand just where I am and with my eyes closed, assume that I am actually standing where I desire to be. Then I remain in this state until it has

1948 Lessons – Lesson 4 – No One To Change But Self

the feeling of reality. Were I now elsewhere I could not see the world as I now see it from here. The world changes in its relationship to me as I change my position in space.

So I stand right here, close my eyes, and imagine I am seeing what I would see, were I there. I remain in it long enough to feel it to be real. I cannot touch the walls of this room from here, but when you close your eyes and become still you can imagine and feel that you touch it. You can stand where you are and imagine you are putting your hand on that wall. To prove you really are, put it there and slide it up and feel the wood. You can imagine you are doing it without getting off your seat. You can do it and you will actually feel it if you become still enough and intense enough

I stand where I am and I allow the world that I want to see and to enter physically to come before me as though I were there now. In other words, I bring elsewhere here by assuming that I am there.

Is that clear? I let it come up, I do not make it come up. I simply imagine I am there and then let it happen.

If I want a physical presence, I imagine he is standing here, and I touch him All through the Bible I find these suggestions, "He placed his hands upon them. He touched them."

If you want to comfort someone, what is the automatic feeling? To put your hand on them, you cannot resist it. You meet a friend and the hand goes out automatically, you either shake hands or put your hand on his shoulder.

1948 Lessons – Lesson 4 – No One To Change But Self

Suppose you were now to meet a friend that you have not seen for a year and he is a friend of whom you are very fond. What would you do? You would embrace him, wouldn't you? Or you would put your hand upon him.

In your Imagination bring him close enough to put your hand upon him and feel him to be solidly real. Restrict the action to just that. You will be amazed at what happens. From then on things begin to move. Your dimensionally greater self will inspire, in all, the ideas and actions necessary to bring you into physical contact. It works that way.

Every day I put myself into the drowsy state; it is a very easy thing to do. But habit is a strange thing in man's world. It is not law, but habit acts as though it were the most compelling law in the world. We are creatures of habit.

If you create an interval every day into which you put yourself into the drowsy state, say at 3 o'clock in the afternoon do you know at that moment every day you will feel drowsy. You try it for one week and see if I am not right.

You sit down for the purpose of creating a state akin to sleep, as though you were sleepy, but do not push the drowsiness too far, just far enough to relax and leave you in control of the direction of your thoughts. You try it for one week, and every day at that hour, no matter what you are doing, you will hardly be able to keep your eyes open. If you know the hour when you will be free you can create it. I would not suggest that you do it lightly, because you will feel very, very sleepy and you may not want to.

1948 Lessons – Lesson 4 – No One To Change But Self

I have another way of praying. In this case I always sit down and I find the most comfortable arm chair imaginable, or I lie flat on my back and relax completely. Make yourself comfortable. You must not be in any position where the body is distressed.

Always put yourself into a position where you have the greatest ease. That is the first stage.

To know what you want is the start of prayer.

Secondly you construct in your mind's eye one single little event which implies that you have realized your desire.

I always let my mind roam on many things that could follow the answered prayer and I single out one that is most likely to follow the fulfillment of my desire.

One simple little thing like the shaking of a hand, embracing a person, the receiving of a letter, the writing of a check, or whatever would imply the fulfillment of your desire.

After you have decided on the action which implies that your desire has been realized, then sit in your nice comfortable chair or lie flat on your back, close your eyes for the simple reason it helps to induce this state that borders on sleep.

The minute you feel this lovely drowsy state, or the feeling of gathered togetherness, wherein you feel- I could move if I wanted to, but I do not want to, I could open my eyes if I wanted to, but I do not want to. When you get that feeling you can be quite sure that you are in the perfect state to pray successfully.

1948 Lessons – Lesson 4 – No One To Change But Self

In this feeling it is easy to touch anything in this world. You take the simple little restricted action which implies fulfillment of your prayer and you feel it or you enact it. Whatever it is, you enter into the action as though you were an actor in the part. You do not sit back and visualize yourself doing it. You do it.

With the body immobilized you imagine that the greater you inside the physical body is coming out of it and that you are actually performing the proposed action. If you are going to walk, you imagine that you are walking. Do not see yourself walk, FEEL that you are walking.

If you are going to climb stairs, FEEL that you are climbing the stairs. Do not visualize yourself doing it, feel yourself doing it. If you are going to shake a man's hand, do not visualize yourself shaking his hand, imagine your friend is standing before you and shake his hand. But leave your physical hands immobilized and imagine that your greater hand, which is your imaginary hand, is actually shaking his hand.

All you need do is to imagine that you are doing it.

You are stretched out in time, and what you are doing, which seems to be a controlled day dream, is an actual act in the greater dimension of your being.

You are actually encountering an event fourth-dimensionally before you encounter it here in the three-dimensions of space, and you do not have to raise a finger to bring that state to pass.

My third way of praying is simply to feel thankful.

1948 Lessons – Lesson 4 – No One To Change But Self

If I want something, either for myself or another, I immobilize the physical body, then I produce the state akin to sleep and in that state just feel happy, feel thankful, which thankfulness implies realization of what I want. I assume the feeling of the wish fulfilled and with my mind dominated by this single sensation I go to sleep. I need do nothing to make it so, because it is so. My feeling of the wish fulfilled implies it is done.

All these techniques you can use and change them to fit your temperament.

But I must emphasize the necessity of inducing the drowsy state where you can become attentive without effort.

A single sensation dominates the mind, if you pray successfully.

What would I feel like, now, were I what I want to be? When I know what the feeling would be like I then close my eyes and lose myself in that single sensation and my dimensionally greater Self then builds a bridge of incident to lead me from this present moment to the fulfillment of my mood. That is all you need do. But people have a habit of slighting the importance of simple things.

We are creatures of habit and we are slowly learning to relinquish our previous concepts, but the things we formerly lived by still in some way influence our behavior. Here is a story from the Bible that illustrates my point.

It is recorded that Jesus told his disciples to go to the crossroads and there they would find a colt, a young colt not yet ridden by a man. To bring the colt to him and if any man ask, "Why do you take this colt?" say, "The Lord has need of it."

They went to the crossroads and found the colt and did exactly as they were told. They brought the unbridled ass to Jesus and He rode it triumphantly into Jerusalem.

The story has nothing to do with a man riding on a little colt.

You are Jesus of the story. The colt is the mood you are going to assume.

That is the living animal not yet ridden by you.

What would the feeling be like were you to realize your desire? A new feeling, like a young Colt, is a very difficult thing to ride unless you ride him with a disciplined mind.

If I do not remain faithful to the mood the young colt throws me off. Every time you become conscious that you are not faithful to this mood, you have been thrown from the colt.

Discipline your mind that you may remain faithful to a high mood and ride it triumphantly into Jerusalem, which is fulfillment, or the city of peace.

This story precedes the feast of the Passover. If we would pass from our present state into that of our ideal, we must assume that we are already that which we desire to be and remain faithful to our assumption, for we must keep a high mood if we would walk with the highest.

1948 Lessons – Lesson 4 – No One To Change But Self

A fixed attitude of mind, a feeling that it is done will make it so.

If I walk as though it were, but every once in a while I look to see if it really is, then I fall off my mood or colt.

If I would suspend judgment like Peter I could walk on the water. Peter starts walking on the water, and then he begins to look unto his own understanding and he begins to go down. The voice said, "Look up, Peter." Peter looks up and he rises again and continues walking on the water.

Instead of looking down to see if this thing is really going to harden into fact, you simply know that it is already so, sustain that mood and you will ride the unbridled colt into the city of Jerusalem All of us must learn to ride the animal straight in to Jerusalem unassisted by a man. You do not need another to help you.

The strange thing is that as we keep the high mood and do not fall, others cushion the blows. They spread the palm leaves before me to cushion my journey. I do not have to be concerned. The shocks will be softened as I move into the fulfillment of my desire. My high mood awakens in others the ideas and actions which tend towards the embodiment of my mood. If you walk faithful to a high mood there will be no opposition and no competition.

The test of a teacher, or a teaching, is to be found in the faithfulness of the taught. I am leaving here on Sunday night. Do remain faithful to this instruction. If you look for causes outside the consciousness of man, then I have not convinced you of the reality of consciousness.

1948 Lessons – Lesson 4 – No One To Change But Self

If you look for excuses for failure you will always find them, for you find what you seek. If you seek an excuse for failure, you will find it in the stars, in the numbers, in the tea cup, or most any place. The excuse will not be there but you will find it to justify your failure.

Successful business and professional men and women know that this law works. You will not find it in gossip groups, but you will find it in courageous hearts.

Man's eternal journey is for one purpose: to reveal the Father. He comes to make visible his Father. And his Father is made visible in all the lovely things of this world. All the things that are lovely, that are of good report, ride these things, and have no time for the unlovely in this world, regardless of what it is.

Remain faithful to the knowledge that your consciousness, your I AMness, your awareness of being aware of the only reality. It is the rock on which all phenomena can be explained. There is no explanation outside of that. I know of no clear conception of the origin of phenomena save that consciousness is all and all is consciousness.

That which you seek is already housed within you. Were it not now within you eternity could not evolve it. No time stretch would be long enough to evolve what is not potentially involved in you.

You simply let it into being by assuming that it is already visible in your world, and remaining faithful to your assumption. it will harden into fact. Your Father has unnumbered ways of revealing your assumption. Fix this in your mind and always remember, "An assumption, though false, if sustained will harden into fact."

You and your Father are one and your Father is everything that was, is and will be. Therefore that which you seek you already are, it can never be so far off as even to be near, for nearness implies separation.

The great Pascal said, "You never would have sought me had you not already found me. "What you now desire you already have and you seek it only because you have already found it. You found it in the form of desire. It is just as real in the form of desire as it is going to be to your bodily organs.

You are already that which you seek and you have no one to change but Self in order to express it.

Now let us go into the silence.

1948 Lessons – Lesson 5 – Remain Faithful To Your Idea

Lesson 5 – Remain Faithful To Your Idea

Tonight we have the fifth and last lesson in this course. First I shall give you a sort of summary of what has gone before. Then, since so many of you have asked me to elaborate further on Lesson 3, I shall give you a few more ideas on thinking fourth-dimensionally.

I know that when a man sees a thing clearly he can tell it, he can explain it. This past winter in Barbados a fisherman, whose vocabulary would not encompass a thousand words, told me more in five minutes about the behavior of the dolphin than Shakespeare with his vast vocabulary could have told me, if he did not know the habits of the dolphin.

This fisherman told me how the dolphin loves to play on a piece of drift-wood, and in order to catch him, you throw the wood out and bait him as you would bait children, because he likes to pretend he is getting out of the water. As I said, this man's vocabulary was very limited, but he knew his fish, and he knew the sea. Because he knew his dolphin he could tell me all about their habits and how to catch them.

When you say you know a thing but you cannot explain it, I say you do not know it, for when you really know it you naturally express it.

If I should ask you now to define prayer, and say to you, "How would you, through prayer, go about realizing an objective, any objective?" If you can tell me, then you know it; but if you cannot tell me, then you do not know it. When

1948 Lessons – Lesson 5 – Remain Faithful To Your Idea

you see it clearly in the mind's eye the greater you will inspire the words which are necessary to clothe the idea and express it beautifully, and you will express the idea far better than a man with a vast vocabulary who does not see it as clearly as you do.

If you have listened carefully throughout the past four days, you know now that the Bible has no reference at all to any persons that ever existed, or to any events that ever occurred upon earth.

The authors of the Bible were not writing history, they were writing a great drama of the mind which they dressed up in the garb of history, and then adapted it to the limited capacity of the uncritical, unthinking masses.

You know that every story in the Bible is your story, that when the writers introduce dozens of characters in the same story they are trying to present you with different attributes of the mind that you may employ. You saw it as I took perhaps a dozen or more stories and interpreted them for you.

For instance, many people wonder how Jesus, the most gracious, the most loving man in the world, if he be man, could say to his mother, what he is supposed to have said to her as recorded in the second chapter of the Gospel of St. John. Jesus is made to say to his mother, "Woman, what have I to do with thee?"

You and I, who are not yet identified with the ideal we serve, would not make such a statement to our mother. Yet here was the embodiment of love saying to his mother, "Woman, what have I to do with thee?"

1948 Lessons – Lesson 5 – Remain Faithful To Your Idea

You are Jesus, and your mother is your own consciousness. For consciousness is the cause of all, therefore, it is the great father-mother of all phenomena.

You and I are creatures of habit. We get into the habit of accepting as final the evidence of our senses.

Wine is needed for the guests and my senses tell me that there is no wine, and I through habit am about to accept this lack as final.

When I remember that my consciousness is the one and only reality, therefore if I deny the evidence of my senses and assume the consciousness of having sufficient wine, I have in a sense rebuked my mother or the consciousness which suggested lack; and by assuming the consciousness of having what I desire for my guests, wine is produced in a way we do not know.

I have just read a note here from a dear friend of mine in the audience. Last Sunday he had an appointment at a church for a wedding; the clock told him he was late, everything told him he was late.

He was standing on a street corner waiting for a street car. There was none in sight. He imagined that, instead of being on the street corner, that he was in the church. At that moment a car stopped in front of him. My friend told the driver of his predicament and the driver said to him, "I am not going that way, but I will take you there." My friend got into the car and was at the church in time for the service. That is applying the law correctly, non-acceptance of the suggestion of lateness. Never accept the suggestion of lack.

1948 Lessons – Lesson 5 – Remain Faithful To Your Idea

In this case I say to myself, "What have I to do with thee?" What have I to do with the evidence of my senses? Bring me all the pots and fill them. In other words, I assume that I have wine and all that I desire. Then my dimensionally greater Self inspires in all, the thoughts and the actions which aid the embodiment of my assumption.

It is not a man saying to a mother, "Woman what have I to do with thee?" It is every man who knows this law who will say to himself, when his senses suggest lack, "what have I to do with thee. Get behind me." I will never again listen to a voice like that, because if I do, then I am impregnated by that suggestion and I will bear the fruit of lack.

We turn to another story in the Gospel of St. Mark where Jesus is hungry.

"And seeing a fig tree afar off having leaves, he came, if haply he might find anything thereon: and when he came to it, he found nothing but leaves; for the time of figs was not yet."

"And Jesus answered and said unto it, No man eat fruit of thee hereafter forever. And his disciples heard it."

"And in the morning, as they passed by, they saw the fig tree dried up from the roots."

What tree am I blasting? Not a tree on the outside. It is my own consciousness. "I AM the vine.". My consciousness, my I AMness is the great tree, and habit once more suggests emptiness, it suggests barrenness, it suggests four months before I can feast. But I cannot wait four months. I give myself this powerful suggestion that never again will I even for a moment believe that it will take four months to realize my desire. The belief in lack must from this day on be barren and never again reproduce itself in my mind.

It is not a man blasting a tree. Everything in the Bible takes place in the mind of man: the tree, the city, the people, everything. There is not a statement made in the Bible that does not represent some attribute of the human mind.

They are all personifications of the mind and not things within the world.

Consciousness is the one and only reality. There is no one to whom we can turn after we discover that our own awareness is God.

For God is the cause of all and there is nothing but God. You cannot say that a devil causes some things and God others.

Listen to these words.

"Thus saith the Lord to his anointed, to Cyrus, whose right hand I have holden, to subdue nations before him; and I will loose the loins of kings, to open before him the two leaved gates; and the gates shall not be shut."

"I will go before thee, and make the crooked places straight: I will break in pieces the gates of brass, and cut in sunder the bars of iron."

"And I will give thee the treasures of darkness, and hidden riches of secret places, that thou mayest know that I, the Lord, which call thee by thy name, am the God of Israel."

1948 Lessons – Lesson 5 – Remain Faithful To Your Idea

"I form the light, and create darkness: I make peace, and create evil: I the Lord do all these things."

"I have made the earth, and created man upon it: I, even my hands, have stretched out the heavens, and all their host have I commanded."

"I have raised him up in righteousness, and I will direct all his ways: he shall build my city, and he shall let go my captives, not for price nor reward, saith the Lord of hosts."

"I AM the Lord, and there is none else, there is no God beside me."

Read these words carefully. They are not my words, they are the inspired words of men who discovered that consciousness is the only reality.

If I am hurt, I am self hurt. If there is darkness in my world, I created the darkness and the gloom and the depression. If there is light and joy, I created the light and the joy.

There is no one but this I AMness that does all.

You cannot find a cause outside of your own consciousness. Your world is a grand mirror constantly telling you who you are. As you meet people, they tell you by their behavior who you are.

Your prayers will not be less devout because you turn to your own consciousness for help.

1948 Lessons – Lesson 5 – Remain Faithful To Your Idea

I do not think that any person in prayer feels more of the joy, the piety, and the feeling of adoration, than I do when I feel thankful, as I assume the feeling of my wish fulfilled, knowing at the same time it is to myself that I turned.

In prayer you are called upon to believe that you possess what your reason and your senses deny. When you pray believe that you have and you shall receive.

The Bible states it this way:

"Therefore I say unto you, What things soever ye desire, when ye pray, believe that ye receive them, and ye shall have them.

"And when ye stand praying, forgive, if ye have ought against any: that your Father also which is in heaven may forgive you your trespasses."

"But if ye do not forgive, neither will your Father which is in heaven forgive your trespasses."

That is what we must do when we pray. If I hold something against another, be it a belief of sickness, poverty, or anything else, I must loose it and let it go, not by using words of denial but by believing him to be what he desires to be. In that way I completely forgive him. I changed my concept of him. I had naught against him and I forgave him. Complete forgetfulness is forgiveness. If I do not forget then I have not forgiven.

I only forgive something when I truly forget. I can say to you until the end of time, "I forgive you." But if every time I see you or think of you, I am reminded of what I held against you, I have not forgiven you at all. Forgiveness is complete forgetfulness. You go to a doctor and he gives you something for your sickness. He is trying to take it from you, so he gives you something in place of it.

Give yourself a new concept of self for the old concept. Give up the old concept completely.

A prayer granted implies that something is done in consequence of the prayer which otherwise would not have been done. Therefore, I myself am the spring of action, the directing mind and the one who grants the prayer.

Anyone who prays successfully turns within, and appropriates the state sought. You have no sacrifice to offer.

Do not let anyone tell you that you must struggle and suffer. You need not struggle for the realization of your desire.

Read what it says in the Bible.

"To what purpose is the multitude of your sacrifices unto me saith the Lord: I am full of the burnt offerings of rams, and the fat of fed beasts; and I delight not in the blood of bullocks, or of lambs, or of he goats."

"When ye come to appear before me, who hath required that at your hand, to tread my courts?"

"Bring no more vain oblations; incense is an abomination unto me; the new moons and Sabbaths, the calling of assemblies, I cannot endure iniquity and solemn assembly."

1948 Lessons – Lesson 5 – Remain Faithful To Your Idea

"Your new moons and your appointed feasts my soul hates: they have become a burden to me, I am weary of bearing them"

"Ye shall have a song as in the night when a holy solemnity is kept; and gladness of heart, as when one goeth with a pipe to come into the mountain of the Lord, to the mighty One of Israel."

"Sing unto the Lord a new song, and his praise from the end of the earth."

"Sing, O ye heavens; for the Lord hath done it: shout, ye lower parts of the earth: break forth into singing, ye mountains, O forest, and every tree therein: for the Lord hath redeemed Jacob, and glorified himself in Israel."

"Therefore the redeemed of the Lord shall return, and come with singing unto Zion; and everlasting joy shall be upon their head. They shall obtain gladness and joy; and sorrow and mourning shall flee away."

The only acceptable gift is a joyful heart. Come with singing and praise. That is the way to come before the Lord . . your own consciousness. Assume the feeling of your wish fulfilled, and you have brought the only acceptable gift.

All states of mind other than that of the wish fulfilled are an abomination; they are superstition and mean nothing.

When you come before me, rejoice, because rejoicing implies that something has happened which you desired. Come before me singing, giving praise, and giving thanks, for these states of mind imply acceptance of the state sought.

1948 Lessons – Lesson 5 – Remain Faithful To Your Idea

Put yourself in the proper mood and your own consciousness will embody it.

If I could define prayer for anyone and put it just as clearly as I could, I would simply say, "It is the feeling of the wish fulfilled."

If you ask, "What do you mean by that?" I would say, "I would feel myself into the situation of the answered prayer and then I would live and act upon that conviction." I would try to sustain it without effort, that is, I would live and act as though it were already a fact, knowing that as I walk in this fixed attitude my assumption will harden into fact.

Time does not permit me to go any further into the argument that the Bible is not history.

But if you have listened attentively to my message these past four nights, I do not think you want any more proof that the Bible is not history.

Apply what you have heard and you will realize your desires.

"**And now I** have told you before it come to pass, that, when it is come to pass, ye might believe."

Many persons, myself included, have observed events before they occurred; that is, before they occurred in this world of three dimensions. Since man can observe an event before it occurs in the three dimensions of space, then life on earth proceeds according to plan; and this plan must exist elsewhere in another dimension and is slowly moving through our space.

If the occurring events were not in this world when they were observed, then to be perfectly logical they must have been out of this world. And whatever is THERE to be seen before it occurs HERE must be "pre-determined" from the point of view of man awake in a three-dimensional world.

Yet the ancient teachers taught us that we could alter the future, and my own experience confirms the truth of their teaching.

Therefore, my object in giving this course is to indicate possibilities inherent in man, to show that man can alter his: future; but, thus altered, it forms again a deterministic sequence starting from the point of interference . . a future that will be consistent with the alteration.

The most remarkable feature of man's future is its flexibility. The future, although prepared in advance in every detail, has several outcomes. We have at every moment of our lives the choice before us which of several futures we will have.

There are two actual outlooks on the world, possessed by everyone . . a natural focus and a spiritual focus.

The ancient teachers called the one "the carnal mind," and the other "the mind of Christ."

We may differentiate them as ordinary waking consciousness, governed by our senses, and a controlled Imagination, governed by desire.

1948 Lessons – Lesson 5 – Remain Faithful To Your Idea

We recognize these two distinct centers of thought in the statement: "The natural man receiveth not the things of the Spirit of God: for they are foolishness unto him: neither can he know them, because they are spiritually discerned."

The natural view confines reality to the moment called NOW. To the natural view, the past and future are purely imaginary. The spiritual view on the other hand sees the contents of time. The past and future are a present whole to the spiritual view.

What is mental and subjective to the natural man is concrete and objective to the spiritual man.

The habit of seeing only that which our senses permit renders us totally blind to what, otherwise, we could see.

To cultivate the faculty of seeing the invisible, we should often deliberately disentangle our minds from the evidence of the senses and focus our attention on an invisible state, mentally feeling it and sensing it until it has all the distinctness of reality.

Earnest, concentrated thought focused in a particular direction shuts out other sensations and causes them to disappear.

We have only to concentrate on the state desired in order to see it.

The habit of withdrawing attention from the region of sensation and concentrating it on the invisible develops our spiritual outlook and enables us to penetrate beyond the world of sense and to see that which is invisible. "For the invisible things of him from the creation of the world are clearly seen."

This vision is completely independent of the natural faculties. Open it and quicken it!

A little practice will convince us that we can, by controlling our Imagination, reshape our future in harmony with our desire. Desire is the mainspring of action. We could not move a single finger unless we had a desire to move it. No matter what we do, we follow the desire which at the moment dominates our minds. When we break a habit, our desire to break it is greater than our desire to continue the habit.

The desires which impel us to action are those which hold our attention. A desire is but an awareness of something we lack and need to make our life more enjoyable. Desires always have some personal gain in view, the greater the anticipated gain, the more intense is the desire. There is no absolutely unselfish desire. Where there is nothing to gain there is no desire, and consequently no action.

The spiritual man speaks to the natural man through the language of desire.

The key to progress in life and to the fulfillment of dreams lies in ready obedience to its voice. Unhesitating obedience to its voice is an immediate assumption of the wish fulfilled. To desire a state is to have it. As Pascal has said, "You would not have sought me had you not already found me."

1948 Lessons – Lesson 5 – Remain Faithful To Your Idea

Man, by assuming the feeling of his wish fulfilled, and then living and acting on this conviction, alters the future in harmony with his assumption. Assumptions awaken what they affirm. As soon as man assumes the feeling of his wish fulfilled, his fourth-dimensional Self finds ways for the attainment of this end, discovers methods for its realization.

I know of no clearer definition of the means by which we realize our desires than to *experience in the Imagination what we would experience in the flesh were we to achieve our goal.* This imaginary experience of the end with acceptance, wills the means. The fourth-dimensional Self then constructs with its larger outlook the means necessary to realize the accepted end.

The undisciplined mind finds it difficult to assume a state which is denied by the senses.

But here is a technique that makes it easy to "call things which are not seen as though they were," that is, to encounter an event before it occurs. People have a habit of slighting the importance of simple things. But this simple formula for changing the future was discovered after years of searching and experimenting.

The first step in changing the future is DESIRE, that is, define your objective . . know definitely what you want.

Secondly, construct an event which you believe you would encounter FOLLOWING the fulfillment of your desire . . an event which implies fulfillment of your desire . . something which will have the action of Self predominant.

1948 Lessons – Lesson 5 – Remain Faithful To Your Idea

Thirdly, immobilize the physical body, and induce a condition akin to sleep by imagining that you are sleepy. Lie on a bed, or relax in a chair. Then, with eyelids closed and your attention focused on the action you intend to experience in Imagination, mentally feel yourself right into the proposed action; imagining all the while that you are actually performing the action here and now.

You must always participate in the imaginary action; not merely stand back and look on, but feel that you are actually performing the action so that the imaginary sensation is real to you.

It is important always to remember that the proposed action must be one which FOLLOWS the fulfillment of your desire.

Also you must feel yourself into the action until it has all the vividness and distinctness of reality.

For example, suppose you desire promotion in your office. Being congratulated would be an event you would encounter following the fulfillment of your desire.

Having selected this action as the one you will experience in Imagination, immobilize the physical body; and induce a state akin to sleep, a drowsy state, but one in which you are still able to control the direction of your thoughts, a state in which you are attentive without effort. Then visualize a friend standing before you. Put your imaginary hand into his. Feel it to be solid and real, and carry on an imaginary conversation with him in harmony with the action.

1948 Lessons – Lesson 5 – Remain Faithful To Your Idea

You do not visualize yourself at a distance in point of space and at a distance in point of time being congratulated on your good fortune. Instead, you make elsewhere HERE, and the future NOW.

The future event is a reality NOW in a dimensionally larger world and oddly enough, now in a dimensionally larger world is equivalent to HERE in the ordinary three-dimensional space of everyday life.

The difference between FEELING yourself in action, here and now, and visualizing yourself in action, as though you were on a motion-picture screen, is the difference between success and failure.

The difference will be appreciated if you will now visualize yourself climbing a ladder. Then, with eyelids closed imagine that a ladder is right in front of you and FEEL yourself actually climbing it.

Desire, physical immobility bordering on sleep, and imaginary action in which Self feelingly predominates HERE AND NOW, are not only important factors in altering the future, but they are also essential conditions in consciously projecting the spiritual Self.

When the physical body is immobilized and we become possessed of the idea to do something . . if we imagine that we are doing it HERE AND NOW and keep the imaginary action feelingly going right up until sleep ensues . . we are likely to awaken out of the physical body to find ourselves in a dimensionally larger world with a dimensionally larger focus and actually doing what we desired and imagined we were doing in the flesh.

1948 Lessons – Lesson 5 – Remain Faithful To Your Idea

But whether we awaken there or not, we are actually performing the action in the fourth-dimensional world, and will in the future re-enact it here in the third-dimensional world.

Experience has taught me to restrict the imaginary action, to condense the idea which is to be the object of our meditation into a single act, and to re-enact it over and over again until it has the feeling of reality. Otherwise, the attention will wander off along an associational track, and hosts of associated images will be presented to our attention, and in a few seconds they will lead us hundreds of miles away from our objective in point of space, and years away in point of time.

If we decide to climb a particular flight of stairs, because that is the likely event to follow the realization of our desire, then we must restrict the action to climbing that particular flight of stairs. Should the attention wander off, bring it back to its task of climbing that flight of stairs, and keep on doing so until the imaginary action has all the solidity and distinctness of reality.

The idea must be maintained in the field of presentation without any sensible effort on our part.

We must, with the minimum of effort, permeate the mind with the feeling of the wish fulfilled.

Drowsiness facilitates change because it favors attention without effort, but it must not be pushed to the state of sleep, in which we shall no longer be able to control the movements of our attention, but a moderate degree of drowsiness in which we are still able to direct our thoughts.

1948 Lessons – Lesson 5 – Remain Faithful To Your Idea

A most effective way to embody a desire is to assume the feeling of the wish fulfilled and then, in a relaxed and sleepy state, repeat over and over again like a lullaby, any short phrase which implies fulfillment of your desire, such as, "Thank you, thank you, thank you, " until the single sensation of thankfulness dominates the mind. Speak these words as though you addressed a higher power for having done it for you.

If, however, we seek a conscious projection in a dimensionally larger world, then we must keep the action going right up until sleep ensues. Experience in Imagination with all the distinctness of reality what would be experienced in the flesh were we to achieve our goal and we shall in time meet it in the flesh as we met it in our Imagination.

Feed the mind with premises . . that is, assertions presumed to be true, because assumptions, though false, if persisted in until they have the feeling of reality, will harden into fact.

To an assumption, all means which promote its realization are good. It influences the behavior of all, by inspiring in all the movements, the actions, and the words which tend towards its fulfillment.

To understand how man molds his future in harmony with his assumption . . by simply experiencing in his Imagination what he would experience in reality were he to realize his goal . . we must know what we mean by a dimensionally larger world, for it is to a dimensionally larger world that we go to alter our future.

1948 Lessons – Lesson 5 – Remain Faithful To Your Idea

The observation of an event before it occurs implies that the event is predetermined from the point of view of man in the three-dimensional world. Therefore to change the conditions here in the three dimensions of space we must first change them in the four dimensions of space.

Man does not know exactly what is meant by a dimensionally larger world, and would no doubt deny the existence of a dimensionally larger Self. He is quite familiar with the three dimensions of length, width and height, and he feels that, if there were a fourth-dimension, it should be just as obvious to him as the dimensions of length, width and height.

Now a dimension is not a line. It is any way in which a thing can be measured that is entirely different from all other ways. That is, to measure a solid fourth-dimensionally, we simply measure it in any direction except that of its length, width and height. Now, is there another way of measuring an object other than those of its length, width and height?

Time measures my life without employing the three dimensions of length, width and height. There is no such thing as an instantaneous object. Its appearance and disappearance are measurable. It endures for a definite length of time. We can measure its life span without using the dimensions of length, width and height. Time is definitely a fourth way of measuring an object.

The more dimensions an object has, the more substantial and real it becomes. A straight line, which lies entirely in one dimension, acquires shape, mass and substance by the addition of dimensions. What new quality would time, the fourth dimension give, which would make it just as vastly superior to solids, as solids are to surfaces and surfaces are to lines? Time is a medium for changes in experience, for all changes take time.

The new quality is changeability. Observe that, if we bisect a solid, its cross section will be a surface; by bisecting a surface, we obtain a line, and by bisecting a line, we get a point. This means that a point is but a cross section of a line; which is, in turn, but across section of a surface; which is, in turn, but a cross section of a solid; which is, in turn, if carried to its logical conclusion, but across section of a four-dimensional object.

We cannot avoid the inference that all three-dimensional objects are but cross sections of four-dimensional bodies. Which means: when I meet you, I meet a cross section of the four-dimensional you . . the four-dimensional Self that is not seen. To see the four-dimensional Self I must see every cross section or moment of your life from birth to death, and see them all as co-existing.

My focus should take in the entire array of sensory impressions which you have experienced on earth, plus those you might encounter. I should see them, not in the order in which they were experienced by you, but as a present whole. Because CHANGE is the characteristic of the fourth dimension, I should see them in a state of flux . . as a living, animated whole.

Now, if we have all this clearly fixed in our minds, what does it mean to us in this three-dimensional world? It means that, if we can move along times length, we can see the future and alter it if we so desire.

1948 Lessons – Lesson 5 – Remain Faithful To Your Idea

This world, which we think so solidly real, is a shadow out of which and beyond which we may at any time pass. It is an abstraction from a more fundamental and dimensionally larger world . . a more fundamental world abstracted from a still more fundamental and dimensionally larger world . . and so on to infinity. For the absolute is unattainable by any means or analysis, no matter how many dimensions we add to the world.

Man can prove the existence of a dimensionally larger world by simply focusing his attention on an invisible state and imagining that he sees and feels it. If he remains concentrated in this state, his present environment will pass away, and he will awaken in a dimensionally larger world where the object of his contemplation will be seen as a concrete objective reality.

I feel intuitively that, were he to abstract his thoughts from this dimensionally larger world and retreat still farther within his mind, he would again bring about an externalization of time. He would discover that, every time he retreats into his inner mind and brings about an externalization of time, space becomes dimensionally larger. And he would therefore conclude that both time and space are serial, and that the drama of life is but the climbing of a multitudinous dimensional time block.

Scientists will one day explain WHY there is a Serial Universe.

But in practice HOW we use this Serial Universe to change the future, is more important.

1948 Lessons – Lesson 5 – Remain Faithful To Your Idea

To change the future, we need only concern ourselves with two worlds in the infinite series; the world we know by reason of our bodily organs, and the world we perceive independently of our bodily organs.

I have stated that man has at every moment of time the choice before him which of several futures he will have. But the question arises: "How is this possible when the experiences of man, awake in the three-dimensional world, are predetermined?" as his observation of an event before it occurs implies.

This ability to change the future will be seen if we liken the experiences of life on earth to this printed page. Man experiences events on earth singly and successively in the same way that you are now experiencing the words of this page.

Imagine that every word on this page represents a single sensory impression. To get the context, to understand my meaning, you focus your vision on the first word in the upper left-hand corner and then move your focus across the page from left to right, letting it fall on the words singly and successively. By the time your eyes reach the last word on this page you have extracted my meaning.

But suppose on looking at the page, with all the printed words thereon equally present, you decided to rearrange them. You could, by rearranging them, tell an entirely different story, in fact you could tell many different stories.

A dream is nothing more than uncontrolled four-dimensional thinking, or the rearrangement of both past and future sensory impressions. Man seldom dreams of events in

1948 Lessons – Lesson 5 – Remain Faithful To Your Idea

the order in which he experiences them when awake. He usually dreams of two or more events which are separated in time fused into a single sensory impression; or else he so completely rearranges his single waking sensory impressions that he does not recognize them when he encounters them in his waking state.

For example, I dreamed that I delivered a package to the restaurant in my apartment building. The hostess said to me, "You can't leave that there," whereupon, the elevator operator gave me a few letters and as I thanked him for them he, in turn, thanked me. At this point, the night elevator operator appeared and waved a greeting to me.

The following day, as I left my apartment, I picked up a few letters which had been placed at my door. On my way down I gave the day elevator operator a tip and thanked him for taking care of my mail, whereupon, he thanked me for the tip.

On my return home that day I overheard a doorman say to a delivery man, "You can't leave that there." As I was about to take the elevator up to my apartment, I was attracted by a familiar face in the restaurant, and as I looked in the hostess greeted me with a smile. That night I escorted my dinner guests to the elevator and as I said good-bye to them, the night operator waved good-night to me.

By simply rearranging a few of the single sensory impressions I was destined to encounter, and by fusing two or more of them into single sensory impressions, I constructed a dream which differed quite a bit from my waking experience.

1948 Lessons – Lesson 5 – Remain Faithful To Your Idea

When we have learned to control the movements of our attention in the four-dimensional world, we shall be able to consciously create circumstances in the three-dimensional world.

We learn this control through the waking dream, where our attention can be maintained without effort, for attention minus effort is indispensable to changing the future. We can, in a controlled waking dream, consciously construct an event which we desire to experience in the three-dimensional world.

The sensory impressions we use to construct our waking dream are present realities displaced in time or the four-dimensional world. All that we do in constructing the waking dream is to select from the vast array of sensory impressions those, which, when they are properly arranged, imply that we have realized our desire.

With the dream clearly defined we relax in a chair and induce a state of consciousness akin to sleep. A state which, although bordering on sleep, leaves us in conscious control of the movements of our attention. Then we experience in Imagination what we would experience in reality were this waking dream an objective fact.

In applying this technique to change the future it is important always to remember that the only thing which occupies the mind during the waking dream is THE WAKING DREAM, the predetermined action and sensation which implies the fulfillment of our desire.

1948 Lessons – Lesson 5 – Remain Faithful To Your Idea

How the waking dream becomes physical fact is not our concern. Our acceptance of the waking dream as physical reality wills the means for its fulfillment.

Let me again lay the foundation of prayer, which is nothing more than a controlled waking dream:

1. Define your objective, know definitely what you want.

2. Construct an event which you believe you will encounter FOLLOWING the fulfillment of your desire . . something which will have the action of Self predominant . . an event which implies the fulfillment of your desire.

3. Immobilize the physical body and induce a state of consciousness akin to sleep. Then, mentally feel yourself right into the proposed action, until the single sensation of fulfillment dominates the mind; imagining all the while that you are actually performing the action HERE AND NOW so that you experience in Imagination what you would experience in the flesh were you now to realize your goal. Experience has convinced me that this is the easiest way to achieve our goal.

However, my own many failures would convict me were I to imply that I have completely mastered the movements of my attention. But I can, with the ancient teacher, say:

"This one thing I do, forgetting those things which are behind, and reaching forth unto those things which are before, I press toward the mark for the prize."

1948 Lessons – Lesson 5 – Remain Faithful To Your Idea

Again I want to remind you that the responsibility to make what you have done real in this world is not on your shoulders.

Do not be concerned with the HOW, you have assumed that it is done, the assumption has its own way of objectifying itself.

All responsibility to make it so is removed from you.

There is a little statement in the book of Exodus which bears this out. Millions of people who have read it, or have had it mentioned to them throughout the centuries have completely misunderstood it.

It is said, "Steep not a kid in its mothers milk."

Unnumbered millions of people, misunderstanding this statement, to this very day in the enlightened age of 1948, will not eat any dairy products with a meat dish. It just is not done.

They think the Bible is history, and when it says, "Steep not a kid in its mother's milk," milk and the products of milk, butter and cheese, they will not take at the same time they take the kid or any kind of meat. In fact they even have separate dishes with which to cook their meat.

But you are now about to apply it psychologically.

You have done your meditation and you have assumed that you are what you want to be. Consciousness is God, your attention is like the very stream of life or milk itself that nurses and makes alive that which holds your attention. In other words, what holds your attention has your life.

Throughout the centuries a kid has been used as the symbol of sacrifice.

You have given birth to everything in your world. But there are things that you no longer wish to keep alive, although you have mothered and fathered them. You are a jealous father that can easily consume, like Cronus, his children. It is your right to consume what formerly you expressed when you did not know better.

Now you are detached in consciousness from that former state.

It was your kid, it was your child, you embodied and expressed it in your world. But now that you have assumed that you are what you want to be, do not look back on your former state and wonder HOW it will disappear from your world.

For if you look back and give attention to it, you are steeping once more that kid in its mother's milk.

Do not say to yourself, 'I wonder if I am really detached from that state," or "I wonder if so and so is true."

Give all your attention to the assumption that the thing is so, because all responsibility to make it so is completely removed from your shoulders.

You do not have to make it so, it IS so.

1948 Lessons – Lesson 5 – Remain Faithful To Your Idea

You appropriate what is already fact, and you walk in the assumption that it is, and in a way that you do not know, I do not know, no man knows, it becomes objectified in your world.

Do not be concerned with the how, and do not look back on your former state.

"No man, having put his hand to the plow, and looking back, is fit for the kingdom of God."

Simply assume that it is done and suspend reason, suspend all the arguments of the conscious three-dimensional mind.

Your desire is outside of the reach of the three-dimensional mind.

Assume you are that which you wish to be; walk as though you were it; and as you remain faithful to your assumption . . it will harden into fact.

QUESTIONS AND ANSWERS

1. Question: What is the meaning of the insignia on your book covers?

Answer: It is an eye imposed upon a heart which, in turn is imposed upon a tree laden with fruit, meaning that what you are conscious of, and accept as true, you are going to realize. As a man thinketh in his heart, so he is.

2. Question: I would like to be married, but have not found the right man. How do I imagine a husband?

Answer: Forever in love with ideals, it is the ideal state that captures the mind. Do not confine the state of marriage to a certain man, but a full, rich and overflowing life. You desire to experience the joy of marriage.

Do not modify your dream, but enhance it by making it lovelier. Then condense your desire into a single sensation, or act which implies its fulfillment.

In this western world a woman wears a wedding ring on the third finger of her left hand. Motherhood need not imply marriage; intimacy need not imply marriage, but a wedding ring does.

Relax in a comfortable arm chair, or lie flat on your back and induce a state akin to sleep. Then assume the feeling of being married. Imagine a wedding band on your finger. Touch it. Turn it around the finger. Pull it off over the knuckle. Keep the action going until the ring has the distinctness and feeling of reality. Become so lost in feeling the ring on your finger that when you open your eyes, you will be surprised that it is not there.

If you are a man who does not wear a ring, you could assume greater responsibility. How would you feel if you had a wife to care for? Assume the feeling of being a happily married man right now.

3. Question: What must I do to inspire creative thoughts such as those needed for writing?

Answer: What must you do? Assume the story has already been written and accepted by a great publishing house. Reduce the idea of being a writer to the sensation of satisfaction.

Repeat the phrase, "Isn't it wonderful!" or "Thank you, thank you, thank you," over and over again until you feel successful. Or, imagine a friend congratulating you. There are unnumbered ways of implying success, but always go to the end. Your acceptance of the end wills its fulfillment. Do not think about getting in the mood to write, but live and act as though you are now the author you desire to be. Assume you have the talent for writing. Think of the pattern you want displayed on the outside. If you write a book and no one is willing to buy it, there is no satisfaction. Act as though people are hungry for your work. Live as though you cannot produce stories, or books fast enough to meet the demand. Persist in this assumption and all that is necessary to achieve your goal will quickly burst into bloom and you will express it.

1948 Lessons – QUESTIONS AND ANSWERS

4. Question: How do I imagine larger audiences for my talks?

Answer: I can answer you best by sharing the technique used by a very able teacher I know. When this man first came to this country he began speaking in a small hall in New York City. Although only fifty or sixty people attended his Sunday morning meeting, and they sat in front, this teacher would stand at the podium and imagine a vast audience. Then he would say to the empty space, "Can you hear me back there?"

Today this man is speaking in Carnegie Hall in New York City to approximately 2500 people every Sunday morning and Wednesday evening. He wanted to speak to crowds. He was not modest. He did not try to fool himself but built a crowd in his own consciousness, and crowds come. Stand before a large audience.

Address this audience in your Imagination. Feel you are on that stage and your feeling will provide the means.

5. Question: Is it possible to imagine several things at the same time, or should I confine my imagining to one desire?

Answer: Personally I like to confine my imaginal act to a single thought, but that does not mean I will stop there. During the course of a day I may imagine many things, but instead of imagining lots of small things, I would suggest that you imagine something so big it includes all the little things. Instead of imagining wealth, health and friends, imagine being ecstatic. You could not be ecstatic and be in pain. You could not be ecstatic and be threatened with a dispossession notice. You could not be ecstatic if you were not enjoying a full measure of friendship and love.

What would the feeling be like were you ecstatic without knowing what had happened to produce your ecstasy? Reduce the idea of ecstasy to the single sensation, "Isn't it wonderful!" Do not allow the conscious, reasoning mind to ask why, because if it does it will start to look for visible causes, and then the sensation will be lost. Rather, repeat over and over again, "Isn't it wonderful!" Suspend judgment as to what is wonderful.

Catch the one sensation of the wonder of it all and things will happen to bear witness to the truth of this sensation. And I promise you, it will include all the little things.

6. Question: How often should I perform the imaginal act, a few days or several weeks?

Answer: In the Book of Genesis the story is told of Jacob wrestling with an angel. This story gives us the clue we are looking for; that when satisfaction is reached, impotence follows.

When the feeling of reality is yours, for the moment at least, you are mentally impotent. The desire to repeat the act of prayer is lost, having been replaced by the feeling of accomplishment. You cannot persist in wanting what you already have. If you assume you are what you desire to be to the point of ecstasy, you no longer want it. Your imaginal act is as much a creative act as a physical one wherein man halts, shrinks and is blessed, for as man creates his own likeness, so does your imaginal act transform itself into the likeness of your assumption. If, however, you do not reach the point of satisfaction, repeat the action over and over again until you feel as though you touched it and virtue went out of you.

7. Question: I have been taught not to ask for earthly things, only for spiritual growth, yet money and things are what I need.

Answer: You must be honest with yourself. All through scripture the question is asked, "What do you want of me?" Some wanted to see, others to eat, and still others wanted to be made straight, or "That my child live."

Your dimensionally larger self speaks to you through the language of desire. Do not deceive yourself.

Knowing what you want, claim you already have it, for it is your Father's good pleasure to give it to you and remember, what you desire, that you have.

8. Question: When you have as assumed your desire, do you keep in mind the ever presence of this greater one protecting and giving you your assumption?

Answer: The acceptance of the end wills the means. Assume the feeling of your wish fulfilled and your dimensionally greater self will determine the means. When you appropriate a state as though you had it, the activity of the day will divert your mind from all anxious thoughts so that you do not look for signs. You do not have to carry the feeling that some presence is going to do it for you, rather you know it is already done.

Knowing it is already a fact, walk as though it were, and things will happen to make it so. You do not have to be concerned about some presence doing anything for you. The deeper, dimensionally greater you has already done it. All you do is move to the place where you encounter it.

Remember the story of the man who left the master and was on his way home when he met his servant who said, "Your son lives." And when he asked at what hour it was done the servant replied, "The seventh hour." The self-same hour that he assumed his desire, it was done for him, for it was at the seventh hour that the master said, "Your son lives." Your desire is already granted. Walk as though it were and, although time beats slowly in this dimension of your being, it will nevertheless bring you confirmation of your assumption. I ask you not to be impatient, though. If there is one thing you really have need of, it is patience.

9. Question: Isn't there a law that says you cannot get something for nothing? Must we not earn what we desire?

Answer: Creation is finished! It is your Father's good pleasure to give you the kingdom. The parable of the prodigal son is your answer. In spite of man's waste, when he comes to his senses and remembers who he is, he feeds on the fatted calf of abundance and wears the robe and ring of authority. There is nothing to earn.

Creation was finished in the foundation of time. You, as man, are God made visible for the purpose of displaying what is, not what is to be. Do not think you must work out your salvation by the sweat of your brow. It is not four months until the harvest, the fields are already white, simply thrust in the sickle.

10. Question: Does not the thought that creation is finished rob one of his initiative?

Answer: If you observe an event before it occurs, then the occurring event must be predetermined from the point of view of being awake in this three-dimensional world. Yet, you do not have to encounter what you observe. You can, by changing your concept of self, interfere with your future and mold it in harmony with your changed concept of self.

11. Question: Does not this ability to change the future deny that creation is finished?

Answer: No. You, by changing your concept of self, change your relationship to things. If you rearrange the words of a play to write a different one, you have not created new words, but simply had the joy of rearranging them. Your concept of self determines the order of events you encounter. They are in the foundation of the world, but not their order of arrangement.

1948 Lessons – QUESTIONS AND ANSWERS

12. Question: Why should one who works hard in metaphysics always seem to lack?

Answer: Because he has not really applied metaphysics. I am not speaking of a mamby-pamby approach to life, but a daily application of the law of consciousness. When you appropriate your good, there is no need for a man, or state, to act as a medium through which your good will come.

Living in a world of men, money is needed in my everyday life. If I invite you to lunch tomorrow, I must pick up the check. When I leave the hotel, I must pay the bill. In order to take the train back to New York my railway fare must be paid. I need money and it has to be there. I am not going to say, "God knows best, and He knows I need money."Rather, I will appropriate the money as though it were!

We must live boldly! We must go through life as though we possessed what we want to possess. Do not think that because you helped another, someone outside of you saw your good works and will give you something to ease your burden. There is no one to do it for you. You, yourself must go boldly on appropriating what your Father has already given you.

13. Question: Can an uneducated person educate himself by assuming the feeling of being educated?

Answer: Yes. An aroused interest is awarded information from every side. You must sincerely desire to be well schooled. The desire to be well read, followed by the assumption that you are, makes you selective in your reading. As you progress in your education, you automatically become more selective, more discriminating in all that you do.

14. Question: My husband and I are taking the class together. Should we discuss our desires with each other?

Answer: There are two spiritual sayings which permeate the Bible. One is, "Go tell no man," and the other is "I have told you before it comes to pass that when it does come to pass you may believe." It takes spiritual boldness to tell another that your desire is fulfilled before it is seen on the outside. If you do not have that kind of boldness, then you had better keep quiet.

I personally enjoy telling my plans to my wife, because we both get such a thrill when they come into being.

The first person a man wants to prove this law to is his wife. It is said that Mohammad is everlastingly great because his first disciple was his wife.

15. Question: Should my husband and I work on the same project or on separate ones?

Answer: That is entirely up to you. My wife and I have different interests, yet we have much in common. Do you recall the story I told of our return to the United States this spring? I felt it was my duty as a husband to get passage back to America, so I appropriated that to myself. I feel there are certain things that are on my wife's side of the contract, such as maintaining a clean, lovely home and finding the appropriate school for our daughter, so she takes care of those.

Quite often my wife will ask me to imagine for her, as though she has greater faith in my ability to do it than in her own. That flatters me because everyman worthy of the name wants to feel that his family has faith in him.

But I see nothing wrong in the communion between two who love one another.

16. Question: I would think that if you get too much into the sleepy state there would be a lack of feeling.

Answer: When I speak of feeling I do not mean emotion, but acceptance of the fact that the desire is fulfilled. Feeling grateful, fulfilled, or thankful, it is easy to say, "Thank You," "Isn't it wonderful!" or "It is finished."

When you get into the state of thankfulness, you can either awaken knowing it is done, or fall asleep in the feeling of the wish fulfilled.

17. Question: Is love a product of your own consciousness?

1948 Lessons – QUESTIONS AND ANSWERS

Answer: All things exist in your consciousness, be they love or hate. Nothing comes from without. The hills to which you look for help are those of an inner range. Your feelings of love, hate or indifference all spring from your own consciousness. You are infinitely greater than you could ever conceive yourself to be. Never, in eternity will you reach the ultimate you. That is how wonderful you are. Love is not a product of you, you are love, for that is what God is and God's name is I AM, the very name you call yourself before you make the claim as to the state you are now in.

18. Question: Suppose my wants cannot materialize for six months to a year, do I wait to imagine them?

Answer: When the desire is upon you, that is the time to accept your wish in its fullness. Perhaps there are reasons why the urge is given you at this time. Your three-dimensional being may think it cannot be now, but your fourth dimensional mind knows it already is, so the desire should be accepted by you as a physical fact now.

Suppose you wanted to build a house. The urge to have it is now, but it is going to take time for the trees to grow and the carpenter to build the house. Although the urge seems big, do not wait to adjust to it. Claim possession now and let it objectify itself in its own strange way. Do not say it will take six months or a year.

The minute the desire comes upon you, assume it is already a fact! You and you alone have given your desire a time interval and time is relative when it comes to this world.

1948 Lessons – QUESTIONS AND ANSWERS

Do not wait for anything to come to pass, accept it now as though it were and see what happens.

When you have a desire, the deeper you, who men call God, is speaking. He urges you, through the language of desire, to accept that which is not that which is to be! Desire is simply his communion with you, telling you that your desire is yours, now! Your acceptance of this fact is proved by your complete adjustment to it as though it were true.

19. Question: Why do some of us die young?

Answer: Our lives are not, in retrospect, measured by years but by the content of those years.

20. Question: What would you consider a full life?

Answer: A variety of experiences. The more varied they are, the richer is your life. At death you function in a dimensionally larger world, and play your part on a keyboard made up of a life time of human experiences.

Therefore, the more varied your experiences, the finer is your instrument and the richer is your life.

21. Question: What about a child who dies at birth?

Answer: The child who is born, lives forever, as nothing dies. It may appear that the child who dies at birth has no keyboard of human experience but, as a poet once said:

"He drew a circle that shut me out, Infidel, scoundrel, a thing to flout. But Love and I had the wit to win! We drew a circle that took him in."

The loved one has access to the sensory experiences of the lover. God is love; therefore, ultimately everyone has an instrument, the keyboard of which is the sensory impressions of all men.

22. Question: What is your technique of prayer?

Answer: It starts with desire, for desire is the mainspring of action. You must know and define your objective, then condense it into a sensation which implies fulfillment. When your desire is clearly defined, immobilize your physical body and experience, in your Imagination, the action which implies its fulfillment. Repeat this act over and over again until it has the vividness and feeling of reality.

Or, condense your desire into a single phrase that implies fulfillment such as, "Thank you Father," "Isn't it wonderful," or "It is finished." Repeat that condensed phrase, or action in your Imagination over and over again. Then either awaken from that state, or slip off into the deep. It does not matter, for the act is done when you completely accept it as being finished in that sleepy, drowsy state.

1948 Lessons – QUESTIONS AND ANSWERS

23. Question: Two people want the same position. One has it. The other had it and now wants it back.

Answer: Your Father (the dimensionally greater you) has ways and means you know not of. Accept his wisdom. Feel your desire is fulfilled, then allow your Father to give it to you. The present one may be promoted to a higher position, or marry a man of great wealth and give up her job. She may come into a great deal of money, or choose to move to another state.

Many people say they want to work, but I question that seriously. They want security and condition security on a job. But I really do not think the average girl truly wants to get up in the morning and go to work.

24. Question: What is the cause of disease and pain?

Answer: The physical body is an emotional filter. Many human ailments, hitherto considered purely physical, are now recognized as rooted in emotional disturbances.

Pain comes from lack of relaxation. When you sleep there is no pain. If you are under an anesthetic, there is no pain because you are relaxed, as it were. If you have pain it is because you are tense and trying to force something. You cannot force an idea into embodiment, you simply appropriate it. It is attention minus effort.

Only practice will bring you to that point where you can be attentive and still be relaxed.

1948 Lessons – QUESTIONS AND ANSWERS

Attention is tension toward an end, and relaxation is just the opposite. Here are two completely opposite ideas that you must blend until you learn, through practice, how to be attentive, but not tense. The word "contention "means "attention minus effort." In the state of contention you are held by the idea without tension.

25. Question: No matter how much I try to be happy, underneath, I have a melancholy feeling of being left out. Why?

Answer: Because you feel you are not wanted. Were I you, I would assume I am wanted. You know the technique. The assumption that you are wanted may seem false when first assumed, but if you will feel wanted and respected, and persist in that assumption, you will be amazed how others will seek you out. They will begin to see qualities in you they had never seen before. I promise you. If you will but assume you are wanted, you will be.

26. Question: If security came to me through the death of a loved one, did I bring about that death?

Answer: Do not think for one second that you brought about a death by assuming security. The greater you is not going to injure any one. It sees all and, knowing the length of life of all, it can inspire the other to give you that which can fulfill your assumption.

1948 Lessons – QUESTIONS AND ANSWERS

You did not kill the person who named you in his will. If, a few days after your complete acceptance of the idea of security, Uncle John made his exit from this three-dimensional plane and left you his estate, it is only because it was time for Uncle John to go. He did not die one second before his time, however. The greater you saw the life span of John and used him as the way to bring about the fulfillment of your feeling of security.

The acceptance of the end wills the means toward the fulfillment of that end. Do not be concerned with anything save the end. Always bear in mind that the responsibility to make it so is completely removed from your shoulders. It is yours because you accept it as so!

27. Question: I have more than one objective. Would it be ineffective to concentrate on different objectives at different periods of concentration?

Answer: I like to take one consuming ambition, restrict it to a single short phrase, or act that implies fulfillment, but I do not limit my ambition. I only know that my real objective will include all the little ones.

28. Question: I find it difficult to change my concept of self. Why?

Answer: Because your desire to change has not been aroused. If you would fall in love with what you really want to be, you would become it. It takes an intense hunger to bring about a transformation of self.

"As the heart panteth after the water brooks, so panteth my soul after thee, O Lord. "If you would become as thirsty for perfection as the little hart is for water that it braves the anger of the tiger in the forest, you would become perfect.

29. Question: I am contemplating a business venture. It means a great deal to me, but I cannot imagine how it can come into being.

Answer: You are relieved of that responsibility. You do not have to make it a reality, it already is! Although your concept of self seems so far removed from the venture you now contemplate, it exists now as a reality within you. Ask yourself how you would feel and what you would be doing if your business venture were a great success. Become identified with that character and feeling and you will be amazed how quickly you will realize your dream.

The only sacrifice you are called upon to make, is to give up your present concept of self and appropriate the desire you want to express.

30. Question: As a metaphysical student I have been taught to believe that race beliefs and universal assumptions affect me. Do you mean that only to the degree I give these universal beliefs power over me, am I influenced by them?

1948 Lessons – QUESTIONS AND ANSWERS

Answer: Yes. It is only your individual viewpoint, as your world is forever bearing witness to your present concept of self. If someone offends you, change your concept of self. That is the only way others change.

Tonight's paper may be read by any six people in this room and no two will interpret the same story in the same way. One will be elated, the other depressed, another indifferent, and so on, yet it is the same story.

Universal assumptions, race beliefs, call them what you will, they are not important to you. What is important is your concept, not of another, but of yourself, for the concept you hold of yourself determines the concept you hold of others. Leave others alone. What are they to you? Follow your own desires.

The law is always in operation, always absolute. Your consciousness is the rock upon which all structures rest. Watch what you are aware of. You need not concern yourself with others because you are sustained by the absoluteness of this law. No man comes to you of his own accord, be he good, bad or indifferent. He did not choose you! You chose him! He was drawn to you because of what you are.

You cannot destroy the state another represents through force. Rather, leave him alone. What is he to you?

Rise to a higher level of consciousness and you will find a new world awaiting you, and as you sanctify yourself, others are sanctified.

1948 Lessons – QUESTIONS AND ANSWERS

31. Question: Who wrote the Bible?

Answer: The Bible was written by intelligent men who used solar and phallic myths to reveal psychological truths. But we have mistaken their allegory for history and, therefore, have failed to see their true message.

It is strange, but when the Bible was launched upon the world, and acceptance seemed to be in sight, the great Alexandria Library was burnt to the ground, leaving no record as to how the Bible came into being.

Few people can read other languages, so they cannot compare their beliefs with others. Our churches do not encourage us to compare. How many of the millions who accept the Bible as fact, ever question it? Believing it is the word of God, they blindly accept the words and thus lose the essence they contain. Having accepted the vehicle, they do not understand what the vehicle conveys.

32. Question: Do you use the Apocrypha?

Answer: Not in my teaching. I have several volumes of them at home. They are no greater than the sixty-six books of our present Bible. They are simply telling the same truth in a different way. For instance, the story is told of Jesus, as a young boy, watching children make birds out of mud. Holding the birds in their hands, they pretend the birds are flying. Jesus approaches and knocks the birds out of their hands. As they begin to cry, he picks up one of the broken birds and re-molds it. Holding it high, he breaths upon it and the bird takes wing.

1948 Lessons – QUESTIONS AND ANSWERS

Here is a story of one who came to break the idols in the minds of men, then show them how to use the same substance and re-mold it into a beautiful form and give it life. That is what this story is trying to convey. "I come, not to bring peace, but a sword." Truth slays all the little mud hens of the mind; slays illusions and then re-molds them into a new pattern which sets man free.

33. Question: If Jesus was a fictional character created by Biblical writers for the purpose of illustrating certain psychological dramas, how do you account for the fact that he and his philosophy are mentioned in the nonreligious and non-Christian history of those times? Were not Pontius Pilate and Herod real flesh and blood Roman officials in those days?

Answer: The story of Jesus is the identical story as that of the Hindu savior, Krishna. They are the same psychological characters. Both were supposed to have been born of virgin mothers. The rulers of the time sought to destroy them when they were children. Both healed the sick, resurrected the dead, taught the gospel of love and died a martyr's death for mankind. Hindus and Christians alike believe their savior to be God made man.

Today people quote Socrates, yet the only proof that Socrates ever existed is in the works of Plato. It is said that Socrates drank hemlock, but I ask you, who is Socrates? I once quoted a line from Shakespeare and a lady said to me, "But Hamlet said that."Hamlet never said it, Shakespeare wrote the lines and put the words in the mouth of a character he created and named Hamlet. St. Augustine once said, "That which is now called the Christian religion existed among the ancients. They began to call Christianity the true religion, yet it never existed."

34. Question: Do you use affirmations and denials?

Answer: Let us leave these schools of thought that use affirmations and denials. The best affirmation and the only effective one is an assumption which, in itself implies denial of the former state.

The best denial is total indifference. Things wither and die through indifference. They are kept alive through attention. You do not deny a thing by saying it does not exist. Rather you put feeling into it by recognizing it, and what you recognize as true, is true to you, be it good, bad or indifferent.

35. Question: Is it possible for one to appear dead and still not be dead?

Answer: General Lee was supposed to have been born two years after his mother, believed to be dead, was buried alive. Lucky for her she was not embalmed or buried in the earth, but in a vault where someone heard her cry and released her. Two years later Mrs. Lee bore a son who became General Lee. That is part of this country's history.

1948 Lessons – QUESTIONS AND ANSWERS

36. Question: How could one who was deprived in his youth become a success in life?

Answer: We are creatures of habit, forming patterns of the mind which repeat themselves over and over again. Although habit acts like a compelling law which drives one to repeat the patterns, it is not a law, for you and I can change the patterns. Many successful men such as Henry Ford, Rockefeller and Carnegie were deprived in their youth. Many of the great names in this country came from poor families, yet they left behind them great accomplishments in the political, artistic and financial world.

One evening a friend of mine attended a meeting for young advertising executives. The speaker of the evening said to these young men: "I have but one thing to say to you tonight, and that is to make yourself big and you cannot fail."

Taking an ordinary fish bowl, he filled it with two bags, one of English walnuts and the other of small beans.

Mixing them with his hand, he began to shake the bowl and said, "This bowl is life. You cannot stop its shaking as life is a constant pulsing, living rhythm, but watch." And as they watched the big walnuts came to the top of the bowl as the little beans fell to the bottom.

Looking into the bowl the man asked, "Which one of you is complaining, asking why?" Then added, "Isn't it strange, the sound is coming from the bowl and not the outside. A bean is complaining that if he had had the same environment as the walnut he, too would do big things, but he never had the chance." Then he took a little bean from the bottom of the bowl and placed him on top saying, "I can move the bean through sheer force, but I cannot stop the bowl of life from shaking," and as he shook the bowl, the little bean once again slid to the bottom.

Hearing another voice of complaint he asked, "What's that I hear? You are saying that I should take one of those big fellows who thinks he is so big and put him on the bottom and see what happens to him? You believe he will be just as limited as you because he will be robbed of the opportunity of big things just as you are? Let's see."

Then the speaker took one of the big walnuts and pushed him right down to the bottom of the bowl saying, "I still can't stop the bowl from shaking," and as the men watched the big walnut came to the top again. Then the speaker added:

"Gentlemen, if you really want to be successful in life, make yourself big."

My friend took this message to heart and began to assume he was a successful businessman. Today he is truly a big man if you judge success by dollars. He now employs over a thousand people in the city of New York. Each one of you can do what he did. Assume you are what you want to be. Walk in that assumption and it will harden into fact.

Chapter 1 -The Coin of Heaven
(From Awakened Imagination & The Search)

Chapter 2 – To Him Who Hath
(From Your Faith is Your Fortune)

Chapter 3 – Consciousness
(From The Power of Awareness)

Chapter 1

The Coin of Heaven

(From Awakened Imagination & The Search)

> "Does a firm persuasion that a thing is so, make it so?" And the prophet replied, "All poets believe that it does. And in ages of Imagination, this firm persuasion removed mountains: but many are not capable of a firm persuasion of anything."
> . . . Blake

Let every man be fully persuaded in his own mind.

PERSUASION IS an inner effort of intense attention. To listen attentively as though you heard is to evoke, to activate. By listening, you can hear what you want to hear and persuade those beyond the range of the outer ear. Speak it inwardly in your Imagination only. Make your inner conversation match your fulfilled desire. What you desire to hear without, you must hear within. Embrace the without within and become one who hears only that which implies the fulfillment of his desire, and all the external happenings in the world will become a bridge leading to the objective realization of your desire.

Your inner speech is perpetually written all around you in happenings. Learn to relate these happenings to your inner speech and you will become self-taught. By inner speech is meant those mental conversations which you carry on with yourself. They may be inaudible when you are awake

Chapter 1 – The Coin of Heaven

because of the noise and distractions of the outer world of becoming, but they are quite audible in deep meditation and dream. But whether they be audible or inaudible, you are their author and fashion your world in their likeness.

> There is a God in heaven . . and heaven is within you . . that revealeth secrets, and maketh known to the king Nebuchadnezzar what shall be in the latter days. Thy dream, and the visions of thy head upon thy bed, are these.

Inner speech from premises of fulfilled desire is the way to create an intelligible world for yourself.

Observe your inner speech for it is the cause of future action. Inner speech reveals the state of consciousness from which you view the world. Make your inner speech match your fulfilled desire, for your inner speech is manifested all around you in happenings.

> If any man offend not in word, the same is a perfect man and able also to bridle the whole body. Behold, we put bits in the horses' mouths, that they may obey us; and we turn about their whole body. Behold also the ships, which though they be so great, and are driven by fierce winds, yet are they turned about with a very small helm, whithersoever the governor listeth. Even so the tongue is a little member, and boasteth great things. Behold, how great a matter a little fire kindleth!

The whole manifested world goes to show us what use we have made of the Word . . Inner Speech. An uncritical observation of our inner talking will reveal to us the ideas

Chapter 1 – The Coin of Heaven

from which we view the world. Inner talking mirrors our Imagination, and our Imagination mirrors the state with which it is fused. If the state with which we are fused is the cause of the phenomenon of our life, then we are relieved of the burden of wondering what to do, for we have no alternative but to identify ourselves with our aim, and inasmuch as the state with which we are identified mirrors itself in our inner speech, then to change the state with which we are fused, we must first change our inner talking. It is our inner conversations which make tomorrow's facts.

> Put off the former conversation, the old man,
> which is corrupt... and be renewed in the spirit
> of your mind... put on the new man, which is
> created in righteousness.

> Our minds, like our stomachs, are
> whetted by change of food.
> . . . Quintillian

Stop all of the old mechanical negative inner talking and start a new positive and constructive inner speech from premises of fulfilled desire. Inner talking is the beginning, the sowing of the seeds of future action. To determine the action, you must consciously initiate and control your inner talking.

Construct a sentence which implies the fulfillment of your aim, such as "I have a large, steady, dependable income, consistent with integrity and mutual benefit", or "I AM happily married", "I AM wanted", "I AM contributing to the good of the world", and repeat such a sentence over and over until you are inwardly affected by it. Our inner speech represents in various ways the world we live in.

Chapter 1 – The Coin of Heaven

In the beginning was the Word.

That which ye sow ye reap. See yonder fields! The sesamum was sesamum, the corn was corn. The Silence and the Darkness knew! So is a man's fate born.

Ends run true to origins.
Those that go searching for love only make manifest their own lovelessness. And the loveless never find love, only the loving find love, and they never have to seek for it.

Man attracts what he is. The art of life is to sustain the feeling of the wish fulfilled and let things come to you, not to go after them or think they flee away.

Observe your inner talking and remember your aim. Do they match? Does your inner talking match what you would say audibly had you achieved your goal? The individual's inner speech and actions attract the conditions of his life. Through uncritical self-observation of your inner talking you find where you are in the inner world, and where you are in the inner world is what you are in the outer world. You put on the new man whenever ideals and inner speech match. In this way alone can the new man be born.

Inner talking matures in the dark. From the dark it issues into the light. The right inner speech is the speech that would be yours were you to realize your ideal. In other words, it is the speech of fulfilled desire.

"I AM That."

Chapter 1 – The Coin of Heaven

> There are two gifts which God has bestowed upon man alone, and on no other mortal creature. These two are mind and speech; and the gift of mind and speech is equivalent to that of immortality. If a man uses these two gifts rightly, he will differ in nothing from the immortals... and when he quits the body, mind and speech will be his guides, and by them he will be brought into the troop of the gods and the souls that have attained to bliss.
> . . . Hermetica, Walter Scott's translation

The circumstances and conditions of life are out-pictured inner talking, solidified sound. Inner speech calls events into existence. In every event is the creative sound that is its life and being. All that a man believes and consents to as true reveals itself in his inner speech. It is his Word, his life.

Try to notice what you are saying in yourself at this moment, to what thoughts and feelings you are consenting. They will be perfectly woven into your tapestry of life. To change your life, you must change your inner talking, for "life", said Hermes, "is the union of Word and Mind". When Imagination matches your inner speech to fulfilled desire, there will then be a straight path in yourself from within out, and the without will instantly reflect the within for you, and you will know reality is only actualized inner talking.

> Receive with meekness the inborn Word
> which is able to save your souls.

Every stage of man's progress is made by the conscious exercise of his Imagination matching his inner speech to his fulfilled desire. Because man does not perfectly match them, the results are uncertain, while they might be perfectly

Chapter 1 – The Coin of Heaven

certain. Persistent assumption of the wish fulfilled is the means of fulfilling the intention. As we control our inner talking, matching it to our fulfilled desires, we can lay aside all other processes. Then we simply act by clear Imagination and intention. We imagine the wish fulfilled and carryon mental conversations from that premise.

Through controlled inner talking from premises of fulfilled desire, seeming miracles are performed. The future becomes the present and reveals itself in our inner speech. To be held by the inner speech of fulfilled desire is to be safely anchored in life. Our lives may seem to be broken by events, but they are never broken so long as we retain the inner speech of fulfilled desire. All happiness depends on the active voluntary use of Imagination to construct and inwardly affirm that we are what we want to be. We match ourselves to our ideals by constantly remembering our aim and identifying ourselves with it. We fuse with our aims by frequently occupying the feeling of our wish fulfilled. It is the frequency, the habitual occupancy, that is the secret of success. The oftener we do it, the more natural it is. Fancy assembles. Continuous Imagination fuses.

It is possible to resolve every situation by the proper use of Imagination. Our task is to get the right sentence, the one which implies that our desire is realized, and fire the Imagination with it. All this is intimately connected with the mystery of "the still small voice".

Inner talking reveals the activities of Imagination, activities which are the causes of the circumstances of life. As a rule, man is totally unaware of his inner talking and therefore sees himself not as the cause but the victim of circumstance. To consciously create circumstance, man

Chapter 1 – The Coin of Heaven

must consciously direct his inner speech, matching "the still small voice" to his fulfilled desires.

> He calls things not seen as though they were.

Right inner speech is essential. It is the greatest of the arts. It is the way out of limitation into freedom. Ignorance of this art has made the world a battlefield and penitentiary where blood and sweat alone are expected, when it should be a place of marveling and wondering. Right inner talking is the first step to becoming what you want to be.

> Speech is an image of mind, and mind
> is an image of God.
> . . . Hermetica, Scott translation

On the morning of April 12, 1953, my wife was awakened by the sound of a great voice of authority speaking within her and saying, "You must stop spending your thoughts, time, and money. Everything in life must be an investment."

To spend is to waste, to squander, to layout without return. To invest is to layout for a purpose from which a profit is expected. This revelation of my wife is about the importance of the moment. It is about the transformation of the moment. What we desire does not lie in the future but in ourselves at this very moment. At any moment in our lives, we are faced with an infinite choice: "what we are and what we want to be". And what we want to be is already existent, but to realize it we must match our inner speech and actions to it.

> If two of you shall agree on earth as touching
> anything that they shall ask, it shall be done for

Chapter 1 – The Coin of Heaven

them of My Father which is in heaven.

It is only what is done now that counts. The present moment does not recede into the past. It advances into the future to confront us, spent or invested.

Thought is the coin of heaven. Money is its earthly symbol. Every moment must be invested, and our inner talking reveals whether we are spending or investing. Be more interested in what you are inwardly "saying now" than what you "have said" by choosing wisely what you think and what you feel *now*.

Any time we feel misunderstood, misused, neglected, suspicious, afraid, we are spending our thoughts and wasting our time. Whenever we assume the feeling of being what we want to be, we are investing. We cannot abandon the moment to negative inner talking and expect to retain command of life. Before us go the results of all that seemingly is behind. Not gone is the last moment . . but oncoming.

> My word shall not return unto Me void,
> but it shall accomplish that which I please,
> and it shall prosper in the thing whereto I sent it.

The circumstances of life are the muffled utterances of the inner talking that made them . . the word made visible.

"The Word", said Hermes, "is Son, and the Mind is Father of the Word. They are not separate one from the other; for life is the union of Word and Mind."

He willed us forth from Himself

Chapter 1 – The Coin of Heaven

by the Word of Truth.

Let us
be imitators of God as dear children

and use our inner speech wisely to mold an outer world in harmony with our ideal.

The Lord spake by me, and His
Word was in my tongue.

The mouth of God is the mind of man. Feed God only the best.

Whatsoever things are of good report...
think on these things.

The present moment is always precisely right for an investment, to inwardly speak the right word.

The word is very near to you, in your mouth,
and in your heart, that you may do it. See, I
have set before you this day life and good,
death and evil, blessings and cursings. Choose life.

You choose life and good and blessings by being that which you choose. Like is known to like alone. Make your inner speech bless and give good reports. Man's ignorance of the future is the result of his ignorance of his inner talking. His inner talking mirrors his Imagination, and his Imagination is a government in which the opposition never comes into power.

Chapter 1 – The Coin of Heaven

If the reader ask, "What if the inner speech remains subjective and is unable to find an object for its love?", the answer is: it will not remain subjective, for the very simple reason that inner speech is always objectifying itself. What frustrates and festers and becomes the disease that afflicts humanity is man's ignorance of the art of matching inner words to fulfilled desire. Inner speech mirrors Imagination, and Imagination is Christ.

Alter your inner speech, and your perceptual world changes. Whenever inner speech and desire are in conflict, inner speech invariably wins. Because inner speech objectifies itself, it is easy to see that if it matches desire, desire will be objectively realized. Were this not so, I would say with Blake,

> Sooner murder an infant in its cradle than nurse unacted desires.

But I know from experience,

> The tongue... setteth on fire the course of nature.

Chapter 2

To Him Who Hath

(From Your Faith is Your Fortune)

Take heed therefore how ye hear; for whosoever hath, to him shall be given; and whosoever hath not, from him shall be taken even that which he seemeth to have.

The Bible, which is the greatest psychological book ever written, warns man to be aware of what he hears; then follows this warning with the statement, "To him that hath it shall be given and to him that hath not it shall be taken away". Though many look upon this statement as one of the most cruel and unjust of the sayings attributed to Jesus, it still remains a just and merciful law based upon life's changeless principle of expression.

Man's ignorance of the working of the law does not excuse him nor save him from the results. Law is impersonal and therefore no respecter of persons. Man is warned to be selective in that which he hears and accepts as true. Everything that man accepts as true leaves an impression on his consciousness and must in time be defined as proof or disproof.

Perceptive hearing is the perfect medium through which man registers impressions. A man must discipline himself to

Chapter 2 – To Him Who Hath

hear only that which he wants to hear, regardless of rumors or the evidence of his senses to the contrary. As he conditions his perceptive hearing, he will react only to those impressions which he has decided upon. This law never fails. Fully conditioned, man becomes incapable of hearing other than that which contributes to his desire.

God, as you have discovered, is that unconditioned awareness which gives to you all that you are aware of being. To be aware of being or having anything is to be or have that which you are aware of being. Upon this changeless principle all things rest. It is impossible for anything to be other than that which it is aware of being.

"To him that hath (that which he is aware of being) it shall be given". Good, bad or indifferent . . it does not matter . . man receives multiplied a hundredfold that which he is aware of being. In keeping with this changeless law, "To him that hath not, it shall be taken from him and added to the one that hath", the rich get richer and the poor get poorer. You can only magnify that which you are conscious of being.

All things gravitate to that consciousness with which they are in tune. Likewise, all things disentangle themselves from that consciousness with which they are out of tune. Divide the wealth of the world equally among all men and in a short time, this equal division will be as originally disproportioned. Wealth will find its way back into the pockets of those from whom it was taken.

Instead of joining the chorus of the have-nots who insist on destroying those who have, recognize this changeless law of expression. Consciously define yourself as that which you desire.

Chapter 2 – To Him Who Hath

Once defined, your conscious claim established, continue in this confidence until the reward is received. As surely as the day follows the night, any attribute, consciously claimed, will manifest itself. Thus, that which to the sleeping orthodox world is a cruel and unjust law becomes to the enlightened one of the most merciful and just statements of truth.

"I AM come not to destroy but to fulfill." Nothing is actually destroyed. Any seeming destruction is a result of a change in consciousness. Consciousness ever fills full the state in which it dwells. The state from which consciousness is detached seems to those not familiar with this law to be destructive. However, this is only preparatory to a new state of consciousness.

Claim yourself to be that which you want filled full. "Nothing is destroyed. All is fulfilled."

"To him that hath it shall be given"

Chapter 3

Consciousness

(From The Power of Awareness)

IT IS only by a change of consciousness, by actually changing your concept of yourself, that you can "build more stately mansions" . . the manifestations of higher and higher concepts. (By manifesting is meant experiencing the results of these concepts in your world.) It is of vital importance to understand clearly just what consciousness is.

The reason lies in the fact that consciousness is the one and only reality, it is the first and only cause-substance of the phenomena of life. Nothing has existence for man save through the consciousness he has of it.

Therefore, it is to consciousness you must turn, for it is the only foundation on which the phenomena of life can be explained.

If we accept the idea of a first cause, it would follow that the evolution of that cause could never result in anything foreign to itself. That is, if the first cause-substance is light, all its evolutions, fruits and manifestations would remain light. The first cause-substance being consciousness, all its evolutions, fruits and phenomena must remain consciousness. All that could be observed would be a higher or lower form or variation of the same thing.

Chapter 3 – Consciousness

In other words, if your consciousness is the only reality, it must also be the only substance. Consequently, what appears to you as circumstances, conditions and even material objects is really only the product of your own consciousness. Nature, then, as a thing or a complex of things external to your mind, must be rejected. You and your environment cannot be regarded as existing separately. You and your world are one.

Therefore, you must turn from the objective appearance of things to the subjective center of things, your consciousness, if you truly desire to know the cause of the phenomena of life, and how to use this knowledge to realize your fondest dreams. In the midst of the apparent contradictions, antagonisms and contrasts of your life, there is only one principle at work, only your consciousness operating. Difference does not consist in variety of substance, but in variety of arrangement of the same cause-substance, your consciousness.

The world moves with motiveless necessity. By this is meant that it has no motive of its own, but is under the necessity of manifesting your concept, the arrangement of your mind, and your mind is always arranged in the image of all you believe and consent to as true.

The rich man, poor man, beggar man or thief are not different minds, but different arrangements of the same mind, in the same sense that a piece of steel, when magnetized, differs not in substance from its demagnetized state, but in the arrangement and order of its molecules. A single electron revolving in a specified orbit constitutes the unit of magnetism. When a piece of steel or anything else is demagnetized, the revolving electrons have not stopped.

Chapter 3 – Consciousness

Therefore, the magnetism has not gone out of existence. There is only a rearrangement of the particles, so that they produce no outside or perceptible effect. When particles are arranged at random, mixed up in all directions, the substance is said to be demagnetized; but when particles are marshaled in ranks so that a number of them face in one direction, the substance is a magnet.

Magnetism is not generated; it is displayed. Health, wealth, beauty and genius are not created; they are only manifested by the arrangement of your mind . . that is, by your concept of yourself . . and your concept of yourself is all that you accept and consent to as true. What you consent to can only be discovered by an uncritical observation of your reactions to life. Your reactions reveal where you live psychologically; and where you live psychologically determines how you live here in the outer visible world.

The importance of this in your daily life should be immediately apparent.

The basic nature of the primal cause is consciousness. Therefore, the ultimate substance of all things is consciousness

Metaphysical / Law of Attraction Books

David Allen - The Power of I AM (2014), The Power of I AM - Volume 2 (2015), The Power of I AM - Volume 3 (2017)

David Allen - The Creative Power of Thought, Man's Greatest Discovery (2017)

David Allen - The Secrets, Mysteries & Powers of The Subconscious Mind (2017)

David Allen - The Money Bible - The Secrets of Attracting Prosperity (2017)

David Allen - Your Faith Is Your Fortune, Your Unlimited Power

The Neville Goddard Collection (All 10 of his books plus 2 Lecture series) (2016)

Neville Goddard - Assumptions Harden Into Facts: The Book (2016)

Neville Goddard - Imagination: The Redemptive Power in Man (2016)

Neville Goddard - The World is At Your Command - The Very Best of Neville Goddard (2017)

Neville Goddard - Imagining Creates Reality - 365 Mystical Daily Quotes (2017)

Neville Goddard's Interpretation of Scripture (2018)

The Definitive Christian D. Larson Collection (6 Volumes, 30 books) (2014)

Looking for more metaphysical/New Thought/LOA authors? Here are a few I would highly recommend.

James Allen
Annie Rix Militz
Anthony Norvell
Catherine Ponder
Charles Brodie Patterson
Charles F. Haanel
Charles Fillmore
Charles Godfrey Leland
Christian D. Larson
Dr. Robert Anthony
Elizabeth Towne
Ella Wheeler Wilcox
Emma Curtis Hopkins
Emmet Fox
Ernest Holmes
Eugene Del Mar
Florence Scovel Shinn
Floyd B. Wilson
Genevieve Behrend
H. Emilie Cady
Harriette Augusta Curtiss
Henry Drummond
Henry Harrison Brown
Horatio W. Dresser
Jack Ensign Addington
James Allen
Joel S. Goldsmith
Joseph Murphy

NOTES:

NOTES:

www.ingramcontent.com/pod-product-compliance
Lightning Source LLC
Chambersburg PA
CBHW031401290426
44110CB00011B/225